About the Author

John is happily married with three grown up children. He has spent his life working in the voluntary sector running various charitable organisations, from outdoor education projects in the north east, a children's charity on the Isle of Man and most recently a large adult hospice in the East Midlands. With an original degree in sport, John has never lost his passion to be outside, seeking any available mini adventure, whether organised or simply made up, he relishes the opportunity to test and understand his own physical and mental resilience.

21/11/22 .

This Wild and Precious Life

John Knight

This Wild and Precious Life

Olympia Publishers
London

www.olympiapublishers.com
OLYMPIA PAPERBACK EDITION

A CIP catalogue record for this title is
available from the British Library.

ISBN: 978-1-80074-268-0

This is a work of non-fiction.

First Published in 2022

Olympia Publishers
Tallis House
2 Tallis Street
London
EC4Y 0AB
Printed in Great Britain

Dedication

For Angela, who has always patiently supported my adventures.

Seven years of KIMM

Well to be absolutely accurate, it should read four years of KIMM and three of OMM — not some mystical Buddist ritual but rather the now infamous two-day fell race which was first run in 1968.

The Karrimor International Mountain Marathon (KIMM) — as many people will have come to know it — was the brainchild of Gerry Charnley. Gerry, it turns out, was a mountaineer and orienteer who wanted to organise an event which would be the true test of orienteering skills in extreme circumstances. His devilish scheming culminated in a race which spanned two days with competitors running in pairs at all times no further than ten metres apart. The early races were simply called 'Mountain Marathons', however sponsorship opportunities and overseas competitors soon saw it become the 'Karrimor' International Mountain Marathon.

True to the intentions of Gerry's original design, today's Original Mountain Marathon (OMM), which has replaced the KIMM, continues the discipline that each team must carry compulsory but minimal equipment with which to 'survive' a wild camping overnight in mountainous terrain and still be able to look after and nourish themselves to cover distances of up to a double marathon.

As the event has evolved — and changed its name with a new sponsor to the 'Original Mountain Marathon'— so have the number of competitors who annually apply in their droves to the lottery of entry with no guarantee of acceptance. The different classes have also multiplied to include everything from 'elite' to 'short score'. It's the elite pairings who cover the mountain terrain at truly incredible average speeds with their kit skilfully compressed into bumbags which defy logic. Every time one of these usually six foot four, nine stone mountain hares, comes whisking past me — I find myself wondering just how all the compulsory kit can fit in to such a small pack and be legal? Perhaps even more importantly, would it be effective when the weather comes in, which is frequently does!

Some of you will instantly recall the Howgill Fells OMM event in 2008 when the weather really did close in with gale force winds and torrential rain. Two thousand, five hundred competitors were out in the hills at the time and it became the first and only time that the event has been abandoned — partly due to the rising pressures of inaccurate media reporting rather than any inability of the runners to look after themselves. It was reported that one thousand, seven hundred runners were missing and unaccounted for. The truth was that many of the 'lost' competitors were actually active mountain rescue team members, they'd just chosen to go running for the weekend! In the end only thirteen competitors were treated for hypothermia and various minor injuries, all the rest either made or found shelter and simply sat the weather out and then made their way back to the start.

In its current format the OMM welcomes some one thousand five hundred pairs to a different mountainous area each year over the October weekend when the clocks go back. It's only recently that it was brought to my attention that the competition areas are carefully chosen for their mixture of runnable terrain — not too much rock and cliff — but with enough wide-open space to ensure sound navigational skills and a wide range of differing route choices through which to gather maximum points without incurring penalty.

The different venues and local running terrain has left me with some memorable moments and some sharp mental images that come vividly back to me whenever I hear or see any sign of a KIMM or an OMM. That's often the windscreen stickers from across the years that you can see in vehicles parked on access paths to hillsides or remote lane tops. They're the sort of vans and cars that have a well-used look, plenty of mud along the topsides and usually the tell-tale signs of an experienced adventurer — maps on the dashboard, old waterproofs, well-thumbed and often damp guide books and a glimpse of assorted warm clothing, not to forget the usual short lengths of thin knotted line not useful for anything in particular but always handy, because you just never know when!

It was 1992 when my Karrimor Mountain Marathon experiences began. It wasn't by design or any well-planned training regime with the event neatly scheduled to come around just when I was reaching peak fitness — my life has never been that organised. What brought me to the start line in the Northern Lakes was that a friend's running partner had had to drop out and he was in desperate need of a substitute. I'm guessing that in his own need to secure a place in the event — should the compulsory lottery for an entry play in his favour — the only accessible person that Chris could think of was me. At the time I was a twenty-eight-year-old keen outdoor enthusiast who'd most probably say 'yes' before even thinking about what he was committing himself to, and Chris was right to choose me because I said yes straight away!

Sitting here some twenty-six years later I can't even recall if we went out on any training runs? I know that at the time I would have been pretty fit. I played regular county badminton for Northumberland and was a committed gym goer. I worked for an outdoor education charity in Newcastle upon Tyne and was spending lots of time in the hills or on the water, but I had little, if any, idea about hill running or orienteering route choices when moving across the hills at speed. I was used to carrying minimal kit and being self-sufficient in the hills but hadn't had to factor in two days' worth of equipment compressed into a twenty-five to thirty litre running sack and how it would feel and be balanced as I both scampered and staggered across the Lakeland terrain chasing my long-legged friend.

Day One of that event remains a blur, but the record shows we collected one hundred and seventy points without incurring any penalty for being late into the overnight wild camp. Chris had entered us into the Short Score — the baby event within the wide array of choices on offer to competitors. The Short, Medium and Long Score events all demand that each pair, staying within ten metres of one another, gather as many points as possible each day within a predetermined time window. As your time allowance runs out you begin to incur a two-point penalty for every minute you're late back to either the midway overnight camp or the second day finish. The Short Score is five hours on Day One and four hours on Day Two — believe me, it doesn't seem that short when you're running it!

The camp in 1992 was at the head of a remote valley in the Northern Lakes and dark was gathering as we made our way into the field to find our pitch for the night. The area was already crammed with hundreds of tents and huddles of bedraggled runners gathered together, sharing their stories of the day, wrapped in down jackets, warm hats and gloves to keep their body warmth in. The additional fashionable arrangement that everyone sports at these events is the improvised shopping bag liner for wet running shoes. This neat fell runners trick enables people to use their wet running shoes in the evening whilst wearing their second pair of much coveted warm, dry socks that have been lovingly transported for five hours across the fells. The newly dressed and warm foot is placed into a thin shopping bag before being inserted back into the wet fell shoe — which must be worn if one wishes to go and seek out friends or more likely pay a visit to the unique toilet arrangements.

And it is the latter, the toilets, that lead me to my two first and most vivid memories of the 1992 Karrimor.

The sea of tents, a mass of green canvas — as they all were 'back in the day' — is made more remarkable by the fact that in the dark virtually every tent looked the same! The classic fell running tent at that time was the much-loved Saunders Space Packer and they must have made up a good forty per cent. of the several hundred tents which were crammed, in no particular order, into the small field system that was to serve as the pop-up home for the night. Even in daylight it was easy to get mislaid, to go to fetch water or check the updated results board only to find that your tent, which was so obvious as you left it, was now perhaps one of many in a particular area of the campsite. Clever running pairs had marked their tents with a coloured ribbon or even a balloon — which was helpful in ruling them out, however this only marginally narrowed the field of options and left many of us novice runners wandering around looking hopefully for familiar signs, clothes or shoes, the top of a rucksack or any other clue that identified the tent as yours! There was of course the option to wander around lamely calling your partner's name — not quite the gritty outdoorsman thing to do, and what if there was more than one Chris in the camp? It wasn't unusual for momentarily thankful runners, thinking they'd found their way home, to be noisily ejected from a tent just as they lowered their body in. The incumbent pair may have been fast asleep or deep in conversation, or listening to music, but whatever they'd been distracted by, they certainly were not anticipating their two-man tent becoming a three-man tent — to entertain a runner from another pair!

My hare-like partner Chris had ventured off into the night muttering something about wanting a pee and leaving me to look after the pan of water which he'd careful placed at the head of the tent. Chris's experience had taught him much over his years of Karrimor events. He had high quality 'kit', a beautiful down sleeping bag, proper fell shoes, Goretex running cagoule and a sporting go faster physique to match. He even had the full mountain beard and the far-away look that proper fell runners have.

Chris had been careful to get his gear ready for his return, his sleeping bag all laid out, turned down in hotel style with the top half neatly folded back to reveal the lofted down inner. It looked perfect, warm dry and comfortable.

The small pan was placed on a precariously tall single gas burner just outside the unzipped inner tent on a carefully but unconvincingly flattened area of grass. The water, when boiled, was destined to make our dessert for the evening, a camper's delight that I remember fondly from those days called Hot Chocolate Crunch. Water plus creamy chocolate powder, whisked together vigorously with a fork and then topped off with lots of pre-crunched digestive biscuits — bloody fantastic and eagerly anticipated as the perfect end to a hard day.

Skilled at these events, Chris wasn't gone long — or it didn't seem a long time before I heard him quietly calling my name. He was somewhere out there in the dark amongst the sea of Saunders Space Packers zig-zagging his way back to me. I remained cocooned in the warm tent and in my own toasty dry down sleeping bag. In his absence I'd been dozing with half an eye on the now close-to-boiling water. As he called out to me to ensure he was homing in on the right tent I sat up hastily on one elbow to welcome him back. Our little oasis awaited him, I replied to his quiet call and simultaneously reached out to turn the gas off and remove the boiling water. My thinking was that it would be helpful of me to ensure that the water was out of the way, off the top of the stove so as to erase any risk that Chris could knock it over as he funnelled himself back into the tent. What I hadn't however factored was that my darting hand, reaching out to turn the gas off, only served to knock the stove over and, my stomach turned and eyes rolled as I watched the now boiling water fall perfectly into the open neck of Chris's carefully arranged sleeping bag!

Oh my God! I have just managed to pour a pint of boiling water into my friend's sleeping bag. The same sleeping bag that he's about to return to, no doubt in anticipation of a bowl of hot chocolate crunch followed by a warm night's sleep! If it wasn't bad enough that I'd slowed him down in the hills all day, that my navigation had been tardy — to say the least — I'd now rounded things off by ruining his night's sleep.

Chris slid his way back into the tent, deftly kicking his wet fell shoes off in the doorway and stretching his leg and foot across the wet grass within the inner tent to make contact with... his wet sleeping bag!

"Errr, Chris," I remember saying, "There's been a bit of an accident, I mean, I've had a bit of an accident, well not me personally you understand, but your bag's soaking, I'm sorry, it's the hot chocolate crunch — well the water for the hot chocolate crunch!"

It's at times like this that you quickly learn who your good friends are! Chris took it all in his stride, refused my offers of swapping bags with him and very quickly rearranged his sleeping set up to protect himself from the not-insignificant wet patch that I had created for him. Being the seasoned mountain man that he was and remains to this day, it really didn't seem to faze him! He politely brushed off all offers from me to exchange equipment and within minutes had changed the subject to something less awkward.

We've run a further two KIMM's together and a Lowe Alpine Mountain Marathon on Mull, so I guess he did forgive me. That said he delights in regularly bring up the mishap when we're in company and he fancies a laugh at my expense.

It might have been that same Karrimor or perhaps the following year at St Mary's Loch in Scotland when my second vivid memory provides a less personal but far more distasteful story.

In today's modern set-up for these events the toilets are those familiar port-a-loo plastic toilet huts which we have all come to know well. In this year's event — the fiftieth running of the KIMM / OMM which was staged out of Langdale in the Lake District, the overnight camp had a good old scutch of these toilets spread around the wild camp site — meaning that for most people a toilet was easily at hand. Whilst these plastic boxes may come with their own individual smell, and are places that we all enter with some hesitation, they are nonetheless private and a decent retreat from the weather even if just for a few moments.

"Back in the day" however the toilets were a very different story. The organisers then went for a low cost and easy-to-organise solution. Whoever came up with the idea clearly didn't pay any regard to health and safety (and why would you) as they simply commissioned two long trenches to be dug out by a JCB on the afternoon of the event and then to be filled back in again the next afternoon when all runners had moved on.

I do recall that, for modesty, the trenches had windbreaks arranged along their length and that also some form of illegible identification was put out to tell competitors which trench was for the women and which for the men. Often this signage deteriorated with the weather and by darkness it was anyone's guess as to who was using which trench, but by then few people actually even cared.

On this particular night I remember feeling very annoyed, lying there in my warm sleeping bag, that somehow, I'd become so well rehydrated after the day's exertions that I now needed a pee. Bloody typical, it's wet and cold outside and in order to sort this pressing need out I now have to find the bags for my feet, find my cold, wet fell shoes in the dark, sit up in a small, confined space, get out my bag and go forth into the night to find the trench. Normally of course we'd all consider the option of simply peeing by our tents, but on these events, there are literally hundreds of tents and peeing next to mine would almost certainly have been peeing onto or into someone else's!

So, I got organised, found my bags and my shoes, put my jacket on and headed out across the field with my head-torch scanning the distance looking for the illuminous tags that denoted the trenches. They were pretty easy to find — for which I was grateful but of course, it wasn't the getting there that worried me, it was the getting back in the dark and finding my own tent without lamely shouting to Chris across the sea of green canvas at this late time of night.

The technique with 'the trench' was to first carefully identify it in the dark and then to even more carefully straddle it with your legs thus enabling yourself to either pee down into the trench or — if absolutely necessary — drop your leggings and squat before performing the necessary activity to fully relieve yourself. The trench was, of course, a perfect JCB bucket width across and most probably one bucket deep.

So, there I was straddling the ditch and taking my late-night pee — nothing too unusual about that. All passed without any mishap to myself. As I was finishing my pee and readying myself to de-straddle the trench, I noticed another person entering the toilet area and making their way cautiously to close by where I was standing. It wasn't clear to me whether this was a man or woman, and I certainly wasn't about to shine my head-torch into their eyes (possibly one of the most annoying novice things that can be done to you) as I guessed it would only aid them to walk straight into the dreaded trench. So, I neatly averted my torch beam and made off into the dark. I hadn't got far, still within the gathered shelter of the wind breaks when I heard a brief but muffled shriek followed quickly by a wet 'sploosh' and a groan of disbelief.

To this day I cannot be absolutely sure as to what happened, however, I left feeling very sorry that the stranger in the night had most probably misjudged their own trench straddle or lost their balance, who knows, but I concluded that the wet splash and groan were almost certain reactions to their short descent into the stinking mire, the effluence of several thousand runners awaiting their landing some four feet down and almost certain to cover them in the worst possible way.

I can only imagine the runner's partner awaiting in the warmth of the tent, all cocooned in their sleeping bag, cosy and comfortable — to then welcome back a wet, poo-covered and very unhappy 'friend' bringing with them the gruesome evidence of the exertions of hundreds of runners. Oh dear, oh dear — it makes spilling water into the neck of a sleeping bag seem so innocent a crime!

Mountain Marathon Days

When I think back now to those early Mountain Marathon weekends and the beauty of the wild and remote places that the courses took you to; The Southern Uplands, The Lakes, The Howgill Fells, Brecon Beacons and St

Mary's Loch. I'm left feeling privileged to have been able to not only go there, but to have been fit enough to run through such places able to lift my head and revel in the environment.

The other slightly quirkier enjoyment comes, for me, from some of the place names that you find yourself homing in on. I've not run a Mountain Marathon in the Merrick Hills, a beautiful cluster of mountains not far from Newton Stewart in Dumfries and Galloway. I did, however, do my summer mountain leaders assessment there and took great pleasure when being asked to navigate the group and the assessor to places such as 'The Murder Hole', the 'Rig of Jarkness' or even the 'Round Loch of the Dungeon'. Who thought of these names, what do they mean and how enticing they are?

Richard Askwith, author of his own inspirational fell running journey "Feet in the Clouds" then goes on to reflect in the second of his books — "Running Free" that we should come to terms with the reality gap between our own ambitions and our actual fitness. He suggests that we need to reconnect with the desire simply to be in the outdoors and the pleasure of running. We should take more time to simply soak up the amazing places and perhaps also those evocative place names that we are able to run to and through, and most of all we must encourage ourselves to stop or slow down, lift our heads and truly appreciate just where we are. Richard's experience is that he has become all the richer for taking this mental step, and is probably only two minutes slower in the race perhaps finishing one hundredth instead of eightieth — his subtle message being 'who really cares, get over yourself.'

The great thing about the OMM for me, as an amateur adventurer, lover of the hills and sucker for a challenge — is the opportunity it presents to actually do okay!

There are various elements that give a limited athlete such as myself a little hope.

Firstly, there is the wide variety of courses, the time expected on the hill and the route choices this allows. Then there are the elements which will take their toll differently across the field of competitors. Some people excel in the cloud and the rain whilst others, perhaps faster across the ground, can simply get too cold and slip quickly into poor decisions and lost time. Experience comes into play, time 'on the hill', and running speed often starts to play second fiddle to the canny sense of route choice, a weather eye and the sensible balance of time allowed, distance travelled and the need to arrive at the overnight camp before penalties start to be imposed.

The 2017 event in proved to have significant quantities of all of the above. Saturday dawned chilly, damp and with a miserable forecast that gloomily predicted rain by mid-morning accompanied by winds of up to fifty m.p.h. on the tops. "Risk of being blown over" was clearly written in chalk on the forecasting board.

My partner Chris and I had once again entered the Short Score event, often viewed as the baby event of the OMM with just five hours of running on the Saturday followed by four on the Sunday.

We had two previous events together under our belts and had shaped up as a decent team. Our inaugural event had been the 2014 Howgill Fells OMM in which we stunned ourselves by finishing fourteenth in class. A year later we'd slipped a little but still managed fifteenth in the Brecon Beacons. Our strength, it seems, is based on the fact that we are great friends with lots of mutual 'water under the bridge'. My running speed and stamina are well below those of Chris' however, my stubborn reluctance to let go of the map and perhaps take a greater lead in the navigation means that, fast or not, Chris politely accepts staying relatively close to me. He also has that canny eye for a fast route!

OMM 2017 Day 1 Short Score Start Area - Myself & Chris happy before the rain & wind.

With a start time of nine forty-five a.m., we had been able to take things relatively easy before arriving at Stool End Farm to park and register, then walking up the valley to the starting area. Once whistled through the opening gate we quickly collected our course maps and, being perhaps a little older and wiser than the young bucks, we calmly found a spot and took a few moments to survey our options and plot in our minds the proposed broad route for the next five hours.

Our choice, which was identical to pretty much every other route option, was one which climbed immediately and steeply out of the end of Langdale.

Oh, how quickly my legs began to burn, and the inner demons began to talk to me:

"Why hadn't I done more training before the event? Why didn't I do those hill-repeat sessions that I'd promised myself? Why hadn't I even carried a heavier pack on the flattest of my runs?"

Could I even last five hours? I hadn't managed more than two in training? Would Chris wait for me this time? — He looks fitter, and I know he's been out a lot — his Strava feed has been intimidating, this is truly going to be awful!"

It was certainly all coming back to bite me now and there was no escape as the hill rose up in front of me and Chris started to show me a clean pair of heels.

Onwards, and upwards we climbed, into the cloud and the gathering wind, light rain turning heavier and the first bits of damp finding their way through my running cagoule. Then quickly past the first two score points before plunging back down out of the cloud and into a remote valley and a prominent stream to then follow onwards towards our second big climb of the day.

Up again into the cloud, properly wet through now but being kept warm by the consistent run, walk, run, navigate routine and the focus upon the next score and the excitement of finding it perhaps on a little rocky outcrop, or a stream junction or a crag foot!

And then at some point in the middle of our five-hour window we find ourselves travelling over Esk Pike, the wind literally stopping us in our tracks, at times pushing us sideways or backwards, the cloud now so thick and visibility so poor that accurate and constant navigation becomes a must. The morning's idea of shorts and a thermal top covered by a lightweight cagoule start to feel like a very dubious decision but then stopping to layer up seems also to not be the sensible option — so we push on, both much less buoyant than before, just getting through it!

Just off the summit of Esk Pike we find our next marker manned by a lonely volunteer marshal who is cocooned in a sleeping bag and further wrapped in a gortex tent outer. He takes our number as we travel through, a chirpy interlude on an otherwise grim and wet traverse. Other runners come and go in the clag but aside from a brief grunt there's little to say, and certainly it's not the done thing to confer about route or admit that you might just be feeling a little disorientated!

Chris mutters that his Raynaud's disease has properly set in, he hasn't had his map in his hands for some time, mainly because he can't feel his fingers and now, he says that the circulation to his feet has become so bad that he can't feel the boulders through his fell shoes and this is making safe navigation across the terrain a real problem. I ponder as I run that it must be both a weird and disconcerting feeling — up here in the cloud and the wind with no sense of touch and feeling strangely disconnected from the very ground that you're running over.

The next check point, at least the one we're aiming to get to, is just over a kilometre away following what should be an obvious ridge line as it sweeps from left to right. To one side there should be a long, steep grassy slope and to the other, our left, a treacherous long crag that would certainly bring our day to a premature end.

Perhaps it was the weather then that took the edge off our judgement, or perhaps that we'd been so accurate up to that last check point in those grim conditions, it now became apparent that we had become complacent and soon found ourselves 'misplaced' (never lost!), running very conservatively and with little positive direction contouring just under the cloud base.

The craggy knoll behind which the next check point was placed — was most definitely not ahead of us and we quickly surmised that we were too low and would need to climb steeply back into the cloud if we were to regain the correct line. But we were both cold, very wet and our motivation was running at a low ebb. The impact of his Raynaud's condition continued to plague Chris and, to be frank, we began to realise that time was now against us. Our best plan was to take a straight-line escape route along the current hillside to first pick up a stream, then a path which would lead us on to a 'virtual' navigational gate at a stone packhorse bridge. If we could do that efficiently then we would be out of the main competition area and facing a final four kilometre run to the overnight camp, maybe we could get there within our time window?

This was now the reality, although it meant that we'd failed to find our last point and had lost this potential score, we would also have to accept that the other scores we'd planned to travel to were now also lost to us, and that the main challenge was to get to the overnight camp on time!

Day One Finish after a wild day on the tops but eleven minutes late!

Charged by this Chris picked up the pace and those clean heels began flashing in front of me. The dull ache soon returned to my legs and the demons once again began to chant their negative messages of weakness and misery in my mind. I chased on, Chris occasionally stopping or looking back from twenty metres ahead with words of encouragement or sarcasm that I think he intended to be helpful.

Day 1 Finish after a wild day on the tops but 11 minutes late!

I'd seen Chris do this annoying antic once before. In 2014 we'd entered an event on the West Coast of Ireland called Gael force West. It was a heavily commercial adventure race with some one thousand, eight hundred people involved travelling sixty or so kilometres up the Irish coastline variously trail running, kayaking and cyclocross biking. I'd managed to keep some sort of credible pace with Chris on the first eight-mile trail run and then endured forty-five minutes waiting with no shelter on the 'fjord-side' for a kayak before paddling about one and a half km. across to the far shore and collecting our cyclocross bikes.

We'd borrowed these bikes from a very helpful Facebook contact in Belfast and therefore had never ridden them in anger. Of course, we'd adjusted seat posts and done the obligatory turn around the car park the night before — but now, as I climbed on and set off across lane and track, I realised that my bike had gearing set up for a superhuman with legs the size of a rugby prop forward. Just turning the crank was a major effort and the hills quickly became excruciating — my cadence dropping to possibly thirty rpm. as I groaned my way up everything that even constituted a gentle slope. Steadily (or perhaps not so steadily) Chris pulled ahead, I couldn't blame him as I was proper slow — and soon I was on my own as the heaven's opened and nature sent with it the cruellest of headwinds across and open moor top. Our destination and next challenge, was the religious peak, Croagh Patrick, famous for pilgrims and standing at seven hundred and forty-six metres high. The idea was that we ran up to the summit before retracing our steps and then cycling on to the finish in Westport.

As I arrived at the foot of the mountain, I could see Chris waiting by his bike looking frustrated as valuable minutes were being lost. I threw my gut-busting-heavily-geared bike to the floor next to his and reached for my fell shoes from my pack.

"You've got to look after yourself better!" started Chris, "You've bonked, get some fuel in you!"

He thrust an energy gel into my hands along with a water bottle with isotonic drink mix.

"Get these in you, come on, we've need to get on!"

I looked up at the formidable slope above me and felt broken — but with Chris waiting like a bouncing puppy there was little else I could do other than dig deep and press on.

"Here," said Chris, "let me take your water bottle, I can carry it for you on the ascent".

With that he grabbed my bottle and set off taking the most direct, and steepest, line up the hill. Within seconds he was metres ahead of me and very quickly the gap widened. Occasionally he turned and shouted backwards — words of encouragement I suspect, but bloody annoying and seemingly oblivious to the fact that he now had my water bottle and I wanted, no I needed, a drink.

I do recall expressing my opinion to him pretty loudly across a hillside of other tired runners and he retreated back to me without saying too much before thrusting my bottle back into my hands!

Back in Langdale, once through the navigational gate there was the final steady climb of the day but now amongst dozens of other competitors all making their way along the marshy path down towards the overnight camp at Cockley Beck in Mosedale. Chris's pace remained relentless, edged more now with a desperation to save points as our cut-off time passed and we still had a final two kms to cover.

In the end we made the Day One finish exactly ten minutes and two seconds late — the two seconds being important as this calculates to eleven minutes late or twenty-two points deducted rather than twenty points had we been three seconds quicker!

And so, the day ended, the tent went up on good, flat, albeit wet, ground, fresh clothes were liberated from dry bags and the essential plastic bags were donned over new dry socks to protect against wet fell shoes. Chris made dinner — he always does and I welcome his generous nature in that respect! We ate and chatted, then spoke to other competitors as the field filled up and began to hear the 'war stories' of many other couples who'd not made it across the high ground that we'd covered or had got lost and wasted significant chunks of available time — some had even just taken a valley route and made straight for the overnight camp with minimal points scored and no intention of going high into the elements.

As we listened on, we began to suspect that perhaps things hadn't been so bad for us after all? Maybe the earlier part of the day and being up high straight away had been to our advantage? Perhaps all was not lost — or that our 'bad' was just that little bit better than other people's versions of 'bad'.

The overnight scores and positions get posted and updated throughout the evening as more and more teams arrive into the camp. It's a regular and sociable short walk from your own tent up to the marshal's tented area, past those convenient port-a-loos (no trenches nowadays) to check on where you are — and to listen and people-watch as others regale their tales of the day. By eight p.m. we were sure that all Short Score competitors must be in and that the latest update would be the final positions for the day — we were eighteenth placed and happy! The forecast was also out and as predicted all was looking good for a total contrast to arrive overnight — beautiful autumnal sunshine was predicted from early morning.

A Karrimor (or OMM) overnight is never a quiet affair, accepting that most people find comfort and warmth in their sleeping bags from the very early evening onwards. As I've previously described, the tents are pitched amorously close together, many actually kissing one another with a cobweb of guy lines neatly arranged to trip any but the most careful night time toilet goer. So, you can lie there in your own tent, feeling quite closely involved in the conversations of those encamped in others just next door, or their snoring or their cooking — and most certainly the releasing of night time gases and groans from a day's over-exertions.

By morning, and the six-a.m. reveille for the early starters, all hope is lost on sleeping any longer. Breakfast routines begin, boiling water for tea and porridge, packing rucksacks with yesterday's still soaking kit and planning how to stay as long in your sleeping bag whilst getting organised for a quick get-away just minutes before your start time (no point in getting cold standing around for too long).

The morning was truly beautiful with the early sun starting to make its presence felt, high up on the fell sides. Our start of eight fifteen a.m. was welcome both as neither too early but then early enough to know that we'd be done by twelve fifteen p.m. and have the rest of the day ahead of us.

This leisurely start was by contrast to our first-ever OMM together in the Howgills where we'd surprised ourselves by finishing well on Day One and being placed something like twelfth or thirteen overnight. There is a starting arrangement used on Day Two of most OMM's called 'The Chasing Start' and it is usually comprised of the top ten teams in each event all starting together at seven a.m. on Day Two. I'm not totally sure of what the logic is for this arrangement suffice to say that Chris and I both considered our overnight position to be well outside of the next morning's seven a.m. chasing start.

So, we slept well and woke in plenty of time for breakfast and the usual early morning routines including the compulsory visit to the toilets. Having made the porridge Chris disappeared off across the wild campsite and I took the opportunity to lie back and lounge in the comfort of an empty tent and the warmth of my sleeping bag and a belly full of hot porridge. It wasn't long before I heard Chris arriving back outside of the tent and detected that he was in a bit of a fluster.

"John, get out, get sorted, quick, quick." I could hear him saying...

"We're in the chasing start and it goes in five minutes."

With no time to question why, I endeavoured to react as quickly as I could, stuffing wet clothes into my rucksack, reluctantly removing myself from my cosy sleeping bag and pushing it in to its own dry bag. You might well know the routine — this was the same as any lightweight camping breakdown but double quick and I was now feeling totally flustered.

Wonderfully, several people from other teams in tents around us started to come to our aid. One guy began unpegging the flysheet of the tent and wrapping up the guy lines. Another rolled our sleeping matts and pushed them each into their own dry bags. They were generous and friendly and clearly enjoyed the distraction — or amusement — of our fluster.

We were going to miss the chasing start but not by long and as we finally pulled our packs on Chris turned to one of the lovely helpful people and thrust our full bin bag of overnight rubbish into his hands and asked if he'd put it in the 'bin' a few paces across the field from where we'd camped. The guy obligingly took the full plastic carrier bag — and we were off, quickly running around tents and jumping guy lines heading for the starting area.

And so, we were away, a little late, missing the infamous chasing start but happy enough to be packed and already getting warm in the first ten minutes of hectic running away from the camp. It was then that Chris started chuckling to himself...

"Did you know that we had to pack out our own rubbish from the overnight camp?" he said to me still chuckling.

"No." I responded with blank expression and still not seeing why this seemed to amuse him so much.

"Well then, I've just given that nice man our full bag of rubbish to carry for the whole day," Chris sniggered guiltily "Poor bugger, oh well!"

My most remarkable memory of Day Two of the Langdale event was just how glorious it was from start to finish. Our navigation went well, route choice was sound, and the ground was covered as well as we could have hoped. Indeed, early on, on Day Two, our slower but perhaps more methodical approach was highlighted as two much younger competitors came quickly past us as we climbed a steep slope up from the valley floor heading for a check point which we'd noted was located at the foot of a large crag. As we dropped behind them in the crisp sunshine, we also noted that they were heading straight for the check point but approaching it across ground leading to the crag top. By contrast as we approach the craggy area we contoured away to the right and then purposefully lost ground so as to then swing around underneath the crag. It gave me great pleasure to then easily find the check point located as noted at the crag foot — and to look up some fifty feet above us and see the two younger runners looking down at us completely unable to reach the checkpoint and having to then re-tread their steps. They passed us some time later but I'm guessing had dropped fifteen minutes through that simple error.

As the day progressed, we were able to find every check point that we'd aim to and even added an extra fifty points which wasn't planned at the beginning (or perhaps Chris had and just never said so). We made a wonderful high-level traverse along a contour around the head of a valley which saved us masses of ground and then scampered across a sun drenched grassy fell side to a final check point. With twenty finals points successfully bagged we began the long steep descent back down to Stool End. Running off — or rather once again chasing a wildly descending Chris — reminded me of other far less enjoyable runs to the finish.

In the Northern Lakes event, possibly it was my first so I'd no idea what to expect, I can recall dropping off the slopes of Blencathra into Threkeld and then picking up the disused train line back towards Keswick. My eager anticipation tricked me, and I simply didn't manage my own expectations very well at all. In my head it was perhaps just a quick ten minutes along the track and we'd be done, but my memory now is of a long drag with tired legs and 'hurry up' drivers that just wanted it to be all done, and it just went on and on as I went slower and slower.

Another memorable — "let's just get back to the finish" run out was in the Brecon Beacons. Here we'd had a solid Day Two in poor weather conditions and pushed hard to successfully find a final check point amongst some wire boundary fences high up on a wild moorland section. It was close to a distinct forest line that would in turn provide us with a convenient handrail along which to run back to the designated course exit and eventually on to the finish. As we turned to retreat from the checkpoint across the moor the rain turned in to driving sleet and the wind picked up dramatically, rattling across the exposed moor but driving, fortunately for us, against our backs.

For the Howgill Fells event the year before I'd purchased a new slightly thicker Montane running waterproof. I'd loved this bit of kit from the start, partly because I found it in TK Max for just fifty pounds, but its extra thickness and protection from the elements were simply superior to anything I'd had before. Now, as we ran ahead of the sleet, assisted by the wind but being stung by the force of the 'wet stuff' against our bare legs, I fell more deeply in love with that amazing waterproof. Every time I pull it out of my bag now, I feel a distinct fondness for it. I find myself nodding appreciatively at others who wear the same jacket — possibly leaving them wondering just why that passing runner was so friendly towards them in particular!

We do all have our favourite bits of kit, I dare say you're thinking of your own right now? Is it for running or cycling or any other activity, open water swimming or triathlons — a pursuit that demands something that will keep you warm, be simply of a superior comfort, that hugs your body, works overtime, or gives you a much needed, psychological lift. Kit is so important, the old adage — 'there's no such thing as bad weather, just the wrong kit' regularly comes to mind. Quite often I find it's a small adaptation or development within the piece of equipment that's so helpful. The longer cuffs on a long sleeve technical feel shirt that allows you to pull it down over your hand and keep it there by pushing your thumb through a pre-placed slit. With the cuff covering your hand, mine even has another slit that allows you to look at your watch without unhooking the cuff.

Back in Langdale we faced our first ever kit check. It felt like being questioned by the Police. You know that you have everything that you're supposed to have, but the very fact that someone is going to ask you to prove it somehow makes you feel guilty or that you'll not be able to produce it when required. Our kit check was a request to see our stove, first aid kit and bivvy bags. This we did, without guilt and were duly signed off and left free to go and find the almost compulsory hot post-run jacket potato.

The sun shone, the teams rolled in, the fells looked stunning and the atmosphere both inside and outside of the event marquee was electric. Stories got told, running partners shook hands and hugged, laughter and loud stories abounded. Somehow the tired legs quickly faded, and plans were already forming for the next event — the 2018 OMM wherever that might be?

Prologue

We finished twelfth overall in the 2017 OMM Short Score event and third Vet Team. A podium finish and one that I'll remain forever proud of. It turns out that those early demons didn't get the better of me and I will live to run another day. Chris already has his sights set on a top ten placing for next time and despite my suggestions that he find a faster partner he remains resolute that I'm the man for him!

Do you know what, with a bit of dedicated training I think a top ten placing is possible!

The Western Isle Challenge
Where it all began…

The truism that everything must start somewhere applies fully to my journey into adventure racing. Quite where my love of the outdoors actually began is harder to define. Perhaps it was the early sailing days being out on the Dee Estuary racing ten feet six-inch-long Cadet dinghies as a four-year-old that has given me a love of wild open spaces that still to this day burns brightly within me. My mother, now close to her eighty-eighth birthday, reflects philosophically as to how little concern she had standing on the foreshore at West Kirby looking out across the Dee estuary at the tiny white sails off in the distance and thinking 'my two sons are out there somewhere' — but she trusted our boat-handling skills and the ability to find our way home safely.

I guess over time that we start to gather around likeminded people. We seek them out and feel comfortable in their presence, sharing stories of adventures past and, more importantly, investing time into plans for the future — things to really live for that pull you to the edge of your seat when you think about them because you're simply not sure what could happen when it all starts.

My good friend John Matthews has been central to these adventures for many years, and it was he who first mentioned to me a multi sports adventure race through the Scottish Western Isles. John and three other friends had done the race the previous year and he was now planning to return describing that first year as simply their 'scouting year'.

John and I first met in the early 1990s when we were both working in the North East. He was initially a volunteer and then later trustee of the charity MOBEX for which I was the Project Leader. Based out of Newcastle upon Tyne, MOBEX (an abbreviation for Mobile Expedition Unit) was a charity that brought adventure education to inner city youth. It did so through the use of a large Mercedes 309 long wheelbase vehicle, that had both the space to carry young people, but also cages for transporting adventure equipment, a roof rack and trailer all to ensure that the 'right kit' was in the right place at the right time. It was a low-key revolution against the traditional outdoor centre, free from the cost of bricks and mortar, Mobex was able to go to where young people needed the support rather than demanding that they travel to a 'centre'.

MOBEX was the brain-child of an inspirational and learned man from Lindale in Cartmel, Cumbria, Brian Ware OBE. I will always consider it to have been one of my life's greatest privileges to have known Brian, it will also be one of my greatest regrets that later in life I never managed to see him during his illness and then death in 2008. Brian typified the British wise old sage. A graduate of Cambridge University he was awarded his OBE for services to geography. Impressively he and a group of students carried a collapsible wooden rowing boat up to every tarn in the Lake District and proceeded to plot the profile of every stretch of water using only a lead line to take soundings at fixed distances across the water. This was all in the aide of studying glacier movement and their pivotal role in forming 'the Lake District'. Brian is perhaps the most influential person that I have ever had the pleasure to know. The briefest of research on the internet finds the following short passage about him:

"It all began through a meeting at the Cambridge University Geography Department. A scientist, Vaughan Lewis, wanted more facts about how glaciers worked. And remember the whole of our Lake District was moulded by glaciers. One of his students, Brian Ware, who had already spent time on the Brathay staff, was asked to take teams of young people into our hills to measure the underwater shapes of all the tarns. Glaciers had helped form these tarns and Lewis believed that glaciers did strange things. How come the overflow lips of these basins were so solid? Did those glaciers once move uphill"?

Brian went on to be the Principle of Brathay, a world-renowned leadership and management school, for seventeen years and was rewarded upon his retirement with a fully expensed trip to Australia. Typical of Brian, it was here that he came across the concept of MOBEX — supporting young students making expeditions across the Simpson Desert. Brian was immediately impressed by the concept and determined to establish MOBEX initiatives when he returned to the UK. Together, he (the brains) and I (the energy) established MOBEX North-East which flourished for more than fifteen years.

Back to 1996 and John Matthews was working for Bass Brewers looking after sales and management in their pubs throughout the region. His heart however actually lay in the outdoors and even more so in leadership development and management training. This love drove him to volunteer for MOBEX and to help organise many an expedition for young adults through which they discovered much about themselves and their own resilience for life and their future.

Perhaps our most notable piece of youth-work was with a group of young unemployed teenagers from an East Durham ex-coal mining community. They were very much on the edge of wildness, involved in petty crime and a law unto themselves. Our mission, through Mobex, was to engage with this group and endeavour to develop their social skills, their personal motivation and ultimately to discover a different, more positive sense of ambition in their lives. Over many weeks we worked with the group and grew to know their personalities and a good deal about the way in which they were living their lives. The ultimate aim for them was to go and stay for a week at a loch-side bothy on the remote Eileen Shona off the west coast of Scotland.

Likeminded and equally passionate about the outdoors, John and I quickly became firm friends and have remained so ever since sharing adventures, races and holidays throughout the UK.

So, for the 1996 Western Isles Challenge John had concluded that he needed a team member who could look after themselves in a sea kayak as well as, if necessary, turning their hand to a stint on a bike or even a short fell run on this relay race hopping across the remote western isles.

The Western Isle Challenges starts on the beautiful island of Barra, made famous worldwide by its tiny Island that utilises the beach at low tide as the landing strip. The race route then takes three days to travel northwards to finish at the Butt of Lewis lighthouse. During this time the team must variously kayak, run, swim and ride across remote and rugged terrain crossing the islands of South Uist, Benbecula, North Uist, Harris and then finally Lewis. The journey is made even more complex by teams having to pass through a number of predetermined checks points whilst also following their own pre-planned route — submitted weeks before — taking in a number of miles 'westings and eastings' that have been stipulated by the event organisers. These miles can be taken at any time during the route north giving teams endless variations as to when to branch off the most obvious main route.

In other words, it is not a straight line drag race to the finish but rather a complex navigational pattern held together by central compulsory check points. To add a further twist every team submits its own route, so at no point are you sure whether the people that you find yourself racing against are ahead or behind you — they may have covered more miles, but there again, maybe not?

Each team needed four members as well as both a support driver and vehicle large enough to carry all the equipment and the people. One team member was the designated kayakist, then there were two runners and finally a cyclist who needed access to both road and mountain bike. The support driver was absolutely essential, as it was, they who needed to transport team members between the different competitive legs whilst also positioning the right outdoor equipment to be in the right place for the next leg, shuffling people and kit around as the race entourage headed generally northwards through the islands. Not forgetting, of course, that this was 1996, an almost forgotten time long before GPS, smart phones and watches that are able to record just about every detail of your athletic life. These were the days of proper paper Ordnance Survey Maps, of compasses and plastic bags to try and keep things dry and having the skills of running with your finger on the map to make reference back to as you covered the ground and mentally recorded navigational features to help to locate yourself, take a bearing then head off again — all in good time!

For those that don't know of the Western Isles, it is an almost impossibly beautiful landscape. Wild and rugged, exposed to the raw elements of the Atlantic Ocean, incredible sandy beaches on the west and craggy, lofty rocky mountain to the east. Endless vistas and peat bogs for miles all around. I had never been there before and was instantly bewitched by the landscape.

Much of the western coastline of the islands is machair, a fertile low-lying dune pastureland. Lewis is comparatively flat, and largely consists of treeless moors of blanket peat. The highest mountain is Mealisval at five hundred and seventy-four metres (one thousand, eight hundred and eighty-three feet) in the southwest. Most of Harris is mountainous, with large areas of exposed rock and clisham, the archipelago's only Corbett, reaches seven hundred and ninety-nine metres (two thousand, six hundred and twenty-one feet) in height. North and South Uist and Benbecula (sometimes collectively referred to as The Uists) have sandy beaches to the west and virtually uninhabited mountainous areas to the east. The highest peak here is Beinn Mhor at six hundred and twenty metres (two thousand and thirty-four feet). The Uists and their immediate outlying islets have a combined area of seven hundred (two hundred and eighty-eight square miles). This includes the Uists themselves and the islands linked to them by causeways and bridges. Barra is fifty-eight point seven five square kilometres (twenty-three square miles) in extent and has a rugged interior, surrounded by machair and extensive beaches.

You're probably by now getting the picture that the Western Isles Challenge was no small undertaking both in time and financial commitment. The Islands themselves are remote even for an event like this where equipment is needed to be carried. The best way to access them is by long drives and multiple ferry journeys. For us, the aptly named 'Conquistadors' leaving from Sunderland early on the Wednesday morning was actually cutting it fine to achieve the Friday morning start. We not only had the long journey north in a tiny Renault Nine to contend with, but then also registration, kit check, briefings, route approval and numerous other formalities before your team became an accepted bona fide entry to the event. Getting 'set up' was almost an event in itself!

Race Day One: Friday

From memory there were about fifty teams in the event, a pretty remarkable entry number really considering just what a logistical juggling act it was to get to the start line.

For the kayak fraternity Day One had actually begun the evening before as we all joined together for a very casual and relatively short paddle across from South Uist to the north beach of Barra landing at Eoligarry Jetty. I say short, but checking the map now I see that the straight-line distance, is around eight kilometres passing just to the west of the tiny islets of Fuday, Lingay and Eriskay, a breathtakingly beautiful paddle in the dying light of the day.

At the time of this event, I'd describe myself as a confident all-round paddler. Most experienced on white water I'd been slowly moving into paddling open boats (often referred to as Canadian canoes) and also getting more and more involved in sea kayak journeys combined with one or two overnight wild camps along the way. The minimum entry requirement for the Western Isles Challenge, was to have your British Canoe Union sea kayaking proficiency — a practical examination standard that required you to demonstrate just what it says on the label. To be proficient in a sea kayak, able to look after yourself in calm to medium weather, coastal paddling, safety and survival with a little navigation thrown in. Being on the water had been a life-long love of mine and so this whole element was well within my comfort zone although the concept of 'racing' sea kayaks had never even entered my mind before the event.

Conscious of the competition, I had been doing some extra gym prep in an effort to be stronger for the event. This had mainly involved using a weird and evil machine I'd found in a gym in Gosforth that simulated the movement of a kayak stroke with light weights attached. Not surprisingly it was the least used bit of kit in the quite posh gym and there was never a problem in just rocking up and getting on it for a thirty-minute session any time of the day. It sorts of felt like, I was gaining some 'specificity' however only time would tell, and that time had finally arrived!

Each team had been issued with a piece of Harris tweed as the team baton to carry and pass along throughout the relay, this came complete with a chunky safety pin. I gamely attached mine to a flap on a pocket of my buoyancy aid readily accessible to unpin and pass to our cyclist (another John — this time John Hargreaves) who would be waiting for me on the shores of Uist when I arrived.

So, the kayakists joint baptism was to sleep next to our kayaks on the beach in readiness for a six a.m. start the following morning. But this was no hardship as the spring weather was absolutely jaw dropping with sun literally unbroken from dawn to dusk, it was dry and beautiful. To add to this heavenly picture, the time of the year coupled with an ongoing fresh sea breeze meant that we did not suffer from the infamous midge at all throughout the three days of competition, a true blessing whilst in Scotland!

With a warm sun slowly setting and a surrounding vista bettered nowhere on the entire planet we glided in great company across the Sound of Barra quietly checking each other out, what 'boat' are you paddling, how smooth does your stroke look and do I stand a bloody chance of staying anywhere near you when things get serious in the morning?

Once on Barra we carried our long sleek sea kayaks loaded with the compulsory safety equipment and our overnight kit high up the beach above the tide line where we would be safe to sleep for the night. As the light faded, we sat in small groups and chatted, many of us full of nervous anticipation for the following morning and some of us with a can or two of beer, or a whisky (as you would do in Scotland) and yet others, perhaps the serious athletes, drinking kinder more gentle fluids. Whatever was in our hands there was no doubt that we were all enjoying a very convivial atmosphere until people started to slowly drift off back to their kayak, their sleeping mat and their warm sleeping bag. A good night's shut-eye was in most people's minds as it was set to be an early start then quickly followed by a day of continuous and vigorous activity.

I have no memory other than sleeping soundly and waking to yet another glorious early dawn at around five a.m. Now, in all these events there is an essential behaviour that we've got to know as 'FAF'. Faffing with equipment is many people's favourite pass-time, checking kit, packing, re-packing, placing it in your sea kayak then taking it all out and packing it again — people can literally lose hours in the pursuit of FAF.

That all said, I am not one of these such people and find it incredible straight-forwards to grab what I perceive to be the necessary kit, throw it together, pack it and then get on with things. Getting ready is a forte of mine — I can do it in no time at all. What I'm less proud to boast about are the number of times that this laissez faire attitude has left me short of the right equipment. The worst occasion perhaps being when I competed in a Trail Quest two-day mountain bike navigation event in and around Kielder Forest in Northumberland. This winter event demanded an overnight at some predetermined wilderness camp. You were required to ride in pairs and carry everything you needed for the overnight ideally either on your bike or in a small pack on your back. The lighter the better and indeed the faster. My partner for this event was a childhood friend Neil Chambers. We duly entered, turned up, packed our kit and set off on day One. We rode pretty well, navigated soundly and, after about seven hours in the saddle, found ourselves at the Day One finish line and the overnight camping spot. As is the done thing in these events, you then want to find your spot to pitch your tent — the flatter the better, preferably dry, near the porta-loos but not too near, a bit of shelter maybe from some trees and also a good place to hang sweaty gear to dry in the wind. So, Neil and I quickly identified our spot and enthusiastically unpacked our backpacks — to discover that neither of us had picked up and packed the tent outer layer (indeed the only layer we were intending to use). So there we were with no tent, it was bloody freezing and rain was forecast. This massive cock-up led to us having to repack our bags and cycle out of the forest back to the starting area where the car was — no short ride in the dark and the deteriorating weather. Not a great outcome after a hard day's riding — and I maintain to this day that it was Neil who forgot the tent, of course it was! Maybe some FAF time might have helped?

Back on the Western Isles in the early morning sunshine we all packed our kit, ate a little and generally readied ourselves for the start time out on the water. There may have been a briefing, I cannot remember, but that said the target was clear — an eight-kilometre mad dash across the Sound of Barra on flat calm water to find our first relay partner and hand over the cherished Harris tweed baton.

Obligatory photos taken, kayaks lined up and muscles loosened we were all ready for the off. The foghorn sounded from the support craft and with varying gusto the paddles were unleashed. Some competitors were immediately thrashing at the water, pumping, hard-focused and determined from the off. There were immediate signs of who were the racing kayakists those that most likely competed every weekend, not necessarily in sea kayaks, but quite clearly who were here because this was their forte, their chosen sport! Others elected for a gentler initial effort coaxing their kayak up to its optimum speed and then maintaining a smooth rhythm that spoke of experience built upon many hours in a sea kayak and a knowledge of the balance between additional effort and limited extra speed. Within all of that bursting energy, I most probably was with the initial thrashing group, kicking up water whilst mentally telling myself that this rhythm and spike of effort was simply unsustainable. A small group started to steadily pull away maintaining their initial rhythm and looking intimidatingly strong. Others fell behind, those perhaps focused on the journey rather than the destination, and so I found myself somewhere in the middle of the field paddling smoothly and telling myself that I must find a pace that could be maintained for a prolonged period of time. Eight kilometres would be less than an hours' paddle and steadily the fleet spread out. With conditions so perfect the single support craft was redundant other than taking pictures and patrolling up and down the increasingly dispersed line of kayaks.

Again, I can only draw on memories — writing this twenty-four years later, but I would be confident to say that I landed on the Uist beach in a position somewhere in the low twenties. Not too bad for a first kayak racing effort which had also provided a suitable insight to the rest of the sea bound competitors. John Hargreaves was waiting at the water's edge eagerly anticipating the Harris tweed baton mountain bike at the ready for a considerable leg north through the hills before turning west for the coast and another longer stretch northwards along the famous Uist machair. Amongst much excitement and shouting from the small crowd he was gone before I knew it leaving me with our support car and driver to load the kayak and head 'up Island' to the next proposed kayak leg.

I fear it would be tedious to work through a description of each and every leg of the day but equally this fantastic event would be short changed if I were not to give some description. The race was underway and as a team we were now very rarely together — not a bad thing with such a small support vehicle. At every planned rendezvous as someone ran, cycled or kayaked in another person left within seconds. And so it should be, we moved as purposefully and accurately as we could throughout the day baked in the welcome sunshine and enjoying the adventure, the terrain and the racing feel all as one glorious big day out. There was plenty of contact with other teams especially at the various mandatory race control points but as each team had designed its own unique combination of westings and eastings it was impossible to say who was winning and who not.

Whilst it was sunny and most definitely warm there was also an ever-present wind that increased in strength as the day continued. One of the kayak legs due to be off the east coast of Benbecula was changed instead to a more sheltered section. I've a clear memory of heading along an ever-widening sea loch paddling furiously into the easterly wind rising and falling to the gathering swell in the company of a small group of other paddlers. The conditions were far from friendly, and it seemed that a subconscious, unspoken pact connected our little group through which we gained a mutual confidence by being in each other's company whilst at the same time pretending to be racing but with no intention of actually losing contact. After a lengthy time of paddling into the elements we rounded a small island and then started the return leg heading back down the loch inland towards the designated 'get out' point and our awaiting team-mates.

The swell by now was considerable with breaking tops, we momentarily wallowed in the troughs between the waves before then being lifted up and surfing along and down the front of the following wave gathering increasing momentum, alternatively paddling then bracing in anticipation of the shape and force that each wave brought to us. It was totally exhilarating and as my confidence grew, I found myself slowly taking ground out of those around me pulling ahead and becoming the boat to chase — just within our little flotilla you understand.

Two Irish Sea Crossings

In a later life when working on the Isle of Man I had the opportunity to sea kayak from the Island to Scotland — sixteen miles or so between the Point of Ayre and Burrow Head, the closest Scottish landfall. We achieved that on a muggy, foggy and docile day before deciding it would be fun to kayak, the very next day, from the Island to Whitehaven the closest landfall in England some thirty-two miles or so distant. That was all good in theory and ultimately, we did achieve our aim, however the weather on day two included a freshening westerly breeze. The combined effect of a strengthening wind and an open sea crossing, once out of the Island's shelter, led to a significant following sea and a long way to go — some twenty-six plus miles from memory. We were just two kayakers together, Craig Whalley and I exposed to the elements and gathering pace with every passing wave.

As the swell grew, I started to lose sight of Craig, if we were both in a trough at the same time it was literally just a sea of grey all around before he would then appear ahead of me on the top of a wave, or I would rise up and glimpse him nearby but below me. At one point during the four-hour crossing I heard him yelping with joy but could not see him. When I finally had the chance to ask him what had motivated his outburst, he told me that his handheld GPS firmly strapped to the fore deck of his kayak had registered a speed of eleven knots as he surfed the front of a prolonger wave hurtling towards Cumbria.

We did have a support RIB that day, however the generous owner of the RIB took the term support with a very casual attitude. He would power ahead perhaps a mile or so meaning that he was a distant dot on the sea ahead of us and then he would just sit and wait until we 'nearly' caught up to him before he would then start the engine and power off again. This did provide us with a 'lay line' for Whitehaven meaning we didn't have to try and navigate however it was really frustrating. Only once on the entire crossing did we actually get alongside the RIB and have chance to hold on for a few minutes to grab a bite to eat and something to drink. The sea was too wild by now to stop actually paddling and, for me at least, to sit comfortably and eat — we needed the RIB to stabilise ourselves.

The Cumbrian coast steadily started to rise above the grey watery horizon and we continued our roller-coaster ride surfing eastwards towards the cliffs outside of Whitehaven. Perhaps half a mile offshore and in an increasingly confused sea we took the decision to say that we'd made the crossing.

Next came the little adventure of precariously holding the side of the RIB and prizing ourselves out of the cockpit and up into the awaiting boat whilst rising and falling on the not inconsiderable swell. Having stayed upright all this way neither of us wanted to have an unwanted bath in the Irish Sea. Safely aboard, and with kayaks stowed each side of the driver's central podium, we turned back into the elements and headed off at speed towards the Isle of Man. What had taken us four hours or so of focused paddling took the RIB less than an hour to cover in a thumping, jolting and spray-ridden straight line — no brace strokes needed on the way back!

Back to the Western Isles Challenge, I had taken a decent lead out of the others and found myself scanning the craggy shoreline ahead trying to identify the 'get out' — it would be a shame to have gained so much ground only to lose it by paddling past the finish! The race organisers though had thought this through, and I easily spotted a distant figure in bright-yellow-foul-weather-gear waving a flag and signalling for us to head towards him. With the following sea and strong breeze, I quickly reached the small pebble beach and found Johnny Hargreaves waiting for me with his road bike ready to take the tweed baton and head onwards.

Day One ended at the very tip of North Uist. It was a running leg, for us at least, to an inconspicuous trig point on a small forty metre summit above the dunes at Aird a' Mhorain. All round we had had a fantastic day without any difficult moments. No one had got lost, I hadn't taken a swim, we hadn't had punctures and our various rendezvous points had all worked well. The team was in good spirits as we stood together at that little spot grinning at the accomplishment of a wonderful journey northwards through this magical part of the world. We were however once again due to be split as the others headed off for the ferry from Port Maddy to Harris and the luxury of a pre-booked B & B whilst I had the joy of a second night sleeping on the beach next to my kayak and making my tea 'en plein air' is, I think, the French saying? As it happened this was no hardship, the weather continued to be absolutely perfect, and with both strong evening sunshine coupled with a steady sea breeze we once again did not have to suffer the infamous midge but rather sat and chatted in small groups swapping stories of the day and enjoying the company of the now familiar faces of the sea kayak contingent.

Day Two

Once again, the race organisers had us up bright and early getting ourselves fed and packed for a six-a.m. start on the water. The sun was most definitely up before us setting the scene for another glorious day, wall to wall sunshine and the by now familiar sea breeze beginning to build. Once again, the wind was from the east and I can recall feeling a little nervous as we faced the biggest open sea crossing of the event — The Sound of Harris. This would be an exposed section of water at the best of times however on this morning we had the Atlantic swell rolling in from our left meeting the freshening breeze from our right. The route, which is a generous description, basically called for us to get to Rodel Jetty on Harris as quickly as possible leaving all the major islets to our left-hand side. After an initial couple of kilometres winding our way out of the Uist narrows we reached open water and headed northeast, the group steadily scattering as the sea picked up. The fast boys, charging ahead with grim determination, impressive as they were with no breaks in their measured powerful paddle strokes. The islands off to our left were nothing more than rocky outcrops sticking above the water but best well avoided as the sea thumped up against them and sent spray into the air accompanied by deep thuds as the water hit the ancient and jagged rock.

I felt like I'd finally started to find my rhythm and settled into it enjoying the trip and feeling comfortable in the elements, this truly was Scotland at its best and it was hard to think of anywhere as being a better place to be. I resisted the racers temptation within me, the inner voice that urged me to be drawn in to racing those that I simply couldn't keep up with. There were paddlers all around — at least within eyesight — but generously spaced and just one support RIB to cover the dispersed field. I recall not seeing much of the RIB at all throughout this leg but did later hear that a kayak had indeed capsized and resulted in the paddler spending a good deal of time in the water waiting for rescue. The other very vivid memory, which will never leave me, was hearing the excited shouts of a kayaker some distance off to my right. I turned to look across the grey seascape towards him and saw two whales cruising along just ahead of him their backs surfacing and then disappearing as they escorted him northeast. It was an incredible sight, enjoyable and memorable from my distance but perhaps just a little too close for comfort for him!

It truly was a glorious morning to remember, and I fared well within the kayak fleet reaching Rodel Jetty without incident and standing at around twelfth place. The pretty little fishing harbour was a flurry of busy activity with paddlers arriving all the time to be greeted by their team-mates, cyclists, runners and support drivers all helping to pull them up out of their boat and quickly pass the tweed baton onwards.

Alongside the other paddlers I looked up at the quayside optimistically expecting to see my own team's familiar faces and anticipating their energised attention, but there were no familiar faces and no shouts of my name and waving of arms and hands towards me!

I landed my kayak and got out, stretching my legs and back before hoisting it out of the water and on to the concrete slipway. Still no familiar shouts, I recruited some help from a bystander, and we carried my long sleek kayak up the ramp and to a small parking area at the top. "They'll not be long," I thought to myself. It seemed a shame that the respectable place I'd managed to attain within the field was now steadily slipping away as more and more kayaks arrived across the Sound then dispatching their team-mate off either on foot or by bike.

And so, I waited, and waited — indeed I out-waited the entire racing field as they all eventually arrived and then left leaving me alone sitting with my kayak at the top of the Rodel slipway.

From memory it was around forty-five minutes later when the familiar grey Renault Nine arrived at speed, bikes on top and full Conquistador team packed inside. They all tumbled out amid a flurry of activity with various clothing and equipment spilling out around them from the back seats. There were raised voices, eyebrows lifting to the sky and emotional gesticulations that gave immediate indication of a story behind the very late arrival.

It was only after the road bike for Johnny Hargreaves was retrieved from the roof of the car and he was pinned with the tweed and fired off at pace up the hill from the jetty, that I began to unpick the story. Apparently, the team had arrived at the relatively luxury of their bed and breakfast the night before and decanted themselves into two different twin rooms. Our leader John Matthews, perhaps the king of FAF, had emptied all of his running kit on to the bed and set about variously sorted through clean gear and dirty gear. Having organised himself, he repacked his clean gear neatly into his rucksack before clumping together all his dirty, wet gear, gathering it in a heap and shoving it into a bin bag and then a separate duffle bag. What Johnny failed to notice was that he neatly gathered up the car keys, left lying on his bed, in with the wet gear and then into the bin bag and duffle. It was in the morning, as they set off the meet me, that he found the keys missing and had absolutely no idea as to where they were. From what I'm told various search strategies failed as incrementally tempers gathered or levels of amusement were worked through. Only as a last resort did Johnny decide to totally empty all of his bags, the keys then obediently tumbling out from the bottom of the last place to be searched!

Back in the race we were once again underway, albeit most probably now in last place and pushing the field along. Johnny had disappeared up the road on his bike and once the sea kayak was strapped to the car's roof rack, we were off to the next rendezvous point to ensure our runner was positioned and kitted up ready to go.

And so, the day continued, variously biking and running.

The journey was dominated by mountain biking and fell running sections through the wild interior of South Harris, most notably A Coileach at three hundred and eighty-six metres right in the heart of the craggy expanse of the island. This section was particularly remote as support vehicles all had to follow the main (!) road up the west coast, a rather circuitous route round to the end of a long run section next to a beautiful sandy bay looking out to the neighbouring island of Taransay. The on-land chunks of adventuring eventually found their way to the relatively populous town of Tarbert, a main ferry port and the start of the next major kayaking section to almost round off day two. This was also a significant milestone in the race as the kayak section, Tarbert itself and the neck of land upon which the little town stands, marks the transition from Harris to Lewis, the final and largest island in the journey.

I have vivid memories of idling on the water in my kayak just off the small beach in West Loch Tarbert waiting for one of our runners to come tumbling into town along the shore path. The loch was sheltered from the easterly wind, a calm, almost tranquil, scene aside from the various shouts as team runners arrived and hailed their kayak buddies to meet them on the little beach. Looking out down West Loch Tarbert a string of kayaks could be seen heading some twelve kilometres in a straight line to the section finish at Amhuinnsuidhe. This was yet another beautiful paddle on a day to relished, to our right were the hills of North Harris, and to our left an opening sea vista across to the relative dot of Taransay, tiny by comparison to its mountainous neighbours. The loch gently opened out and with the breeze pushing us along there was no threat from the conditions, only the physical challenge of catching the team ahead or fending off the chasing team behind. Closer to the finish, in the last four kilometres the route entered Soay Sound and squeezed between some rocky islets and into Loch Leosavay and finally the beach, once again bathed in bright sunshine.

The whole of my team was there, waiting, cheering and clapping as I arrived — a wonderful reception and with the day almost over I just needed to pass the tweed baton to Johnny Hargreaves waiting on his road bike and ready to cover the relatively short ten-kilometre road section almost time trial to the true day end of day two at Hushinish.

Less than thirty minutes later we were all back together properly for the first time in days. The morning's tribulations were long behind us as Johnny Hargreaves cruised into the finish at the road head and we celebrated another well-coordinated day's travelling through such incredible scenery. That said we were all pretty smelly, I was salty, and they were all sweaty and muddy. There was a definite need for some hot showers and a good deal of FAF time to re-organise kit whether it needed it or not! In great spirits we packed the car and headed off for our overnight accommodation in a nearby B & B which for me especially was going to seem like sheer bloody luxury after two nights on the beach!

Day Three

Another early start but once again bathed in sharp morning sunshine, all the teams assembled back at Amhuinnsuidhe, the beautiful fishing cove that I'd paddled into the previous evening.

Johnny Matthews had planned a slightly different

strategy for us this morning, still needing to get some 'westing miles' in, he'd got two of us heading off simultaneously in different directions. For me this early morning was to be taken up by a relatively short run up and through a hilly pass and then dropping down back to the coast before a short mountain bike section. My route headed northwest whilst a second runner, Johnny Matthews himself, headed off north-eastward on a far longer and mountainous route over several significant Lewis peaks, firstly Cleiseval (five hundred and eleven metres), then Ullaval (six hundred and ninety-nine metres) and finally Stulaval (five hundred and seventy-nine metres). This was to be a truly committed run across some of the island's most remote high land and taking in various compulsory check points along the way. Open moor navigation would be essential and route finding amongst very mixed terrain.

Mountain names have long fascinated me — how great are those names on Lewis that I've just listed? Some years later, after the Western Isles Challenge, I did my Summer Mountain Leaders training in the Merrick Hills of Dumfries and Galloway. The five-day assessment involved a two-day expedition with one night out 'on the hill' to allow for plenty of night navigation. We saw a lot of the Merrick Hills, zigzagging our way, practicing navigation and attempting to prove our prowess in hill-craft, there was a lot of time on our feet. But it was the names that enchanted me — The Rig of Jarkness, Round Loch of the Dungeon, The Murder Hole and The Neive of the Spit. These were places that, irrespective of being assessed for navigation, I simply wanted to go and see and to walk across. Years earlier these Gaelic names of the Lewis mountains had a similar impact upon me.

My morning run at this start of Day Three was absolutely beautiful. Steadily climbing away from the tiny fishing village, the well-defined bridlepath ran up an open valley with a babbling brook to our left. The climb, for what it was, didn't have much back to it and quickly peaked at just two hundred and twenty metres above sea level before then descended for four kilometres along the side of a twinkling loch to reach the beach at Loch Cravadale. We had left a mountain bike there the evening before and so I quickly transitioned from running to cycling and sped as quickly as possible firstly across the beach and then along a coastal bridle path to Hushinish, which had been the end point of Day Two. There my journey ended without any handing over of the baton, the team car was waiting, and we quickly packed the bike before heading off to meet the others and see how Johnny had been getting on in his long leg over the mountains.

We were at Aline Lodge well before he arrived in, this was our planned meeting point just north of Vigadale Bay on the west coast of the island and the shores of Loch Seaforth, an impressive body of water running deep into the interior of Lewis. It was from here that Johnny Hargreaves was to use his road bike for a long ride northwards heading into Stornaway, the capital of the whole area and a compulsory race control point in the grounds of the castle. This long ride took us well North and it started to feel like we were well on the way to finishing. The various remaining legs were either on well-trodden drover's roads or indeed back on tarmac allowing for a fast pace and getting good ground covered. There was one final compulsory check point, RC Romeo, as it's marked on my old map, which was a small hut on the shores of a tiny loch in the heart of the peaty wilderness of northern Lewis. This was Mick Whelan's last running leg and he faced it with tired legs and a deteriorating afternoon's weather. It was a long time ago, but I recall that the drizzle had now set in, and visibility had dropped accordingly. Mick set off across the barren terrain, faced with a true navigational challenge of using lochans, stream junctions and the occasional identifiable change in topography to find his way to Loch Foisnavat. From here, having confirmed his arrival with the awaiting race marshals, he then had to head westward to re-connect with the main road at an agreed point where we would take the baton from him. After that there was only the final cycling leg to the finish. I do not think that any of us envied Mick, the best of the day was now long gone, his legs must have been fatigued and it was not a run that anyone would make by choice. But true to his nature and the years of fell running events he had behind him, he calmly set off, good natured and seemingly unperturbed by the remoteness of the challenge ahead.

The rest of us climbed back in the car, crammed in with wet kit and bags, and set off for the short drive around the moorland expanse to the meeting point, SC Seventeen, where in theory Mick would emerge a few hours later. Our mutual destination was the tiny hamlet of Five Penny Borve high up north on the west coast, boasting a little scutch of houses and even a post office which was impressive for this remote part of the world.

I've long forgotten just how long Mick took to do that run — and however long it was I do not blame him — but it was long enough that we started to drive up and down the road hoping to spot his lonely figure emerging out of the drizzle across the moorland to find us. It did not matter under the race rules whether we met him exactly at the point we'd planned, he simply had to go via the check point and then return to civilisation. A long time passed, and we did several journeys south and north — a few kilometres either side of the hamlet eyes straining into mizzle. On one hand it was an impressive sight, the baron remoteness, the peat hags at the side of the road, the mountain backdrop shrouded in the dreik Scottish weather, such a shame after so many long days of glorious sunshine. Eventually we spotted a yellow cagouled figure away in the distance, sometimes in our sight and then suddenly falling out of sight. We quickly realised that the peat moor was criss-crossed by rain gullies which demanded sudden plunges downward and short climbs back up on heavy sticky peaty mud — energy sapping, rhythm breaking and remorseless.

Tired and dirty Mick spotted the car and changed his bearing to run directly towards us. Now was no time for us to drive back along to Borve. I think that might well have pissed Mick off, so we parked in a tiny passing space and awaited his arrival, road bike already unloaded and ready to go. Mick staggered in tired and dirty but wearing his usual high spirits, smiling from ear to ear.

I'd been given the honour of bringing the team home, cycling the final leg north to the Butt of Lewis Lighthouse, the finish line and the end of three pretty amazing days journeying through such incredible terrain. My recollection was that the thin road seemed simply to go on forever. I'd made the schoolboy error of creating a false mental image that the race was all but over. Of course, it wasn't, and I toiled physically northwards cursing the poor condition of the tarmac, every undulation and the freshening breeze straight into my face. Like many rides I've been on, it seemed to go on forever.

Lighthouses seem to add their own character to that 'forever' effect. The Point of Ayre lighthouse at the northern most tip of the Isle of Man is a light that I've sailed away from or towards many a time heading across the North Channel to Scotland or rounding 'the point' on the way to Northern Island. In poor weather it's a welcome light, a handrail in the gloom and signal of something solid and safe. In more fair weather it's a never-ending reminder that you're not getting anywhere fast and, heading south towards it, you start to wonder if you'll ever arrive.

I once supported a team of swimmers raising funds for the children's charity I ran on the island. They alternatively swam one mile each from Burrow Head in Scotland back to the Point of Ayre. In a straight line it was sixteen miles, but their incredible relay lasted for over seventeen hours. My job was to sea kayak next to the swimmer whilst following the lead boat, a powerful cabin cruiser, which navigated the best route taking into account the strong tidal cross currents. The swimmers in fact swam a massive S shape, being first swept west by the currents then back east and final back west again. The straight-line distance was never going to be possible with all that time in the water and they swam far further, most probably more than twenty miles in total. The one constant however, the permanent norm throughout that whole day was the Point of Ayre lighthouse and its lower lying partner Winkie sitting on the stony beach just below. I stared at that light literally for hours and wondered if we were actually getting any closer!

I could see the Butt of Lewis lighthouse far in the distance from my bike on the single-track road. It too played with my head, dragging the distance out, teasing me with its illusive distance and sucking the final energy from my already heavy legs. Head down, I just kept turning the pedals and thinking that the rest would simply take care of itself. The light got closer, painfully slowly but of course eventually I climbed the last gentle slope into the courtyard of the lighthouse cottages and the finish line marked by waving flags and the almost compulsory inflatable arch.

There were claps and cheers from a small crowd of onlookers, various other teams had arrived at a similar time and yet others were scattered around their support vehicles organising and packing equipment. It was an underwhelming end to the race but then after three days of magical weather, incredible scenery, open water crossing, wildlife and sporting camaraderie the end perhaps wasn't really what it had all been about. It's often said that it's more about the journey than the destination and this race had absolutely captured that sentiment. Maybe the clue was in the name, the Western Isles Challenge — that's challenge not race, and it had been very much that from the very start. The route planning had been a challenge, the logistics of people, kit, vehicles, travel and staging. It was never going to be simple. More than any other event I've entered this was one that you really had to want to do.

That evening we attended the post-event ceilidh at a hall in Stornaway and slept soundly full of beer and haggis in our nearby bed and breakfast. It had been an adventure well done, leaving vivid memories imprinted in my mind to this day.

The 1997 British Three Peaks Yacht Race
"That's marketing, we're operations!"

By 1997 the run of 'adventure events' that John Matthews and I had been annually challenging each other to had begun to establish a pattern and was escalating in complexity and endurance. It had started with the Western Isles Challenge in 1995 (another story featured in my adventure memoirs) and had continued through the Lowe Alpine Mountain Marathon on the Scottish Island of Mull, to then be followed by my suggestion of the British Three Peaks Yacht Race in 1997.

I had long been a very keen sailor having first been tipped into a 'pram dinghy' by my father at the tender age of four (with a friend called Andrew Robinson who, as I recall, later competed in the Cadet World Championships). From dinghies I'd graduated to keelboats and had always been a competitive club racer, enjoying many a regatta and the occasional trophy along the way. By 1997 I was living in Newcastle upon Tyne working for a charity called MOBEX North East and owned a twenty-six-foot Swedish yacht of the Albin Express class — called Skoosh!

I campaigned Skoosh out of Blyth Yacht Club, just North of Newcastle, where there were five Albin's all berthed together and a really competitive race scene as well as some great sailing camaraderie. Blyth Yacht Club was awash with good sailors and the summer NECRA Series (North East

Cruiser Racer Series) saw us all racing up and down the coast at weekends as far as Whitby to the South and Dundee to the North. So, distance sailing had become familiar territory and several of us had sailed in events on the Scottish West Coast such as the annual Scottish Series out of Tarbert on Loch Fyne as well as the Scottish Islands Peaks Race.

As a significant step up, The British Three Peaks Yacht Race is a truly iconic event and was one that my adventure appetite had long aspired to gain an entry to.

The Barmouth to Fort William Three Peaks Yacht Race is a unique event combining sailing, running and a little cycling that has become known as one of the toughest long-distance events in the world. The following history and event description is lifted directly from the website and very succinctly captures the essence of an event that is now etched into my adventure memory:

The adventures of <u>H.W. (Bill) Tilman</u>, the climber and sailor who lived in Barmouth, was the inspiration behind the idea, which was conceived by his doctor, Rob Haworth. Rob spent many hours talking to Tilman about his adventures, and as a result came up with the idea of spending his holidays doing a "mini Tilman", sailing from Barmouth to Fort William and en route reaching the top of each of the highest peaks in Wales, England, and Scotland by foot.

The idea of making it into a race came from Rob Haworth's partner, Dr Merfyn Jones. Sitting around the kitchen table on a winter's evening in 1976 Rob recounted his idea for his holidays. Merfyn heard him out and then said, "wouldn't it make a marvellous race". They set out a rough map using kitchen utensils, with bottles to represent the mountains, and worked out the logistics. Merfyn spent his spring break checking out the course, a committee was formed from local people interested in sailing and Bill Tilman was invited to be the race president. This was a fortunate choice since it was Tilman who, when the race rules came up for discussion said, "why not let them just get on with it". There were some rules of course, crews were limited to five, the use of yacht engines was not allowed except when entering or leaving harbour, boots had to be worn on the land sections and no additional transport was allowed.

Seven teams took part in the first race in 1977, and it took those entrants just over five days to sail three hundred and eighty-nine miles, climb eleven thousand feet and walk or run seventy-three miles. Unusually monohulls and multihulls raced together without handicap for the first eleven years. In 1980, HTV made an hour-long documentary about the race, which did much to spread the word; and entries were thereafter limited to thirty-five due to restrictions in the harbours used. At this time the race finish was moved to Corpach.

After several years, the multihulls began racing in their own class but since 1999 the race has been restricted to monohulls only. In 2000, the Port of Whitehaven, an alternative in the first years of the race replaced Ravenglass as the port for Scafell.

Being further away, bicycles may now be used for the first fifteen miles to the mountain: but the runners are then faced with an extra two-thousand-foot-high mountain pass! Incidentally Tilman was also into cycling, having cycled across Africa in the early thirties!

For the sailors, the Race includes many seamanship problems not normally associated with yacht races: the crossing of Caernarfon Bar, the treacherous Swellies in the Menai Straits, the rounding of the Mull of Kintyre, the whirlpools of the notorious Gulf of Corryvreckan, and finally the narrows at Corran where the ebb will stop the boat dead in the water. Thus, a well-found boat is needed and much meticulous planning and preparation is required for success. Yachts are not designed for rowing and to get the best out of oars, which many boats carry, special fittings are needed. The talents of the runners and the sailors must be combined — teamwork is essential.

The runners, both gentlemen and ladies, include some of the finest fell runners and marathon runners in the country. Generally, marathon runners don't much care for running up and down hills and fell runners are equally averse to running on roads. The mountains present problems of their own; there is always snow on Ben Nevis, even in June; wind, rain and mist can make conditions atrocious. Added to which many have to do their running in the dark and for those who suffer from sea sickness they do not even start the runs feeling at their best. The faster the yacht sails, the quicker the runs come around. For the leading boats the runners usually have to do the first two runs, twenty-four miles and forty-eight miles respectively during one twenty-four-hour period.

The Race is a journey through much of the finest scenery in Great Britain. Barmouth itself lies at the mouth of the Mawddach estuary described by Wordsworth as "sublime". The Race has attracted competitors from all over the UK, Finland, Sweden, Belgium, Eire, Norway, the United States, Canada, Germany, New Zealand, South Africa, and

Australia; and has spawned other three Peaks yacht races not only in the UK but also Australia, Hong Kong, and other parts of the world so that today, Three Peaks yacht racing has become a genre of its own.

Every type of yacht has taken part from eighty-eight-year-old prawners to expensive trimarans specially built for the race; even the stars of the BBC series 'Howard's Way' — Barracuda of Tarrant and Alien. Gareth Owen, a three-time winner of the race, was a national, European, and world champion in dinghies, when not at work as a Merseyside policeman. Several skippers have skippered yachts in round the world races, and many others have sailed round the world. Robin Knox-Johnston was another past competitor, as was Brian Thompson who is said by many to be Britain's top offshore multihull sailor. On shore many of the runners have international honours in long distance racing. Helene Diamantides holds the world record for the race from the Everest Base Camp to Katmandu at something over three days! She was the first lady to share a King of the Mountains title with a gentleman — and achieved this in the Australian race.

There can be no doubt that The British Three Peaks Yacht Race is truly an inspirational event and one not to be sniffed at — as we were to find out in 1997!

Pulling a crew together for the 1997 event was, I recall, pretty straightforward. John Matthews, fellow adventurer, was an automatic choice for a fell runner — of course he would be, having dragged me to the Western Isles Challenge in 1995 and the Lowe Alpine Mountain Marathon on Mull the very next year. John needed a running partner, and I didn't have to look far to identify my own fell running friend Chris Dunning. Chris and I had notched up a few races together, Karrimor Mountain Marathons and the Lowe Alpine Event, so I knew him as a strong runner, very savvy in the hills and great company when trapped in small spaces often feeling tired, wet and hungry. This all seemed to fit perfectly with the thought of four to five days on a yacht with four other people.

I needed the skills of an experienced skipper, able to run a yacht well in all kinds of conditions but equally be prepared to push hard and have a real desire to race consistently over several days. For several seasons I had had the pleasure of crewing for Tony Van Hee, an exceptionally accomplished sailor campaigning yachts out of Blyth. Tony owned his own transport and logistics business and had many years of sailing all kind of yachts, winning races, crossing oceans and generally being Mr. Yachtie. He was also great company with a wicked sense of humour and a story for every occasion. Tony and I got on really well, he'd often sit on the back rail of the yacht we were campaigning (usually his own) and allow me to helm. He meanwhile would be observing the racecourse around us, the wind patterns, the changing weather, the tactics of other yachts and the tides, eddies and currents which might work for us or against us. In other words, he was a master tactician and was very often the brains behind a yacht finishing at the front, or near the front of the fleet. He'd often observe the racecourse and the changing conditions before gently suggesting that we tack and head back to the coast or in another certain direction where he thought an advantage could be gained. More often than not we followed Tony's advice and quite often we'd find ourselves at the front of the fleet.

It didn't take me long to convince Tony that the Three Peaks Yacht Race would be a great event and he quickly signed up as Skipper. We then jointly turned to the need for a third sailing crew member and agreed that the likely candidate needed to be a first-class navigator — primarily to help route plan the yacht through various navigational challenges not least the famous Swellies on the Menai Straits, around the Mull of Galloway, rounding the Mull of Kintyre and then the tight squeeze through the Corran Narrows into Loch Fyne on the final drag put to Fort William. There was indeed a lot of 'pilotage' and variables that any navigator would need to take into account.

Whilst I didn't know him well myself, Tony recommended a young sailor called Rory who was a student at the time, and so able to free up the necessary time out to join us for the event. We were then five, and after a few persuasive phone calls, our mutual commitment to a race entry was solidified.

Team Sunsail

By 1997 I had spent some eleven years in the world of the voluntary sector and had become well versed in asking others for support and resources. My career journey and some unexpected twists and turns had, by now, involved me heavily in writing funding bids and shaping appeals to a wide range of corporate organisations to support the work that I was delivering with disadvantaged young people from inner-city Newcastle upon Tyne.

Accepting the above, it didn't seem a big ask to write

directly to major yacht charter business 'Sunsail' in order to make the proposition that they lend us a yacht at no cost and adopt us as their 'Team Sunsail' for the British Three Peaks Race. Looking back now, but perhaps in a more sophisticated world, I'm impressed with myself that the proposition gained traction and that I convinced the marketing team of Sunsail to say yes and agree the loan of a 'race prepared' Beneteau 36' yacht from their marina base in Largs close to Glasgow on the west coast of Scotland.

Of course, Largs is a long sail from the 'Three Peaks' start line at Barmouth in Wales, so we needed to incorporate a delivery trip into our itinerary and ensure that we had both the time and hopefully the weather to get the yacht delivered, provisioned and meet up with our runners the day before the race actually started.

Whilst I will be eternally grateful to Sunsail — and particularly their marketing team who embraced the opportunity to sponsor an entry into the event — I look back on the occasion of collecting the yacht with memories of deepening frustration. The 'race prepared' Beneteau 36' actually turned out to be anything but race prepared. With tired sails, no spinnaker and few, if any, spares. The boat looked every bit the seasoned charter yacht that most probably had just returned the previous day from another week being thrown around the Irish Sea. Collecting the yacht actually turned in to working our way through a hurried list of chores and testy interactions with the Largs shore base staff of Sunsail. We begged access to their sail loft in order to find some better sails including a choice of head sails for different wind conditions. We hunted out a spinnaker, sheets, guys and a spinnaker pole, none of which were on the boat and we took off no end of unnecessary equipment in an attempt to lighten the boat and increase our chances of competing against the rest of the fleet.

I have one very clear memory of challenging the shore team of Sunsail, telling them that we'd been promised a 'race prepared' yacht only to be told in no uncertain fashion that "they're marketing and we're operations" — in other words you're getting what you get and communication within the business didn't account for any sponsored crews wishes! Indeed, they also informed us that the yacht was out to charter the following week and as such needed to be back at Largs by Tuesday evening — no questions asked, unless of course we fancied paying a week's charter fee and keeping her!

We left Largs on a grey and grizzly afternoon, I think the Scottish describe it driek, but with a good following breeze we set sail first heading past Ailsa Craig then on down along the Galloway coast before crossing the North Channel between the Mull of Galloway and the Point of Ayre on the Isle of Man. Overnight the wind dropped, and we resorted to motor sailing along in a sloppy sea which didn't make any of us feel much good. We also determined that we would need to find a harbour to re-fuel at the southern end of Mann. We needed to be sure that we had enough fuel to use the engine if required as we headed past Anglesea and on down across Barmouth Bay and our liaison with the runners in Barmouth. Time was of the essence, and we needed to push on, maximising the speed of the boat whether under sail or under motor.

Port St Mary at the southern end of Mann, was the logical stop to get fuel. It required us to round the Calf of

Man, a sizeable island that is separated from the main island by 'Calf Sound'. This notorious channel of fast-moving water has ferocious tides, swirling eddies, standing waves and whirlpools, all of which persuaded us to use the most southerly route around the Calf itself avoiding the sound before then heading north for a few miles up to the harbour. Of course, as they do, a damp sea fret came out to play obscuring all hazards and demanding that we gingerly navigated the yacht into the harbour and alongside the break water eventually tying up to a fishing boat.

Tony set off in search of fuel — assuming that there would be a 'fuel dock' with ready-to-pump diesel and we'd be filled and away within the hour — at the very worst. We hadn't however factored that marine diesel on the Island, in 1997, was supplied via a mobile bowser service which required ringing the owner who would then drive to the harbour at his next convenience. If, of course, he happened to be at the other end of the Island fuelling a different boat then, well, we'd just have to wait!

In 1989 and 1990 I had taken a year out from my work with inner city youth to travel with my wife as an extended adventure for our year-long honeymoon. We made our way through mainland America, the Hawaiian Islands, Fiji, Australia then back to the UK via Singapore, Thailand, Malaysia, Hong Kong, China and eventually home. I have wonderful memories of all of those places for a whole raft of different reasons.

In Fiji — pertinent to this story — we became used to the colloquialism 'Fiji time' which we quickly came to realise meant 'whenever, not sure, sometime in the future, maybe never' or all of the above and many more things as well. What 'Fiji time' didn't mean was that anything would happen anytime soon and there was no use in worrying about it — it was simply the way in which their beautiful Island worked, and one was best to just relax and go with the flow.

The Isle of Man has a similar saying — Tres de lieur — or 'all in good time', and this was exactly how we were to experience the delivery that early morning of our much-needed diesel as we sat in the cold and damp of the Irish Sea fret waiting, waiting, waiting and worrying about the rest of our delivery voyage and the time pressures which were now steadily mounting. We had just over twenty-four hours to go until the race actually started and we were in the wrong country, on the wrong side of the Irish Sea with too little fuel left to press on.

As these things go, the fuel did eventually arrive in a big red mobile bowser towed by an impressive four by four and driven by a jolly Manx man who then took great joy in charging us well above the going rate to fill the yacht — all at his own speed of course! I feel amply qualified to make this judgement of that days' experience as since then I came to live on the Isle of Man for a period of fifteen years and grew to know and love it for its rugged beauty and its people and their stubborn independent charm.

What happened next has become a blur over the years since this adventure, but I do know that we got to Barmouth by late afternoon and picked up a swinging mooring amongst other yachts lying off the town. No sooner were we tidied up, than a water taxi arrived and we were whisked ashore to register our presence with the sailing committee. As with all of these events whether running, sailing, cycling or triathloning there is the process of registration. Whilst it's a pretty straight-forward ritual where you or the team collect race numbers and instructions, it is also always like the actual 'start' of the event. Butterflies begin to gather and flutter around one's stomach, the energy lifts whilst also those physical niggles seem to show their face once more — is it just me or does my knee hurt just a little!

Back in Barmouth we were keen to make contact with John and Chris who had been waiting some time with not just their own running kit but also the yacht's provisions for our predicted four-day race time.

John and Chris were very much the fell running pair and a sinewy athletic sight to behold as we came alongside the Barmouth harbour wall. Both well over six foot tall, with light weight torsos and a stride length to match a running emu, they fitted perfectly into the surrounding race scene. Adorned in their navy blue 'Team Sunsail' rugby tops and baseball caps they were doing a good job of promoting 'the brand' and generally adding an air to proceedings that gave us some credibility and even perhaps the impression that we knew what we were doing — or about to do! Sailors and runners mingled along the quayside — swapping stories, carrying equipment and striding meaningfully towards awaiting dinghies. Many of the sailors, easily identified in their foul weather gear, stood holding pints of beer and variously gazing out to sea towards the gathering fleet of race yachts and laughing loudly at the latest wisecrack from their gathered friends. There were a handful of multihulls 'dried out' on the mud below the quay, impressive speed machines that had a small class of their own in the event. Their performance on the water meant that they would finish hours if not days ahead of the monohulls, but the strain would potentially tell on their runners who would get significantly less rest between the running legs as the yachts greedily gobbled up the sea miles.

Having done our own envious survey of the multihulls we took the opportunity to join the majority of the other sailors at the local hostelry for a 'planning meeting' whilst also sampling a good, few Welsh beers.

Suitably charged we then grabbed our own kit and loaded the water taxi with everything that we needed before heading back out to the yacht which was patiently waiting, gently swinging on its mooring in the fading evening light. Once there, a flourish of activity saw us stowing food and equipment, allocating berths, running though how the heads worked, briefing John and Chris about the workings of the yacht and having a hot brew before settling down for the night. Our bravado no doubt masking the fact that we would all most probably then simply lie awake contemplating the massive adventure that lay ahead and how we would fulfil our own part in what was to come.

In my own head I was turning over the fact that I was not just one of the three sailing crew, I was also the spare runner should anything happen to either John or Chris. Now similar to other fell running events that I'd competed in with this pair, I knew I could run, I was fit and played sport every week to a good level — but I couldn't run as fast or as far as either John or Chris. The thought of setting off on one of those long arduous mountain legs, of chasing a lanky figure for hours on end and only gaining respite when they stopped to check a map — to be frank, it terrified me and I was lying there praying that the situation would not arise!

Team Sunsail (1997) & assembled multihulls in Barmouth

And so the morning of the race dawned bright and calm. Everyone emerged from their restless slumber and, in good shipshape fashion, immediately packed sleeping bags and other equipment away. The sea-going regime needed to be quickly established including the fact that everything would be stowed safely or otherwise get quickly scattered around the cabin and sole of the boat as it pitched and rolled. There after followed a lazy morning as we anxiously waited, drinking tea and chatting, for the formal proceedings to start. One of the great things about life on a yacht is that there are always jobs to be done, messing around with 'stuff' is simply a part of the life and we easily made up jobs to kill time, whilst also exchanging our own stories and catching up for lost time. Thinking about this now, it's probably one of the reasons that sailing suits me so well as I'm a serial 'unable to sit down for long' sort of character — having endless tasks to do suits me just fine as long as they're not too complex!

Leg One: Barmouth to Caernarfon and the summit of Snowdon, sixty-two sea miles and twenty-four running miles

The Race Committee had set an early afternoon start time with a mandatory pre-start procession of all the racing yachts heading out to sea past the harbour wall. A good-sized crowd had gathered to witness the spectacle and the organisers had a plan of rousing music being blasted out to the unsuspecting crowd and race crews alike. The result however was far less dramatic as the sound emerged through speakers which struggled to deliver the required volume and consequently the desired effect. Instead, so I recall, it resulted in a rather crackly somewhat distant musical effect that was more a reminder of an old British Pathe Newscast at the cinema. It was only missing a well-spoken English accent to make the announcements — but then that would have definitely not been suitable for this very Welsh setting.

Four multihulls and seventeen monohull yachts gathered around the starting area as the ten-minute preparatory signal sounded and we readied for the off. There was little if any breeze across Barmouth Bay and, with sails limply sagging and flogging from side to side in the long gentle swell, our main effort was to stay somewhere near the start line and stem the tide which threatened to push us away. Some more seasoned competitors broke out their oars and sent crew members to their well-organised rowing stations so as to keep the yachts 'on station' in the best possible position for the start.

The British Three Peaks Yacht Race rules allow for yachts to be equipped for rowing. Most crews have well thought-through and purpose-designed rowing machine stations that can be quickly assembled on their decks with rollocks being attached to the yacht's toe rail for maximum efficiency. The aim of course being to give forward propulsion to a heavy displacement yacht. On Team Sunsail we too had rowing stations — two borrowed and somewhat out of date rowing machines which we intended to tie to the deck when needed and also fashion a rowing point for the oars which I had scrounged from Durham Rowing Club. None of this design had been tested as we simply hadn't had access to the yacht until the previous day and our first experience of setting up the rowing stations resulted in much hilarity, as we realised just how ergonomically ridiculous they were. There was little chance that we could get any physical traction from our position high up on the deck line and with inefficient rowing machines the potential to transfer any real energy through long oars down into the water was limited to say the least. It was unlikely that we would be able to propel the three tonne yacht forwards and that was on a calm sea with fresh bodies! Oh well, we concluded that this was an adventure, and we'd simply have to make do.

Fortunately, as we all gently rolled around and the start gun sounded, there was some semblance of a breeze filling in and the fleet started to make progress across the bay and out towards the first major navigational point which involved sailing between Bardsey Island and the Llyn Peninsula. It certainly wasn't exciting sailing and progress was slow, intermittently both rowing (inefficiently) and sailing alongside the dawning realisation that our heavy charter yacht and poor sail wardrobe was better suited to heavy weather conditions.

By early evening we had got past Bardsey and were heading north making for Caernarfon where we were to set down John and Chris for their first run across to the summit of Snowdon and then back again. Full of excitement at finally being underway they stayed up on deck and played a full role in sailing the boat, or rowing, making tea and generally being 'handy'. As night fell, they prepared dinner and sat with us as we now used the spinnaker to run with the gentle breeze. On any other occasion this would have made for a pretty ideal cruise up the Welsh coast — calm and warm, good company and a well provisioned boat. However, as this was The British Three Peaks Yacht Race and we were on a tight time agenda, the conditions only served to frustrate us.

Caernarfon lies at the southern end of the Menai Straits and is easily accessed from the sea once the main channel marker and 'safe water' is identified. The town is dominated, indeed made famous, by its impressive castle and the put down point for the runners was against a large wooden jetty just near the castle ramparts. After a slow overnight passage, I recall that we arrived at the channel marker buoy in the very early hours of the morning. The Menai Straits opened up in front of us and, having passed the mark, we were allowed to put the engine on and motor across to put John and Chris ashore. Many of the other yachts were already there, well ahead of us they had deposited their runners and were variously tied up to visitor mooring buoys or were pottering around under motor looking for somewhere away from the jetty to anchor and await their runners return.

After such a long, slow night passage, the sudden rush of activity — dropping sails, starting engines, approaching a jetty, ropes and fenders, avoiding other yachts and putting runners ashore — preferably without tying up and as quickly as possible — all came as a short lived and welcome frenzy. And then they were gone — into the early morning dampness, John and Chris bid us farewell and then sped away for a twenty-eight-mile round-trip including summiting on Snowdon at one thousand and eighty-five metres!

Over the years, and recounted in other stories I've recorded, I've done the Scottish Island's Peaks Race twice and was familiar with what comes next in these events. After dropping your runners ashore, you know that they'll be gone for a significant period of time — estimated in hours but hard to say with any accuracy when they've not done that specific run before. The weather and terrain is unpredictable and the runners' bodies have just had a night at sea and are out of sync with any home comforts and domestic pre-race routines. As a sailing team member, you need to find a safe place to moor or anchor the boat, do any jobs that have appeared, get some food into yourself, organise a meal for when the runners return and then, importantly, get some sleep! It's the sleeping bit that I find the hardest — not that I dislike sleep at all — but it's a mixture of the guilt of sleeping knowing that your team are out there running a monstrous distance and also the unknown time frame that's being worked to. An additional consideration back in those days was the limited mobile phone coverage and therefore ability to track your runners' progress and get any accurate information as to when they might return.

With John and Chris quickly gone in to early morning chill we set about picking up a handy mooring buoy and then organising the yacht, preparing some food for ourselves and getting some much-needed sleep after the long and rather slow overnight sail. We had only a rough idea of how long they would be and even less of a clue as to just how gruelling the run would be, never mind the ascent of Snowdon right in the middle of that formidable distance. So, we waited and variously chatted, ate, slept and scanned the shore line for any sign of their return. Eventually, at about the right estimated time for their return, I ventured ashore using the dinghy and opted to wait for them inside the race marshals' small marquee. John and Chris would have to pass through this to 'dib' back in and possibly to have their kit rechecked before I could then ferry them back to the waiting yacht.

Eventually they arrived, all long legs and sweat and high energy — a rush of life in to an otherwise dull scene! Once through the check point they were allowed to join me, lifejackets on, in the dinghy for the short row back out to Tony and Rory who had already slipped the mooring and got the sails up, flapping but ready to go.

With John and Chris safely back on board we turned north to sail through the Menai Straits. The race rules here allow teams the choice of either sailing through the Straits, and under the Menai Bridge, which have a fearsome reputation for navigational challenges including plenty of rock hazards and fast currents. These culminate in a section known as 'The Swellies' which involve whirlpools and overfalls at particular states of the tide and all of which demand exacting navigational skills when taking a yacht through. The other option is to sail back out of Caernarvon, heading very briefly south and then west to sail around Anglesey. This choice involves a greater distance but comes with the potential advantages of better wind and far less involved navigation.

For us however, and for Rory in particular, this was a sailing challenge to be relished. Rory had done his homework and was totally confident about his passage planning. In addition, the lighter airs that we had already suffered all of the previous night didn't indicate that a seaward passage would be of any advantage — greater distance and no guarantee of breeze — only confirmed that our wish to go through the Straits was also the right choice.

The gentle breeze took us slowly north as the Straits started to narrow and the early navigational bouyage and transits started to appear. Tony was on the helm, I was tacking the headsail and when necessary, playing the mainsail in an effort to maximise propulsion whilst Rory stood in the companion way, head out of the yacht with binoculars intensely surveying ahead for navigational indicators, but with his legs on the steps ready to retreat back into the cabin to the chart table and his passage planning notes. The yacht picked up speed as the channel narrowed and the current quickened creating a massive marine conveyor belt carrying us along regardless of our size and weight, we were now committed unless we chose to use the engine and suffer disqualification.

Up ahead we started to make out the shape of a few yachts, all of them ahead of us in the race and all of them considerably 'racier' than our heavy displacement cruising yacht. Significantly however the ones that we could see had got their navigation wrong and were now either aground on the mud, keels stuck fast until a rising tide picked them off, or the less fortunate ones, were aground on a rock perch, healed over precariously as the tide fell away but their keels and hulls remained wedged on some rocky outcrop which they'd misjudged. Whilst we cringed at their predicament, I think we also relished these moments as we sped past on the current remaining in deep water and in absolute respect for Rory's careful pre-planning that was serving us well.

I recall at one point Rory standing in his companion way position waiting for a transit post on the shore to align with another transit post on a rocky ledge in the channel. He had pre-warned us that as these transit's aligned then we needed to tack, quickly and efficiently to avoid some rocks not much further downstream. As the posts aligned, he called that tack, Tony swung the helm across and I followed with the sails, winches whirling and clicking, ropes thudding on the deck and the sail slapping the mast as it was pulled across from the old tack to the new one. The breeze was by now strong enough to propel us forwards and away from the rocks, retaining the deep water and our steady progress north and out of the Straits. It was a memorable moment, the grin on Rory's face as all came good and we continued unhampered down the channel — out past Bird Island and into Liverpool Bay.

John & Chris in Wales & Rory navigating us under the Menai Bridge

Odd to recall now, but I think that section of sailing was so intense, so satisfying and so well 'called' by Rory that I have no recollection of where John and Chris were throughout. I do not for a moment think that they were in their bunks below, tucked up in sleeping bags or even sat at the galley table eating — I fully expect that they were equally involved in the sailing and the excitement of that important passage — but I simply do not recall.

Onwards then, into the fading light at the end of an exciting and successful day, but out now across the wide expanse of Irish Sea that forms Liverpool Bay. Whatever they had been doing throughout the afternoon, it was time now for John and Chris to get some rest and to leave this next night-time passage to the sailors. It shouldn't be overlooked that by this time they'd been up most of the previous night, run some twenty-eight miles and climbed over three thousand feet as well as helping to crew the yacht through the Menai Straits. The sailors meanwhile had benefitted from a hot meal whilst sat at a mooring, got some valuable sleep and all whilst they'd been out running. The next brutal leg they were preparing to face was an even more demanding thirty-two mile round-trip out of Ravenglass including the ascent of Scafell Pike.

Tony, in Tony's own way, sat calmly at the stern of the yacht surveying the scene that lay ahead. The weather remained calm and in the far distance we could see the twinkling lights of several off-shore oil rigs and their supply vessels. All of these needed avoiding but without taking too far a detour from our desired straight-line course to Ravenglass. In the modern day British Three Peaks the course has been amended to Whitehaven as the second port and runners are now permitted the use of bikes to cover the distance from the harbour to Wasdale from where they ascend Scafell. Whitehaven has a trendy new marina and excellent yacht facilities, warm showers and local pubs.

In 1997 however, the route was as originally designed with yachts having to make a good tide into Ravenglass to then set down their runners and find a suitable mooring to await their return. The additional challenge at Ravenglass is however that the bay completely dries out at low tide and thus all fin-keeled yachts (as racing yachts are) either have to 'lie down' on their sides as the water recedes or they have to carry aluminium legs which are bolted to the side of the yacht and allow it to stand up on its keel even though that water has gone.

Of course, it almost goes without saying that we on Team Sunsail did not have artificial legs to enable the yacht to stand up whilst the tide went out and so we prepared to have her slowly lie down. Stowing any loose gear, emptying the heads fully, ensuring lockers were closed and locked, gas turned off and goodness knows what else, we fussed round endeavouring to think just what could happen when a thirty-six-foot, three-ton yacht lays on its side. In a fit of enthusiasm, I tied all of our fenders along the guardrail on the side of the yacht, that would eventually lie on the mud. In my mind they would make a better 'soft' bed for the boat to lie on, however I hadn't reckoned for the fact that all the fenders simply floated away from the yacht with the outgoing tide — still attached by their lines they slowly formed an aesthetic line away from the boat and were therefore of no use whatsoever, more an embarrassment to myself. It was a well-intentioned but complete waste of time.

When we knew everything was safe and the yacht was lying comfortably, we retreated to the local pub in search of hot food and perhaps a Cumbrian ale or two. We didn't have too long because of course the tide would eventually return and we needed to be around to witness the yacht come back to life as the new tide lifted her upwards.

In the meantime, good old John and Chris were slogging out the miles through the West Cumbrian lanes. Their approach run was fourteen miles before the actual two mile fell ascent of Scafell from Wasdale Head. The summit of Scafell stands at three thousand, two hundred and ten feet and as the runners literally start at sea level it's not difficult to calculate their ascent as being well over that height, taking into account the road hills and undulations they'd be tackling on their way up to Wasdale Head.

We, of course, had no idea as to where they were, how they were doing and indeed how long they would be. This was now properly unknown territory to us all and so waiting was all that we could do. What we needed, the ideal outcome for this section, was for John and Chris to be back within twelve hours thus allowing to us to escape Ravenglass on the next full tide and head on to leg three, the long two hundred-and twenty-seven-mile sail to Fort William and the final seventeen-mile mountain run up and down Ben Nevis.

To collect the runners at Ravenglass we, like all other yachts, needed an inflatable dinghy on board so as to access the quayside without risking having to bring the deeply drafted yacht into the shallows. This latter manoeuvre may well have been possible at high water however it was highly unlikely that runners would be so cooperative as to both leave the yacht and then return perfectly aligned to high water times. So, at what started to feel like the right time for Chris and John to return, I headed off in the dinghy to pick them up. From memory it was also around this time that the adventure began to unravel!

Chris's wife, Helen, was and remains a Cumbrian GP and as they lived near Penrith, she had decided to head across and see her husband and offer some support whilst they did the run. After pursuing them through a variety of country lanes she eventually tracked them down well into the return leg to Ravenglass. Worryingly, she found Chris still moving but clearly struggling with the distance and the residual punishment of the previous Snowdon leg and both the approach run and ascent of Scafell. Indeed, Chris, my gritty friend of several mountain marathons, was truly in a bad way. When he limped into Ravenglass he did so using a branch from a tree improvised as a crutch, soaking wet, bedraggled and absolutely exhausted.

Helen cross-examined him and touched his lower legs where through gritted teeth he indicated the pain was emanating from. She could barely touch his shins, he winced in extreme pain as she initially began her first once over and continued to do so even as her ministrations became gentler. In the round then it wasn't a giant leap or surprise for any of us looking on when she announced her diagnosis as severe shin splints. We stood around on the pavement of a street somewhere near the outskirts of Ravenglass for only a brief time swapping thoughts as to 'where do we go from here'. Helen predicted (correctly) that Chris would not be running again for some time and that he should not in any circumstances be persuaded by his team mates to 'grin and bear it'. Reluctantly she accepted that we needed Chris back on to the yacht and that we had to catch the now falling tide out of Ravenglass in order to get away up Fort William. In my own head the reality was beginning to dawn that it would now be me who would undertake the final run with John. "Oh joy" I found myself thinking, but it was both a part of the deal that I had created and also an enticing challenge to picture chasing the tall and athletic figure of Mr Matthews up Scotland's highest peak.

So with a very sore Chris Dunning safely deposited back onto the yacht and having sent both runners straight below to get a hot wash and plenty of pre-prepared food into them, the sailing crew stowed the dinghy and efficiently slipped anchor. The rules allowed us to motor directly down the Ravenglass channel and, once again, out into a very calm Irish Sea.

Leg Three: Ravenglass to Fort William and the summit of Ben Nevis, two hundred and twenty-seven sailing miles and seventeen running miles.

Early evening passed as we endeavoured to sail the heavy yacht in very light airs away from the Cumbrian coast. We needed to make significant westerly miles across the Irish Sea passing the Isle of Whithorn, through the North Channel sandwiched between the Isle of Man's Point of Ayre and the Scottish headland called the Mull of Galloway. At that point we would continue further westwards to pass the Mull of Kintyre and then turn north for the long haul up to Fort William.

As I mentioned earlier, I have since lived on the Isle of

Man and came to sail several times across the North Channel between the Point of Ayre, Mann's most northerly point, to round the Mull of Galloway some sixteen miles distant. The North Channel presents a number of challenges even in good weather. Strong tides sweep west to east and then back again, commercial shipping is frequent and fast moving and there are tidal overfalls off the Mull to be avoided if a comfortable passage is to be had.

On this evening however the weather remained quiet, indeed the wind completely died and we tried in vain for some time to fashion the rowing stations and oar lashings so that we could at least try to row. At one point we celebrated as we saw half a knot register on the yacht's electronic readout but then that was momentary, the reality was that we were most probably being pushed back by the tide and no amount of short-term effort would overcome the relentless force of the tidal escalator which was intent on taking us in the wrong direction.

Eventually and to our great relief Tony made the call. It was dark but not late, he asked that we prepare the anchor which was stowed over the bow of the yacht with anchor chain and warp ready to play out from within the bow locker. His suggestion was to anchor away from the main channel but still in relatively deep water and wait out the foul tide until it turned and could then be used to our advantage. So we furled the big headsail to make room on the foredeck before carefully lowering the anchor, chain and then warp to hold us in position.

The Irish Sea was absolutely flat calm and the anchor immediately did its' job, holding the yacht steady 'on station' against the east bound tide. Sitting in the cockpit Tony lit a cigar and relaxed back against the guardrail looking up wistfully at the stars as they emerged and the summer night darkened. We prepared a cup of hot tea and chatted for a while, frustrated at making no progress and realising that our time was fast running out. If the yacht needed to be back in Largs by Tuesday evening — and we had yet to sail up to Fort William, have the runners go ashore, run up and down Ben Nevis — before then sailing the yacht back to Largs — then we needed wind, preferably lots of it and even better if it were to push us north. The reality however was that the forecast was not suggesting any change. Light winds remained and it was now Sunday night and here we were at anchor on the North shore of the North Channel.

With heavy hearts (not to mention heavy legs where the runners were concerned) we accepted Tony's offer of heading to our bunks whilst he took first anchor watch.

For me there is nothing quite like sleeping onboard a yacht. On a calm night there's the sound of the water lapping against the hull, knowing that just a few inches of fibreglass, separates you from the sea. When the boat is underway the lapping becomes a swishing rushing sound as millions of tons of water is separated by the shape of the hull as the boat drives forwards. Up above the rigging creaks and the yacht heels, the sails draw the breeze and provide the power to move the hull forwards. On windy nights the hull rises and falls, sails flap and vibrate, the rigging sings and the wind rushes past whistling as it goes. The hull shudders as the sea demands that it accommodates the passing waves, peaks and troughs that bring the boat to life. In every element being aboard a yacht under power and at night is simply exhilarating!

Recently, in the summer of 2018 I chartered a Jeanneau 42 with group of friends out of Largs in Scotland. After a first peaceful night at anchor in Lochranza we then sailed for the day before running for Tarbert on Loch Fyne. A storm was due in from the Atlantic with fifty mile per hour gusts, not the sort of weather to be out in an unfamiliar yacht with a novice crew! Later that night, or early the next morning, safely tied up to a pontoon in Tarbert harbour, I lay awake listening to the gusts hurtle across our deck driving rain like hard pellets against the topsides, the rigging joining in with hundreds of other masts as the halyards clanked against metal and created a harbour-wide song that was almost impossible to ignore. But safe and warm, snug in my berth wrapped in a down-sleeping bag and knowing we were safely tied up — it just created a wonderful atmosphere to experience and relish.

Back in the North Channel on our Three Peaks adventure, my memory is of being woken by the slow rhythmic clanking sound of the anchor chain coming up over the bow roller. There was however no other sound, no wind in the rigging, no swishing of water passing the hull — we were still becalmed with the only compensation being that the tide had now turned, and we would be being pushed westward with the current. By the time we had all scrambled from our sleeping bags and made it on to the deck Tony had single-handed hauled the anchor up and was heading back to the cockpit to take up the lifeless helm. He smiled in a weary way, how generous he had been to sit there alone since around midnight ensuring everything and everyone was safe.

So we gathered together, the five of us, Tony tired from a long but eventless night, Chris with painful severely bruised blue shins, John Matthews all smiles but with seventy miles of running already in his legs, and then there was Rory and I!

What to do, it was early Monday morning, and we were making no real headway against the race-course. There was no indication of a breeze, and it remained a long passage even to get to Fort William never mind the mountain run and return trip around the Mull to deliver the boat back to Largs. So we pondered our options, go straight to Largs and have the boat back early, perhaps sail south to a port on the Isle of Man or maybe motor sail westwards and across the Irish Sea to Belfast and Bangor Marina where a pint of Guinness would be easily found. In the end we decided with heavy hearts to retire from the race and instead to head west until we rounded the Mull of Galloway and then north up past Ailsa Craig and onwards through Kilbrannan Sound, the wide expanse of water that separates the Mull of Kintyre from Arran. We decided to focus upon reaching Carradale, a small fishing harbour on the west side of the Sound protected from the elements by a high-built stone pier with room alongside for only a few local trawlers and one or two visiting yachts.

Retiring from the event was straight-forwards. It only required a mobile phone call or VHF message to the race organisers to announce that firstly we were safe but secondly heading home to Largs via a different route than first planned. Time and weather were simply both against us and taking the decision to retire now meant we could do some other enjoyable things rather than sit hoping for the breeze to fill in.

So we took our time and slowly motor-sailed our way across to Carradale arriving by late afternoon after an uneventful day typified by tired sailors and runners intermittently chatting and snoozing as the boat ambled across an Irish Sea mill pond. We passed Ailsa Craig, indeed I've sailed past this impressive rock several times but only discovered in 2017 that it is famous across the world as the island quarried for its rare type of micro-granite which is used to make stones for the sport of curling. As of 2004, sixty to seventy per cent. of all curling stones in use were made from granite from the island and it is one of only two sources for all stones in the sport, the other being the Trefor Granite Quarry in Wales.

By early evening we were tying up alongside the pier wall in Carradale only to then almost immediately untie and move away to make room for a local fishing boat returning with his catch of the day. Perhaps it was because we looked so weary, or because we moved with no fuss that there quickly came a knock on our deck and a rusty skinned fisherman handed across a bucket of fresh prawns caught only hours — perhaps minutes — before in the waters of Kilbrannan Sound. We sat in the cabin of the yacht whilst John Matthews set to and cooked the prawns which he then managed to serve with a garlic butter dip which he rustled up from somewhere within the provisions now left on the yacht. I have a picture somewhere of my crew mates, all rosy cheeks, each lowering a tasty-looking prawn into their mouths illuminated only by the background light of the cabin.

I don't recall that we stayed up long that night mostly due to the fatigue of the previous days and also mindful that in tiny fishing harbours such as Carradale it is usual to be woken at the crack of dawn, if not earlier, by the fishing boats wanting to cast off and head out for the day. So sleep beckoned us in the probable knowledge that we would be up again around five a.m.

Sure enough, the sound of heavy sea boots on wooden decks woke me early the next day and we assembled as a crew in almost meditative silence to cast off our lines and let the fishing boats slip out from between us and the harbour wall. In a working harbour, as opposed to a yacht marina, it is usual for the heavy and longer boat to sit against the wall. Being longer there is less chance that they would literally crush the lighter and shorter boat against the stone wall, particularly if a swell is running. The downside of this arrangement, as you now know, is that when they want to go you have to be up. I've heard many a tale over the years of sleepy yachts people coming on deck after ignoring the shouts of the 'inside' fishing boat to find themselves adrift or aground as they'd literally been cast off and left to their own devices by the departing fishing crew.

Being early up on deck and having waved the fishing boats off to their day of trawling up and down the local waters, we made a light breakfast and enjoyed the peace of the harbour. Tony and I decided to run out of Carradale and take the coast road which headed North towards Skipness Point and the route back to Largs. The others were happy to motor along the shoreline and to retrieve us from a beach using the dinghy at a point when we were happy with our own meagre running effort.

And so it was that the morning passed, it turned out to be a beautifully sunny morning run, we trotting along a thin coast road looking out across the Sound our right and seeing the yacht ambling along with three people sitting in the cockpit drinking tea and chatting, keeping a look out for our wave which would mean they should stop and send a dinghy ashore.

I have no idea, no memory of the distance that we ran. It wouldn't have been too far — Tony wasn't a big runner, and even then, had plenty more years under his belt than the rest of us. Perhaps five miles in we called it a day and hailed the others to come and fetch us. Once back on board we motored more assertively towards the head of Kilbrannan Sound and across the open stretch of Loch Fyne to gain the entrance of the beautiful Kyles of Bute and the final run home to Largs.

It had been a wonderful if frustrating adventure. The disappointment of the yacht when we arrived to collect it, the excitement of reaching Barmouth and joining the jamboree atmosphere on the quayside, the night passages, the attempted rowing, the incredible navigation by Rory and the constant anticipation of John and Chris heading off on such massive runs. If only there had been some wind — but then I'd have had to run up Ben Nevis with John Matthews and that wouldn't have been pretty!

1997:
1 Royal Marines Commando Nic Bailey Tri 40ft J Heal
2 Sola Squawk Dragonfly 800 Tri 26ft A Parritt
3 Micro Station Modeler Farrier F-27 Tri 27ft P Newlands
4 Triharda Farrier F-27 Tri 27ft G Owen

1 Myriad IV Tilman Bull 7000 26ft J Thompson
2 Insanity X119 40ft M Dawson
3 Slate Queen Pocock 38ft M Ellis

4 Still Desperate Beneteau Europe 36ft D Williamson
5 Universal Hart Beat Swede 75 52ft J Harding
6 Maverick Owen Clarke Open 30ft C Manzoni
7 Highwayman Beneteau First Class 8m M Slack
8 Jailbird J-80 26ft D Bursnall
9 Galahad Contessa 38ft I Jones
10 Spirit of Casares Freedom 35 33ft B Metcalf
11 Aratapu Koonya steel cruise 38ft H Clay
12 Assent Contessa 32ft W Ker

Retirements (6): Catriona (R Carter), Shining Dancer (N Murray), Lodestar (I Hudson), Uphill Racers (D Hearsey/P Curtis), **Sunsail (T Van Hee),** Joint Venture (B Porter)

The Wild Man of Peanmeanach

I first came to know "Peen-mune-ack" in the late 1980's when, after leaving Newcastle Polytechnic with a Bachelor of Arts Degree in Sports Studies, I started working for a small local children's adventure organisation. The sole aim of the charity was to get children and young people out of the 'priority areas' of the city and into the beautiful countryside of Northumberland, the Scottish Borders and The Lake District.

"Newcastle Children's Adventure Group" (NCAG) organised Adventure Days and Adventure Weekends throughout the school term and a willing group of trained and vetted volunteers readily gave up their time to take and look after the children in no end of wild and remote places — planning their adventures and trying their very best to give the young people fantastic memories.

I had never heard of the concept at the time — but I believe that building 'a reservoir of happy memories' is a recognised and valued therapeutic tool and equally applicable to all of us, young and old, to build up and carry with us as a hidden tool of resilience for all our years.

In its own way, this simple and small charity was helping those children to create some semblance of their own reservoir. They got to sleep in village halls with their friends, play in mountain streams, build dens in the forest, climb hills and watch sunsets from the top, swim in lochs and tarns and spend time with people who knew and understood the power of the outdoors and the impact that a sound adult role model could have upon those that perhaps hadn't had the best start in life.

As the charity grew and became more sophisticated, we started to add week-long adventure holidays to more remote locations, as well as coaching the children in specific outdoor skills such as camp-craft, climbing, river kayaking and sea kayaking. These were introduced in the knowledge that they would make a 'journey' possible using those new skills. Journeying in the outdoors is powerful and provides an ever-changing medium through which young people and adults alike can discover important qualities in themselves, independence and interdependence, coping skills, determination and an understanding of beginnings and endings.

In time we took many groups away. There were the teenagers who went white water kayaking to France in the Ardeche Gorge, the Tarn and the Lot rivers. We travelled to Norway several times — sea kayaking many miles and sleeping rough on the fjord banks at night before walking high up on to the Hardanger Vidda plateau and sleeping out for several nights in sub-zero temperatures.

We journeyed by minibus and trailer to Romania, not long after the overthrow and eventual execution of dictator Nicholae Ceaucsescu, and worked for two weeks at a children's orphanage decorating and endeavouring to improve the environment for the children living in desperate circumstances. I witnessed tears from street hardened 'unemployable' Geordie teenagers as they left those Romanian orphans behind, realising just how fortunate they actually were to be returning to their council flats in some of the North East's most disadvantaged communities, but nevertheless better off than any Romanian orphan.

We even managed to go to the Algonquin National Park north of Toronto and lived for nearly three weeks out of open canoes in the remote wilderness with bears and cougars, and with that, not many sounds nights' sleep! There were just eight young adults on that trip — four able bodied and four with considerable disabilities. We all canoed together and shared every chore and task over the time. My strongest memory is of just how resilient the young people with disabilities were compared to their able-bodied friends. They were far better at adapting to their new wilderness environment and to the hardships of canoeing all day, sleeping on remote beaches, cooking over an open fire that they had to gather and make themselves, packing out everything you packed in and tolerating the highs and lows of expedition life in which they got to see and know people in the most intimate of circumstances. My canoe mate was a young woman named Maria who had spina bifida but was able to sit on the front canoe seat partially propped up so she could paddle. Most days Maria sat there in a splendid sunhat not doing too much paddling but rather commentating on the day, the sights, the group and just being the fantastic character that was 'Maria'. I began to think of her as Audrey Hepburn from The African Queen — sitting there floating along holding court — and so started our wonderful friendship 'Audrey & I' throughout three weeks of amazing wilderness paddling — treasured memories!

Somewhere amongst all of these adventures I began to hear tales about this wild and remote Scottish Bothy, West of Fort William. Rumour had it that it was only accessible by foot or boat, sitting on the Ardnish peninsula in the Western Highlands. Challenging to get to, but once there it's position was rumoured to be breathtaking standing proudly against the elements raised above a beautiful beach looking out across The Minch towards the Island of Eigg and in the further distance to the Ardnamurchan peninsula.

The Scottish Mountain Bothies Association has managed and maintained these remote buildings for many years. Their aim is to preserve the integrity of the buildings ensuring that they are watertight and have rudimentary sleeping platforms within them to afford adventurers at least a dry overnight stop in some of the wildest parts of both Scotland and England. They have become destinations in their own right with people shaping their weekends around reaching and spending a night or two in them, ticking them off almost like train spotting — but better!

I knew early on that I wanted to visit Peanmeanach. Wild places have always called out to me and particularly those that are on the coast, the draw of water, beaches, cliffs and surrounding wilderness are an intoxicating mix that I've found hard to refuse for as long as I can remember.

Friends within NCAG regaled stories of walking and sea kayaking into Peen-mune-ack before spending heady days there in bright Scottish sunshine — happy being cut off from everyday realities engaged mostly in creating your own world of exploration, adventure and close living with like-minded individuals indulging in a brief and wonderful basic existence.

Only now have I had the time to research that Peanmeanach is in fact Gallic for 'middle farm' and that in its day there was a small community of one hundred and fifty people there forming a fishing village including being the post office for the whole of the Sound of Arisaig area. The villagers also kept black cattle and sheep and no doubt had a hardy existence in surely one of the UK's most idyllic locations — on a good day!

Quoting directly from The Bothy Bible (Geoff Allan 2017) "Pean derives from *peighinn* meaning 'pennyland': twenty of these each within a farm, made up an 'ounce' of land, an acreage capable of producing an ounce of silver in rent. *Meanach* simply means middle... in the late nineteenth century the bothy was the post office for the whole area around the Sound of Arisaig. The village's demise followed the completion of the railway in 1901, which bypassed the peninsula and focused trade on Mallaig.

But sadly, in my days with NCAG, the time and

opportunity didn't arise and I never got the opportunity to drive north with a group of young people and to make that journey across the Sound to the bothy. The name however remained etched in my mind as were the old grainy pictures that got passed around of that beautiful spot on the Scottish west coast.

Peanmeanach Bound

It was in the late summer of 1999 that the opportunity finally arrived for me to travel north and visit Peanmeanach. The August Bank Holiday weekend lay empty until two friends, Simon and Tracey, suggested we go for a few days' sea kayaking. These two were and remain the ultimate outdoor couple. Their strong emotional bond includes a seemingly never-ending enthusiasm for adventure, they're both joined at the hip and pretty much up for anything that takes them outdoors and into the wilderness. It didn't take me long to accept the invitation and begin to assemble my own kit.

As with all such trips and like many thousands of other weekend adventurers, we bolted out of work on the Friday to pack the car with the necessary selection of outdoor kit, kayaking equipment, tents, sleeping bags, stoves and food for the weekend. Peanmeanach was firmly targeted as the destination with at least one night reserved to sleep over in that iconic bothy.

All these years later my memory is vague as to what actually prevented us from leaving that same evening, but I do know that in the end we stayed at Simon and Tracey's in Hexham and treated ourselves to a few Friday night beers, always good preparation for a weekend away (or it was in those younger years!) We drove up to Scotland early the next morning with the aim of reaching the launching point for our kayaking trip, Glenuig, by early afternoon. In theory this would leave us time to get organised, pack our kayaks and paddle across the Sound of Arisaig and on to the beach just outside of Peanmeanach around tea-time, perfect!

And that's nearly how things went. We set off early and made good time up to and through Fort William before heading further west to the tiny village of Glenuig which lies across the Sound from Peanmeanach. The village is a collection of just a few cottages, a village hall and importantly a pub which is huddled down into a cove not far above the waterline but sheltered from the prevailing westerlies by a bluff of heather strewn land.

It was when we arrived, that things started to change, as the weather wasn't looking too good. There was a strong easterly wind blowing down the Sound and a sea was starting to build. The forecast was for it to worsen as the afternoon went on.

Tracey was instantly clear and very vocal that she didn't fancy the paddle in those conditions particularly in a loaded kayak and the wind blowing at ninety degrees across the necessary route to the bothy. Those of you who paddle will know that kayaking either straight into the wind or heading straight downwind is pretty manageable — but paddling across the breeze is far more challenging. If you add a cross sea, then things can start to get really interesting!

So, logic being as it is, we retreated into the pub and soon found a seat close to the open fire which, despite the summer month, was roaring away almost as if it had been prepared in anticipation of the impending storm.

Simon and I were both Guinness drinkers and the Glenuig Inn served a quality pint. The intoxicating mix of a warm pub, roaring fire, weather closing in and cold Guinness was fantastic. So, we indulged in more Guinness and occasionally took turns to go outside and inspect the weather, updating one another on just how much things were improving out there — perhaps there was a window of opportunity?

With growing optimism (or perhaps Guinness-fuelled bravado) we surmised that if we were quick, we could make a hasty get away and beat the forecasted storm, get ourselves across to Peanmenach and have the night that we'd planned.

And so, we did. We unloaded our kayaks from the car roof-rack, packed all that we needed equally balancing the load in to the fore and aft lockers before tightly sealing them with their waterproof hatches and carrying the boats down to the shoreline. The trip was on and we were off!

The journey across was, from memory, pretty straight-forwards. I recall that there were some tears from Tracey as the swell grew and the occasional gust of wind did its best to unbalance us all, a hasty low brace stroke being needed to just ride out the passing wind and regain full balance before paddling on and maintaining the momentum needed to keep the kayak stable.

For those that don't sea kayak — the long and relatively narrow design of a sea kayak makes it most stable when it has momentum and also when it is well packed to sit low in the water but preferably in balance with an even waterline along its whole length. A heavily laden sea kayak can take quite a few initial powerful strokes to get the boat up to speed but once momentum has been gained the kayaker can relax a little and just paddle to maintain that speed. Paddling style is slightly different to that used on white water as the sea kayaker uses their upper body more with straighter arms rotating through the strength of their back using the latimus dorsae muscle group. This approach allows prolonged paddling as sea journeys can clearly go on for some time.

We arrived at Peanmeanach in deteriorating weather but the bothy stood in a well-sheltered spot, hunkered down behind a small hill, for that day's wind direction. We glided gently on to the beach with just small waves to help us carry enough momentum to drive the kayaks' noses gently up just high enough to allow an exit from the boat without getting too wet, feet and ankles dipping into the chilly Atlantic water. In good kayaking fellowship we then helped one another carry the boats up the beautiful sandy beach, through seaweed and ocean debris at the high-water mark to the tussock platform in front of the bothy.

Setting the boats down we moved almost in unison to the front door, all of us eager to see what lay within, who else might be there and to make an initial assessment of just how comfortable or uncomfortable the night was going to be in this wild and beautiful location. Not that we really had much choice at that moment as it would be a brave person, in the rising wind with worse weather forecast, who'd chose to paddle away at this time of the early evening.

It's important at this stage to attempt an accurate description of the layout inside Peanmeanach.

The door sits at the centre of the building with rooms to both the left and the right. As you enter through the front door there is, immediately ahead of you, a heavy, steep and wide wooden step ladder that goes up through a hatch cut through the rafters of the 'ceiling' that allows people to then sleep up in the roof space on a well-made floor below the sloping roofing tiles.

Downstairs, with stone flooring throughout, the room to the left has a good large open fire and an elevated sleeping platform along the back wall and wooden benches set along the front wall running underneath the window that looks out to sea. The room to the right was the same (from memory) but without the luxury of the open fire and so potentially much colder. As with all bothies there is a large chest within which non-perishable food can be left by those that might have been to the location and moved on, without the need for all the food they've carried in. The generally accepted bothy law, if there is such a formally written thing, is to leave food for others and to always leave wood and kindling for those who might arrive next so that they can build a fire even on a wild and wet night to get warm.

But for us, in the dwindling light, there was no such problem as the fire was already set, gently crackling away. Whilst the bothy was empty, there were signs that one or perhaps more people were already in occupation and well settled in. A sleeping bag was laid out on the platform, a small axe lay next to some freshly cut wood, a saw was hanging on the wall and a rucksack was propped up with various clothes either hanging to dry or laid next to the sleeping bag. Pretty standard bothy behaviour really and we smiled to think that we had company for the night and every chance of a good chat with a new 'friend' in the making.

Having got the lay of the land we went back outside to empty our boats of the necessary kit needed for the evening.

Sleeping bags, roll mats, food, stoves, dry clothes, head torches and the ever-essential bottle of whisky and wine that seem to fit so neatly through the hatches of a sea kayak and, of course, weigh almost nothing to transport with you on all occasions! We then rolled the boats over in a line against one another to firstly stop them getting any overnight rain-water in, and secondly to make a heavier object for the wind to buffet against, left tight against the bothy wall but out of the way in case any further adventurers happened to arrive in the growing dark.

We re-entered the bothy and began to get ourselves organised — opting to sleep 'up in the rafters' primarily out of respect for the fact that someone was already there and may not want us all 'crashing' on the platform next to them without at least meeting them first.

I can't recall just how long we'd been settling in before the door burst open, heavily swinging back on its hinges and banging noisily against the stone of the door surround. I momentarily glimpsed the rain, now lashing down in the fading light of the evening, before the entire doorway was filled with an absolute bear of a man. Long scraggly hair soaked from the rain, a thick dark beard hiding weathered skin and a physique which reminded me of contestants I'd seen in the "World's Strongest Man" competitions when you can't quite work out if they're overweight or simply muscle bound around a massive skeletal frame. Whatever the case — this Peanmeanach wild man was very big!

From our perspective we were sitting next to 'his' fire, taking our warmth from wood that he'd collected and left generously burning away in the stony hearth. With that in mind we were, of course, quick to our feet and to walk the few paces across the bothy to the doorway in order to greet him almost like a long-lost friend returning from the cold. With a smile he stretched out his hand, as big as a frying pan and dwarfing mine, to shake hands and make our acquaintance. All these years later I have no recollection of his name but do recall him as a quiet man, a gentle giant and immediately generous to offer seats around the fire and the suggestion that we could all eat together sharing the warmth of the flames and good company on this now stormy Scottish west coast evening.

And so, the true story begins…

We prepared food, cooked and ate together happily chatting and sharing stories of adventures, sea kayaking, hill walking and mountaineering, the west coast and wild places that we'd visited or would love to visit. Of course, we opened the wine and shared it around — somewhat disappointed that we only had one bottle and when shared between four of us it offered little more than a glass each! I say glass — but to be accurate it was actually a blue plastic camping beaker with a distant taint of tea or coffee or even perhaps soup — remnants of other adventures and times when a hot drink had been very welcome perhaps sheltered behind a rock or on a river bank and drinking some hot offering made much earlier that day in readiness for the lunch stop.

As the evening drew on the rain increased in intensity drumming on the roof driven harder by the wind, which must have swung around to the west and was now rattling the windows as if it wanted to join us by the soft glowing warmth of the bothy fire. With the wine gone we opened the whisky and our Scottish friend welcomed the first few drams that we offered him, his cheeks beginning to glow whether it was from the fire or, more likely, the effect of the alcohol which was flowing freely and lubricating the conversation in a very convivial way. There really can't be many things better than a wild stormy night, a warm bothy, good craic and a quality Scottish malt — we were all aglow and very happy to be just where we were.

Now well lubricated our friend began to talk more freely, describing how he had walked into Peanmeanach via the six-mile hill path and had done so some several weeks earlier. His intention, which was now the reality, was to live in the bothy for the entire summer season. By day he went out beach combing, collecting wood and wandering along the shorelines local to the bothy, his primary activity though was collecting cockles and winkles along the coast.

He told us that he would fill his sixty-five-litre rucksack with this shellfish hoard about once a week before then heading off back across the hill path to the nearest road which ran north and south, north to the fishing village and port of Mallaig or south to Arisaig. Once at the road he'd endeavour to hitch a ride and then sell his beachcomber booty to the fish yard in Mallaig. On a good day he could make around sixty pounds, give or take, depending upon the price being paid at the time. He'd then head straight to the local Co-Op store and invest his fishy winnings in food supplies for the coming week, carefully wrapping them in plastic bags to prevent them from becoming totally 'fishy-fied' on the return journey back by foot, car and ultimately hill path to Peanmeanach.

He'd been living this routine now for close to eight weeks and seemed very happy with his lot. He said that few people had been through during the summer, the odd walking group who might stay just for the afternoon and enjoy the peace and tranquillity of the spot, a few more committed hikers who would stay over for the evening and the occasional small group of sea kayakers who'd stop for the evening or just paddle on after having a brew up on the beach. It all sounded very tranquil, almost idyllic but also quite lonely.

So I asked him why? It seemed like the obvious question. Why did he choose to spend his time here, in this remote place mostly cut off from others and exposed to the extremes of the elements from beautiful sunrises to westerly storms and quite probably all and everything in one single day?

His answer took us all by surprise.

Our new friend told us that he was in fact a self-medicating schizophrenic from Bell Size Park in Glasgow. Some time ago he'd taken the decision that the city and his life there weren't helping him and that his heart actually lay out in the wilds. He knew of Peanmeanach from boyhood adventures and so decided to remove himself from Glasgow and retreat to a better place. An integral part of the plan was for him to stop taking his medicine and live a better and more healthy existence away from the pressures of bad influences and mundane city routines where being unemployed and bored didn't help him feel worthwhile.

The only issue he told us, looking slightly embarrassed, was that his mental health challenges and his moods, indeed his whole new non-medicated routine, were only ever put at risk through indulging in alcohol!

The room fell silent. Simon, Tracey and I simultaneously

glanced sideways at one another, this revelation had come a little too late for us to do any more than smile somewhat nervously and mutter some muted and ineffective responses. It was useful of course to know that we were now holed up with a bear sized self-medicating schizophrenic, who'd had a good deal to drink and who had various sharp instruments hung around the walls of this remote bothy where no one else was going to arrive certainly now, on this rain and wind-swept evening!

So the mood had suddenly changed, our enthusiasm for sharing the expensive Scottish malt had dried up as had the attraction of the warm fire. We now seemed united in extracting ourselves subtly but swiftly with a view to a tactical retreat to three warm sleeping bags up in the rafters of the building.

Again, time has dulled my memory as to how we removed ourselves from the company of 'the wild man'. I don't recall that it was difficult or indeed that our friend was in anyway aggressive or inappropriate, but remove ourselves we did and I expect we giggled our way up the steep step ladders to the 'relative safety' of the platform above.

The square hole cut in the floor gave way to nothing more than an expanse of wooden floorboards with the tiled and uninsulated roof sloping down to the four corners. It was a dusty, and draughty space, the tiles clinked and rattled a little as the stronger gusts of wind blew along the sloping face of the building.

We had lined our toasty warm duck down sleeping bags up, all on thermarests — those wonderful sleeping mats that revolutionised sleeping outdoors doing away with the impact of cold floors and hips, bad backs and all-over dull body aches in the morning. My bag was next to the hatch and step ladder, followed by Tracey in the middle, and then Simon last of all, furthest from the hatch. Looking back, this seems almost like a chivalrous act, having Tracey somehow protected in the middle, but I can't even now think that that was the intention just more likely how the arrangement fell in to place on that particular evening.

So we all snuggled down and whispered jokes about the evening and the 'wild man of Peanmeanach', trying not to giggle too loudly and disturb him downstairs. We heard him readying himself for bed, going outside — to pee no doubt — and then coming back in causing a rush of cold air up the step ladder and into our sleeping space. The fire still crackled away downstairs and certainly I felt a pang of envy at the thought of him settling down on the sleeping platform next to the fire and dozing off with the warmth of the flames on his face.

In my modern-day life, of work and travel, of 'corporate' responsibilities and of sometimes waking at night churning and turning over mental challenges around issues that need considered decisions where personalities might clash or funds may be jeopardised — I make mental reference back to nights such as that then in Peanmeanach. I think of the wind howling outside and the rain clattering on the roof, but then of being warm within my sleeping bag and feeling drunk and mellow and falling to sleep so content. I can imagine myself back there and feeling so cosy and tired — and it helps me remove myself away from my modern day worries and to fall back to sleep, in my mind back in a bothy all warm and toasty, despite the storm outside!

It was sometime in the early hours that my sleep became disturbed, my first semi-conscious senses detecting a dull dripping sound but then, as my mind untangled itself from the cobweb of sleep, the very light splashing of water on to my face. I lay there on my back now fully awake and waiting somewhat optimistically in the hope that the drip was just a one off. Of course, it wasn't and only seconds later another drip fell from the tiles just feet above my head and landed perfectly upon my exposed forehead — light but cold, a perfect west coast version of Japanese water torture and all arranged just for me! How could I possibly have chosen this spot so perfectly aligned to possibly the only small hole in the roofing tiles and most probably the only drip for absolutely miles around — on my forehead!

It was like waking in the early hours, knowing that you need a wee, but having the dilemma of whether you get yourself out of bed and take that wee — and by doing so you fully wake up and have the hassle of the short journey to the bathroom — or of turning over and ignoring the urge in the hope that you can get back to sleep and make it through to your proper waking up time? You know in your head that you should get up but then your heart wills you to stay put, to stay warm and persuades you that you can make it through to the alarm.

So there I was, my dripping dilemma was similar — I could cover my head and face in the hope that I could get back to sleep but then I didn't want a wet sleeping bag and I felt sure that the dull thud of each drip would only consolidate my frustration and what's more, I'd be waiting for that next dull thud!

I wrangled with the dilemma and stayed put for some

minutes, now counting the drips, moving a little to one side only to realise that the drip landed on my thermarest and then ran down underneath my sleeping bag to wet me from beneath.

Hurrumphing to myself I eventually did the right thing, reaching out to unzip the side of my bag and folding my legs out in to the cold of the night air. As quietly as possible — so as not to wake Tracey or Simon — I extracted myself from the sleeping bag and dragged it and my thermarest across the floor to a dark corner furthest away from the hatch opening and remote from Tracey and Simon.

Once there I reorganised myself and climbed back into the residual warmth of my bag. No sooner was I back in that enveloping comfort than I was back to sleep silently congratulating myself on having the motivation to sort the situation and content that I could now sleep soundly until first light…

"Tracey, Tracey… where's John? He's gone, he's been taken! Tracey, its John… he's gone. I think the wild man's taken John, he's gone!"

I awoke to the hushed but frantic voice of Simon who'd clearly woken up and realised that I was no longer there lying next to Tracey as I had been when we'd fallen asleep several hours earlier. Silently, and tucked away in my dark corner I smiled to myself — this was going to be fun, let's just keep quiet and see what happens.

Tracey didn't respond at first, still groggy, cocooned in her sleeping bag and toasty warm against the chill of the night air. Simon however was wide awake and began shaking her, "Tracey, wake up, John's gone. There's nothing there — see where he was lying, his sleeping bag and everything have gone!"

There followed a good deal of shuffling which I could only imagine was Simon extracting himself from his own sleeping bag in a desperate attempt to look down through the hatchway to the stone corridor below. So focused was he on his own misperception that 'the wild man of Peanmeanach' had dragged me down through the hatch in the dark of the night — that he never once looked up and around himself. There I was, no more than five metres away, stifling my giggles and peering into the dark to see just what he was doing.

"I'll have to go down there and see what's happening," said Simon. Tracey was now just about reconnecting with the world and mumbled that, in her view, I'd probably just got up to go outside for a pee.

"If that's the case, then why would he have taken his sleeping bag Tracey!" exclaimed Simon — who was by now sounding impressively worried about me. In my dark little hiding place, I began to feel a real affection for this friend of mine who was clearly very worried indeed thinking that I'd been snatched by a self-medicating schizophrenic whom we'd innocently plied with alcohol.

"Right, I'll need something to defend myself with," said Simon with an edge to his voice, "what have we got that I can hit him with?"

So, now came the dilemma — to keep quiet and witness my good mate Simon descend through the hatch armed only with the battery pack of a Petzl head torch to defend himself with against a bear of a wild man — or to speak out now and save him the humiliation of going in search of me downstairs only to find our friend fast asleep next to the dying embers of the fire?

"Simon, I'm here you bloody idiot, over here in the corner! What's all the fuss about?"

In all my years I don't think I've ever heard such initial relief in someone's voice so quickly followed by an edge partly made of amusement and partly of embarrassed anger, "John, thank God you're there, I thought you'd been taken — I did really, and you've been there all the time — you bastard, and you never said a word!"

The bonds of friendship are formed in many ways often through sharing experiences that create memories that will never be lost. Simon, Tracey and I were all friends already and had shared many adventures in all sorts of weathers and adventurous situations — but that night at Peanmeanach has become special in our own tight-knit web of folklore.

We saw the wild man once more during our long weekend along that coastline. True to his word he was hitching out of Mallaig with a fully packed rucksack, no doubt freshly filled with supplies ready for another week at Peanmeanach. We, by contrast, were driving with the sea kayaks loaded on the roof and heading south. The wild man stuck his thumb out at us and crouched slightly, as if peering in through the front windscreen. He had a hopeful look on his face — willing us to stop and take him down the road to the mountain path along which he could regain the bothy.

I looked at Simon and Tracey, and they looked back with a twinkle in their eyes. Would we stop?

Would we hell!

Can you come back now?
A sailor's story

Crackajax was my beautiful Swedish X95, quite a sexy yacht in her day at thirty-one feet long (nine and a half metres) with running back stays a very bendy mast and all the go faster racing gear assuming you knew how to use it.

Living as we were on the Isle of Man, I'd rather conveniently bought her from Liverpool Marina having been immediately smitten by her good looks, trailing stern, low coach roof and voluminous hull which provided not just for a classy half tonne racing yacht but also the potential to be a spacious weekend family cruiser. I'd managed to sell my previous boat, Skoosh, at a handsome profit, not something that readily occurs in the second-hand yacht market so I found myself with cash in my pocket and the ability to borrow a little to upsize from the twenty-six feet that Skoosh had been.

Helped by three friends I delivered Crackajax back to Douglas on the Isle of Man from Liverpool Marina on an overnight voyage which, when I now think back to it, was a courageous thing to do in its own right. Totally strange yacht, overnight passage, untested crew and thick fog to boot. We reached Douglas in the early dawn and had to stand off the harbour entrance as the Steam Packet freight ship The Ben My Cree left for Heysham. We never actually saw her in the fog but rather listened to the dull thud of her engines as she passed somewhere close ahead of us. I guess they could see us on their radar, but we certainly never saw them!

That season I quickly learnt that Crackajax was a seriously powerful yacht. Her mainsail demanded the entire strength and attention of one strong man even with a six to one purchase main sheet system. The running back stays required a second crew member and certainly a further three were required to handle the one hundred and fifty per cent overlapping headsail as well as foredeck duties.

Alex, my daughter, was still relatively young and Angela — my long-suffering wife — quickly recognised that we'd never be able to gently sail this pedigree racing yacht alone on a family cruise to Scotland or Northern Ireland. So, racing it was, and the crew slowly got used to her foibles, ensuring the windward backstay was released just as we tacked and the leeward one wound on as we came through the wind and powered up into the new tack. There were always rope ends everywhere — mainsheet, head sail sheets, backstay lines and quite often the port and starboard spinnaker sheets, the cockpit could be mayhem. One thing did however become apparent and that was if you got her 'set up' right, back stays wound on just so, main sheet at a matching and certain spot on the traveller and the headsail tight but not too tight — then she went like a rocket. It wasn't often that we got all of those dynamics lined up in harmony but when we did, she truly performed and left most other yachts of her size standing.

I campaigned her around the Isle of Man for a season or two before entering Bangor Race Week in Northern Ireland. There we certainly never found our racing pace and ended up at the back of the fleet pretty much every day. Crackajax's handicap was hard to compete with, never mind that we couldn't often find that illusive slot when everything was just right, so ultimately, we were rubbish but nevertheless enjoyed living onboard and plenty of social Guinness to ease the pain of daily defeat.

By this time, two seasons into owning Crackajax, I'd replaced her sails with a beautiful new main and number one headsail from Robbie Storrar's loft in Windermere. Interestingly I'd thrown a chunk of money at the new sails and ordered them with Angela's children's clothes business name stitched to them. 'Jellybeans.co.im' adorned the sails and I incorrectly believed that this would be enough to avoid the VAT element of the invoice. Of course, I'd never bothered to check this, and our rather officious accountant soon corrected me that VAT could only be avoided on the element that was for actually advertising i.e., the stitched letters only and not the actual sails!

In the winter of 2007 and with a regular crew now formed and the 2008 season lying ahead, I posed the idea of entering Scottish Series on Loch Fyne to the team. There was immediate enthusiasm and our commitment was such that we not only entered Crackajax into the regatta, but also booked a static caravan at West Loch Tarbert so as to ensure we could campaign her as stripped out and light weight as possible, no bags onboard and only the emergency essentials to fulfil the racing instructions.

I'd done Scottish Series three times before, twice with Skoosh my beautiful Albin Express of Swedish pedigree and an absolutely fantastic all-rounder, and once aboard a metal hulled yacht called Tumbling Dice owned and skippered by the wonderful Tony Van Hee from The Royal

Northumberland Yacht Club. Tumbling Dice — or Tumbling Teabag as we affectionately called her due to the impressive number of tiny pin sized holes in her hull — was as complex a yacht to race as Crackajax was. She too sported running back stays, multiple winches and lines coming at you from all around the deck. Tony had, of course, kept us in contention during that particular series, his extensive seafaring wisdom coupled with years of racing nouse, had him place us in the right place at the right time whether it be on the start line, up the first beat or the right gybe to be on coming down wind. There was never a better man to sail with.

As the early season shake down races got underway and Scottish Series 2008 approached, I did the usual Isle of Man thing and asked around at Douglas Bay Yacht Club as to who else was going. It transpired that there was just one other yacht, a Sigma 33 attractively called Seapie of Cultra owned and skippered by Jerry Coleman and competitively raced at Tarbert every year for as long as people could remember. I knew Jerry well as we both lived in Ramsey at the north end of the Island and so took it upon myself to call him and see whether he fancied sailing Sea Pie and Crackajax up together in company. It's always pleasant to sail with others, not to mention the additional safety considerations and as the two yachts were well matched for speed there'd be little holding each other up.

As with any big boat regatta there's a good deal of pre-planning and organising to be done to get your yacht ready and delivered on time to the venue. Of course, 'delivered' has a whole different context for sailing yachts as seldom are they uplifted and delivered by truck, more often it's the organisation of a crew and passage planning to sail to the destination. Scottish Series was no exception, indeed for the average working person it was a serious commitment not just in the time needed to get the yacht there — full of anticipation and pre-regatta excitement — but more so in bringing her home again after several days of racing, beer drinking and late nights! In the build-up, there's making sure that all the sailing gear, rig and hull fittings are working to their optimum. That the right sails are onboard as often owners will keep their best racing sails off the yacht and bring them on board only for regattas. Then there's the utility stuff, gas, engine fuel and other essentials for the delivery trip. Even organising the crew to bring the right kit and all be together on the pontoon at roughly the same time can become a task in its own right. For many of them it's taking annual leave and getting the ever essential 'pass out' from loved ones at home.

Living in Ramsey at the northern end of the Isle of Man the delivery trip to Tarbert on Loch Fyne is around one hundred miles. The passage entails sailing up what's left of the east coast of the island before rounding the Point of Ayre and heading northwest towards the Mull of Galloway. From there the choice is to either hug the Scottish coast before turning to round the north end of Arran and into Loch Fyne or to take in some early westward miles and sail up past Alisa Craig and on through Kilbrannan Sound leaving Arran to starboard and Campbeltown to port. There's not much to choose between the two and often people would decide depending upon the weather and the preferred scenery.

The format of Scottish Series, as I recall at that time, was to race from the Saturday morning through to the Monday lunchtime. At one time some years before there was actually also an overnight delivery race from Inverkip Marina around various marks between Arran and Troon which eventually brought yachts into Tarbert early on Friday morning. I'm guessing the theory went that this then gave crew members a 'lay day' to recover before racing proper started on the Saturday. I recall twice doing that race, once on Tumbling Dice and once aboard a friend's Albin Express "Expresso". Both times it was a long overnight passage and not something I remember fondly. The other factor I recall was that no matter how tired we were when we reached Tarbert we always made straight for the multitude of harbour side hostelries and that then led to an equally long day drinking with an increasing number of sailors coming in after their own overnight racing adventures. This wasn't great pre-regatta preparation but the innocence and energy of youth carried us boldly on ultimately in ignorance of the inevitable hangovers.

The overnight delivery race has stopped now, most probably as less and less yachts were entering it opting instead to deliver their yachts in their own time and be fresh come the first race of Saturday morning. That option stands for the local Scottish yachts from Largs, Kip, Troon, Tarbert and Campbeltown but it is not an option for those coming up from the Isle of Man, Belfast, Ardglass or Dublin. We, by contrast, had a passage to cover and needed to factor being into Tarbert by Friday afternoon or evening at the latest. Then there were the tidal considerations and even the necessity to factor in getting out of Ramsey which itself is a tidal harbour — accessible only two hours either side of high water.

All of those considerations dictated that for the crews of Sea Pie and Crackajax the ideal departure would be on the

Thursday morning rising tide giving us plenty of time for the passage north and most probably arriving into Tarbert sometime early morning Friday.

The weather however had very different ideas as, bang on time, a southerly force eight gale was forecast and was set to blow for several days right across our intended delivery window. Jerry and I had been speaking throughout the week pondering our options. We'd agreed to be in Ramsey harbour tied up alongside ready for the Thursday departure, but we also had equally been recognising that it wasn't looking promising.

For me, as Skipper of Crackajax, there were a multitude of emotions running. On one hand there was the frustration of wanting and needing to get to Tarbert — we had after all paid our significant entry fee and there was the promise of great racing. Then there was an overriding sense of responsibility for the crew, many of whom would simply look to me to make the decision as to whether we should go — total trust, which could be unnerving. Of course, there were my own inner voices, the cycle of "you should just go", set against the next wave of "do not put people's lives at risk". It was a real dilemma and not a decision to be trifled with. Jerry and I had a few quiet skipper-to-skipper chats and certainly I looked to his numerous years of taking Sea Pie to Tarbert as a source of wisdom that I didn't have.

The tide rose and with it the wind howled ever louder through the yachts rigging even in the relatively sheltered outer harbour. We didn't go as we'd planned at the earliest point of the tide but instead stayed alongside nervously pacing the harbour wall and hoping to sense that the wind was abating, but it didn't. The crews made tea and chatted on board then variously disappeared into Ramsey to see friends or have a coffee. I ventured up to our shop on Parliament Street to see Angela who innocently asked why we hadn't gone, again total trust that, as always, everything would be just right. I was riddled with "what ifs"!

The tide flooded and at high tide the yachts and local fishing boats (interestingly none of which had ventured out) tugged impatiently at their mooring lines. Gusts whipped around the harbour setting rigging clanking against masts and lines creaking as they stretch to take the weight of the hefty fishing fleet. There was no let-up in the weather.

As the tide started to drop, and I'm not sure motivated by what or whom, Jerry appeared from the cabin of Sea Pie and made purposefully towards Crackajax.

"We're going" he announced with great certainty, "Are you coming?"

It was as straight forwards as that, after more than four hours of deliberations there was a decision and "yes" he could be dead sure that we were going too, it was now or never.

I got back on board Crackajax and asked the crew to gather around. Great friends they all were, Matthew McSevney, a dear friend of many adventures and his father-in-law Ian McCauley, Stephen Dickson and Ian Jeffers both from Northern Ireland and who'd flown in especially for the delivery and the regatta. Ian was there primarily as he'd a fully paid-up place on the entire BT Global Challenge due to go the next year and was after every sea mile he could get.

I asked them if they were happy to go and was honest about the forecast as if they didn't know already! Southerly force eight certainly set to blow all night and then predicted to die off in the early hours. The passage included overfalls off the Point of Ayre locally known as 'the screws' and then a tidal race off the Mull of Galloway. It was going to be pretty wild and most certainly wet not to mention dark for the majority of the passage. The saving grace was that it would be downwind all the way and to that end potentially quite forgiving.

Were they happy to go? Of course, they were!

I asked them to clip on the number 3 headsail — the smallest that Crackajax carried aside from the storm jib, and to prepare for a triple reefed mainsail. That 'sail plan' felt right for the conditions and as many a sailor knows, it's easier to shake out a reef than it is to put one in during heavy weather. We agreed it was good to head out to sea as an under canvassed yacht. The crew set to, stowing things tightly, prepping sails, putting on their own favoured wet weather gear configuration and making their quick calls home to confirm that we were off.

Fifteen minutes later and both yachts were untying their lines, casting off and turning towards the short channel out into the Irish Sea. With the tide dropping there was now limited time to get safely over the sand bar which lies across the entrance to Ramsey fairway, so we motored out assertively as if the decision to actually go now had to be compounded by getting out as quickly as possible before any doubts could turn our minds.

There is something that raises the adrenalin as a yacht responds to that first rise and fall of a sea's swell. The bow lifts as it meets the first long rounded wave of the open water and then dips into the following trough. Pushed by the engine the sharp leading edge of the yacht parts the oncoming water waiting with almost tangible enthusiasm for the fluttering sails to be hoisted. More often than not the mainsail is already up but jammed tightly amidships waiting for the moment when the helm can be turned, setting course and enabling the main to be eased and the headsail to quickly join it as both are trimmed to power the yacht forwards. Within seconds the engine is turned off and the throttle pushed into reverse to fold the propeller and afford minimum drag under the hull.

As we went through this familiar routine, I surveyed the wild scene ahead of me. Across the sea straight out from the harbour channel were the distant peaks of the Lake District. Their skyline was clear more than thirty miles distant but set as if in a blue green seascape across a boiling confusion of white caps and occasional foam. Now clear of the protective channel walls we became fully exposed to the elements. The wind was truly whipping across Ramsey Bay and here, still in the relative shallows, there was a short steep sea with waves either breaking naturally or through the wind whipping their tops away as it hurried northwards.

Ahead of us Sea Pie had already turned downwind and was running quickly under a small headsail and reefed main. We immediately gave chase no more than a few hundred metres astern, the sail plan we'd discussed was now set, the cockpit of jumbled halyards and sheets neatly stowed away and the hatch cover and boards all closed to prevent any spray or breaking water entering the cabin. Having done their respective jobs, the crew now settled down sitting together snuggly in the cockpit, myself at the helm and the others sitting cosily next to one another along the cockpit seats as we too headed north. Crackajax's speed was quickly up at between seven and eight knots, occasionally higher, as we surfed down the front of a larger wave surging forwards before the bow dug into the wave ahead and the yacht braked against the force of slower water.

Those early miles up the Manx coastline were both exhilarating and reassuring as Crackajax settled into a rhythm and we contented ourselves that the yacht could handle the elements especially as we were being pushed downwind in effect 'running' with the weather rather than trying to fight against it. Within minutes of leaving the shelter of Ramsey Harbour we were surfing waves past my house 'Whitestones' which stands proudly on Mooragh Promenade looking out across the Irish Sea to the Lakes and the Cumbrian coastline. I got a distinct sense that the adventure was now truly on as I watched the house and a potential warm bed for the night slip by only several hundred metres away from us.

Quickly onwards chasing Jerry and the crew of Sea Pie, passing Cranstal Point and on then to the Point of Ayre and our first decision of the late afternoon and of the passage in general. Our two options were to either stay tight to the shoreline and round the point alongside the stoney beach and well inside of 'The Screws', or to run further offshore and pass the boiling water to the north before then turning westward towards the Mull of Galloway.

The Screws — their local name as far as I know — is an area of turbulent racing water that is created as the two currents running along the west and east sides of the Island collide just off the Point of Ayre. The collision produces a field of large standing waves that are uncomfortable in a yacht and certainly very challenging in a sea kayak. Several years before this current sailing trip I'd organised a sea kayaking fundraiser for The Children's Centre which entailed kayaking from the Point of Ayre across the North Channel to Scotland at Burrow Head, some sixteen miles in a straight line. Fortunately, on that day the weather had been very kind, calm seas, no wind and an eager morning sunshine endeavouring to pierce the sea fret which blocked out all visibility. Craig, my trusty fellow paddler, and I paddled on a compass bearing for most of the day listening intently for the rumbling sound of any ships engines as they plied their trade between Northern Ireland, Scotland and England. Nothing untoward happened, we just didn't see a single thing all day and spent six hours navigating the strong currents that sweep through the North Channel demanding that we in fact paddle an S shape as the tides forbid any direct route between the two countries.

So, on this day, and perhaps as much to stay near the shoreline, we chose to round The Point inside of The Screws. We turned westward, sheeting in our sails to start the long twenty-six mile reach across to the Mull of Galloway and a section of the voyage which immediately proved to be wetter as Crackajax drove through the waves powerfully sending spray up across the decks and occasionally into the air dumping heavy downpours of cold seawater around our heads and shoulders.

We thumped along for goodness knows how long, the years since have dulled my memory of the time, however I can clearly recall that at some point mid-channel my mobile phone rang and I hurriedly dug it out of the pocket of my soaking foul weather gear. Why I had left it in there I have no idea but fortunately it was still working and even more impressively we still had a reception out here perhaps thirteen miles from the nearest land.

The call was from Angela, my wife, who did away with any pleasantries and instead asked where we were. She of course was back in Ramsey and still in her shop getting ready to close up for the day but listening to Manx Radio and the recurrent weather forecasts that are an essential part of Island life.

"They've cancelled all the ferries for the rest of the day and overnight, the forecast is for a Southerly Force eight all night" she blurted out, "Don't you think you should come back?"

Of course, holding a conversation with Angela wasn't going to be a prolonged affair as the howling wind, the rain, spray and bucking yacht all served to shorten any conversation. I explained as calmly as I could that turning back was simply not a sensible option as it would mean heading upwind back to the Island and recrossing the rough and busy North Channel. At this point, even with twilight not long away, it was more sensible to continue running on downwind and taking our chances of conditions moderating as night fell.

That was the last conversation I ever had on that phone as not long later my drenched foul weather gear and watery pockets killed the phone for good. Any reassuring calls to Angela throughout the night would have to come from someone else's phone!

We rounded the Mull of Galloway in the fading evening light, another area of boiling water needed avoiding but with plenty of open water this wasn't a problem and Sea Pie — always within eye sight and not far ahead — made for a great moving way mark to follow, not least as Jerry had sailed this route on many, many occasions before.

A gybe was necessary to round the Mull. For non-sailors, this is the point at which you turn the stern of the boat through the wind and has the potential if uncontrolled to send the main sail with heavy metal boom swinging angrily across the deck and cabin top. Worse still on Crackajax was the potential of the boom catching the 'lazy' running back stay thereby placing heavy strain on to the upper sections of the yacht's mast and snapping it — quite literally! In other words, gybes are to be respected, planned for and executed in a controlled way.

So, we discussed the gybe well in advance, again with plenty of open water there was no need to rush, and the crew united in their purpose and roles to sheet the main sail in and control its passage across the deck, to release the current windward side backstay and take up on the new backstay as the boat came through the wind. As skipper and also steering Crackajax, my intention was to bring her through the wind slowly giving clear instructions and allowing the crew plenty of time to undertake their tasks. The gybe went smoothly, and we set ourselves on to the new course running directly downwind along the west coast of the Mull of Galloway.

In good seaman-like manner we were sailing with the VHF Radio turned on to channel sixteen in order to listen out for coastguard warnings and hear relevant news of other marine traffic. From memory Steve and Ian had gone below to make a hot drink and were therefore next to the radio in the relative calm of the cabin when a Mayday call came through from a yacht in the Irish Sea some miles behind us but equally bound for Tarbert. Steve relayed the breaking news up into the cockpit. The distressing fact was that they were sinking having had some initial problems with their rudder which then escalated to the point when their metal stock had snapped and, in the violence of the seas, had then come back through the hull of the boat. They were taking on water and had launched their life raft whilst calling for assistance. It was most probable that we were indeed the closest sailing yacht to them — I figured maybe fifteen miles downwind of them (to their North).

What to do? We could and should turn upwind and, although it would be wet and uncomfortable not to mention quite some time, make our way back towards them to offer help. There are many stories of yachts facing similar situations perhaps most famously British skipper Pete Goss in the Vendee Globe Singlehanded Round The World yacht race.

The 1996/7 race turned Pete into a national hero overnight for the dramatic rescue of fellow competitor Raphael Dinelli in hurricane-force winds. Pete, who scuppered his own chances of winning the race in order to save Dinelli, was awarded the MBE by HM The Queen and the Legion d'Honneur by the French President for his actions.

Pete also became nurse to Dinelli, who suffered from hypothermia and was so stiff with cold he could not move for days. Pete made him sweet tea and gave him physiotherapy while he made his slow recovery. The pair became firm friends, vowing to sail together and toasting their future on New Year's Eve with a bottle of champagne Dinelli had had the incredible foresight to bring aboard! Dinelli, realising what was important to him after his ordeal, asked his girlfriend to marry him using Pete's fax machine and — after she accepted — asked Pete to be best man at his wedding.

We on Crackajax were of course nowhere near hurricane force winds but equally we were not in a professionally prepared open ocean racing yacht. A discussion quickly gathered momentum as to the sense of turning upwind. I think that I wanted to go and started preparing the crew to turn the boat into the wild conditions. We'd need all hands up on deck and prepared for a wet, few hours as we battled south. But then even as we were having this discussion there were further radio calls being made, a lifeboat launched from the Irish coast and a freighter diverted to where the yacht was and the life raft with crew on board. So, we were stood down as quickly as we might have 'stood on' — and just thanked our own lucky stars that we were by comparison heading north in relative control and comfort.

Darkness had now fallen, and we began to discuss our night time routine for the overnight passage. I had been steering for several hours and was feeling both cold and wet. With nine to ten hours of darkness ahead I elected to hand the helm over to Matthew, good friend and the next most experienced sailor on board. We discussed the course to sail and the yacht's set up including the absolute imperative to not allow an unplanned gybe, if anything sailing slightly higher than dead downwind would be sensible. This course would eventually track us back to the coast of Galloway however we would have plenty of time to then gybe away again.

With that I headed below for some rest and to get warm in my sleeping bag.

Now, I've sailed since I was four years old and have sailed on all sorts of dinghies and yachts in quite a few parts of the world and many varying conditions, but I have never been good in a cabin when the sea is rough. My strategy, developed over those years, is to get below, get undressed quickly and get horizontal in my sleeping bag ASAP! That seems to work and allows me to get some rest without being overwhelmed by sea sickness and the debilitating fog that it descends over your body and mind.

So as Crackajax surged northwards I dived below and got myself horizontal. Two other crew members did the same and whilst the cabin was somewhat wet it was also warm by comparison to the outside environment. The sounds of the wind and the sea were muffled by the thick fibreglass hull, replaced to a greater extent by the swishing and gurgling of sea water rushing along outside and the occasional clunk of blocks and other rigging hitting the deck or mast as a squall blew through. Crackajax was set up for the night, she seemed solid, and I soon fell asleep content that all was as good as could be.

Some time passed, I'm not sure how long, but I was awoken by a loud crash from up on deck and the yacht aggressively pitching from one side to the other. There were shouts from various crew members and the violent flapping of sails — clearly, we were out of control and I suspected that an unplanned 'crash' gybe had occurred taking all on deck by surprise and goodness know what toil on the rigging!

Sure enough, Matthew had allowed Crackajax to gybe and the boom had indeed caught the lazy running back stay. This to some degree had helped to arrest the swing of the boom across the deck and had resulted in the mainsail being pinned closer to the centre of the yacht. The pressure of the mainsail was now however being put through the backstay and onwards then into the higher sections of the mast. It was a potentially disastrous situation as the power of the sail, especially in such extreme wind conditions, had the potential to bring the entire rig down. To this day I'm amazed that it actually hadn't and can only think that Matthew had allowed the yacht to drift so close to 'dead downwind' that when the gybe happened the main sail was not in fact fully powered up.

The situation needed rectifying quickly. I took the helm back from Matthew and briefed the crew on deck that we needed to sheet the main sail into the centre of the yacht and take the pressure of the sail off the running back stay. Then we would wind on the windward stay and loosen the leeward or downwind stay before then letting the main back out. All of this of course as the yacht surged ever onwards in the darkness of the night, the wind howled, and the seas constantly chased us as we ran ahead of them and their breaking foaming tops.

The manoeuvre went smoothly and with the situation sorted I looked at Matt to see that he looked pretty shocked — possibly the severity of the situation dawning upon him. Bizarrely it struck me that he needed to get back on the helm as quickly as possible and to re-engage the feel of driving the yacht at a safe angle downwind being aware of the potential to gybe but holding the yacht a few degrees higher into the wind to stop this from happening. He needed to connect with that first sense of the power coming out of the mainsail as an indicator that a gybe was becoming imminent and he needed to do so on a night that was so dark that it almost had to be done by feel rather than sight.

So, Matthew took back up on the helm and I decided to get dressed again in to my foul weather gear and stay on deck lying along one of the cockpit benches curled up as best I could out of the conditions.

The crash gybe had changed our course to now be slowly tracking away from the coastline and out across the Irish Sea towards Ailsa Craig and the southern end of the Isle of Arran.

Occasionally and through binoculars we could see the masthead light of Sea Pie and it seemed that they were electing to stay close to the mainland coast running up towards the Clyde Estuary past Ardrossan and Troon. This option would then see them eventually gybing and heading to Tarbert across the North and East coasts of Arran whilst our new course would take us through Kilbrannan Sound between the Mull of Kintyre and the west coast of Arran. It mattered not, we were not in touch with them, and I suspect that they, like us, had plenty to deal with on their own without worrying about us.

By now and most probably due to the relentless attack of the elements our electrics had all gone down. We had no navigation lights, no cabin lights, no instruments — indeed the only working item was the VHF radio which kept dutifully reporting to us other events happening around the Irish Sea. So our navigation strategy had become using a hand held torch to illuminate the compass as and when necessary and to make reference to Ian's hand held Garmin GPS — which by the way was low on battery power so we only switched it on around every twenty minutes to check that we were going in the right direction and where on the passage we'd actually got to. I know, I know... piss poor preparation — but there we are, that was it and we were managing!

Another distinct memory of that night was my first and only experience of a large wave catching up with Crackajax and dumping directly into the cockpit. It was pitch black throughout that night as the force eight storm raged around us and we ran downwind under a minimal sail plan. For that reason, I certainly didn't see the wave coming and only heard it at the very last moment as a wall of foam came from behind us, higher than the yacht and dumped down upon us, tonnes of water, into the cockpit and filling it to overflowing. The wave was gone as fast as it arrived leaving us staring at one another caught between shocked laughter and relief that the boat had withstood the watery onslaught. The water drained away quickly through the cockpit scuppers and Crackajax lifted herself back into full life charging on undeterred into the darkness. For those of us on deck, we peered back into the night and wondered what other walls of water might be gathering themselves somewhere back in the Irish Sea and thundering north to take their chance with our little yacht.

In the early hours, perhaps around four a.m., the conditions started to relent. We'd run past Ailsa Craig in the depths of the night keeping well clear and not really ever seeing it in the heavy darkness. Ailsa Craig has mystical qualities — it is a mere twenty-four and a half acres and stands just three hundred and thirty-eight metres out of the Irish Sea but its precious rock, reibickite, is the source of seventy per cent. of the world's curling stones and historically the Island's quarry has opened just once every four years to allow the cutting of special granite.

As conditions improved and once again the yacht felt safe, I retreated back to my sleeping bag and spent a couple of restless hours lying on a bunk pinned in by a convenient lee-cloth to stop me from rolling out.

When I next properly woke, I was disorientated by the fact that Crackajax was now wallowing in a dead calm and the sea had quickly become a long steady line of rounded smooth swells that rolled the yacht in a calming fashion after such a wild night. As I emerged through the hatch the sun was just breaking out and Kilbrannan Sound was a real picture of Scottish beauty with the craggy and imposing mountains of Arran off to our right and the lower but impressive hills of the Mull off to our left.

The crew's spirits were high, a kettle was fizzing away on the stove and there was talk of bacon sandwiches not to mention a variety of newly developing 'war' stories from the previous night and a passage which we'd all not be forgetting in a hurry. Crackajax was though in a bit of a sorry state especially considering that we were delivering her to a three-day regatta and she needed to be in prime racing condition. The tiller extension had come away at some point in the night, all the electrics were down and the 'traveller' across which the mainsheet block system moved had been partially ripped from its anchor. Down below literally everything was wet and any personal gear that hadn't been properly stowed by a crew member was now liberally spread around the cabin.

As conditions were now close to flat calm, of all ironies, we decided that it would be best to fire up the engine and motor the remaining ten miles or so up the Sound and around Skipness Point and then along Loch Fyne and into Tarbert. So, with teas and coffees served and bacon sandwiches in the making we got the engine going and dropped the headsail. It was still only sometime around six a.m. but it felt special to be where we were, all together and safe, heading for our intended destination.

My final abiding memory of that fantastic, exhilarating, eventful and at times scary night at sea was pulling alongside the pontoon in Tarbert and being greeted by the harbour master.

"You're here early boys" he shouted in his thick Scottish accent, "Where have you come from?"

"The Isle of Man, overnight" we all stated back in a variety of voices and confidence.

"The Isle of Man, overnight, in that weather?" he threw back at us clearly impressed by the achievement. "What was it like, it must have been wild!"

Simultaneously our chests puffed out and shoulders moved backwards a sense of pride washing over us at hearing just how impressed the harbour master seemed.

"It was pretty rough and wet" I heard a voice say, "But not all that bad, hey boys?"

"No, not bad at all" came the united reply alongside some sheepish looks and grins!

Gaelforce West — Connemara, August 2013

The name drew me in from the very first moment that I spotted it on sleepmonsters.com — perhaps the most extensive adventure racing website in the world!

Gaelforce spoke to me of the sea, the wild elements, wind-blown spume skittering across the Atlantic wave tops and past nervous decisions as to whether to leave a safe harbour to brave the gale force winds that awaited.

And then there's the 'west'! Something that draws you on, the wide-open spaces and of course that atmospheric line from Stairway to Heaven' — *There's a feeling I get when I look to the west and my spirit is dying for leaving'*.

I was instantly sold, I simply had to do this race.

Chris and I had been looking for something different to do, an event off the Isle of Man and one that fell into the summer school holiday weeks that he had off. It needed to be fairly close by, not too expensive and no more than three days off the Island. Choices were limited but Gaelforce was a match and we were booked within hours!

Quite often Chris and I had found ourselves squeezing in a race in the UK by leaving on the Thursday evening ferry (Chris getting special permission from his headteacher to escape a Friday teaching at Foxdale School) or even by me being already across in the UK at a conference or other meeting but able then to collect Chris from the closest airport to the event. I can recall several late Sunday afternoon drag races with only minutes to spare heading back to Bristol Airport, or Liverpool to ensure he was on the last flight home — ready to be back teaching on the Monday morning. It always seemed amazing when we did it as to just how much you could squeeze into a weekend.

Chris has always been a planning 'officianardo' leaving no stone unturned, flights, ferries, car hire, equipment carried or delivered in advance — he relishes getting the very best deal and ensuring everything is neatly in place well before the event. In the build up to our first Original Mountain Marathon (OMM) I can recall being very impressed when Chris summoned me to his garage one evening and proceeded to brew a cup of tea on his trangia stove. His aim was to very specifically measure the amount of meths required to boil a pan of water sufficient for two hot drinks and then to multiply this carefully up for the OMM race weekend to ensure that we carried only just enough meths in our backpacks — saving unnecessary weight being his ultimate aim. He was of course absolutely right to do so, I was just impressed that he could even be bothered!

Gaelforce West was however going to be very different from our annual mountain marathon exploits. It was first and foremost a commercial adventure race attracting literally thousands of entrants from all over the UK. I recall something like one thousand, six hundred people entered the year we went which most definitely detracted from any sense of remoteness. The upside was the venue near Westport in Southern Ireland, the beautiful county of Connemara, the wild Atlantic coast, mountains and ever-changing elements.

The race route totalled sixty-six kilometres including twenty-two kilometres of trail and mountain running, forty-three kilometres of cyclocross style riding and a one-kilometre double kayak paddling section across a sea fjord. You know I never knew until this trip that the Southern Irish called their arms of Atlantic water 'fjords'!

To get set up and 'situated' for the race there were various things to put in place and true to form Chris was immediately on the case. He posted on Facebook that we needed to borrow two cyclocross bikes however, as we were landing in Belfast to collect a van for the drive to Westport, they needed to ideally be easily collected along the way. Of course, within twenty-four hours and the powers of social media a very kind Belfast-based rider offered us two bikes and my great friend Stephen Dickson loaned us a small van as ideal transport. Things were quickly coming together and within days Chris had then booked accommodation in Westport, coach transfers to the start and post-race meals. All sorted! How great to have a friend and race partner that just loves to be organised!

There were many things that we hadn't anticipated about this event, I'll list them now and then expand upon them as the story unfolds. From memory they go in this particular order:

1. Never borrow a bike from a stranger for an event.

2. Nowhere is close by on the west coast of Ireland.

3. Never ride that bike for the first time in anger during the event.

4. Nutrition and hydration are vital during a long day out.

5. Even good friends can get mad at you.

6. Even good friends do stupid things in anger.

We left Belfast mid-afternoon in our 'O2 Guru' mini-van and headed off in the sunshine to drive the one hundred and eighty miles to Westport where we were then due to register at an outdoor centre, Killary Adventure Centre, near the start of the race. After that we 'only' had to drop our bikes off in the transition pen on the far side of Killary Fjord before finally heading back to our bed and breakfast accommodation in Westport. Easy enough, or so it seemed, in fact we were so relaxed that we stopped with cyclocross man in Belfast for a lovely cup of tea (you will, you will, you will!) as he ran through the bikes and asked us all about the event. A very pleasant hour or so past in amicable conversation and then we were off, van loaded and excited to be finally on our way in the bright Irish sunshine.

I'll spare us all any detailed recollection of the road trip save to say it was mostly on slow urbanised roads that were both busy and winding — Westport began to seem like a very long way away and the time lost in Belfast chatting amicably might well have been better spent heading west.

After a long, long drag we eventually arrived in Westport. It was twilight as we homed in on our very cute bed and breakfast perfectly situated close to the town centre (well done Chris!) Losing little time, we checked in and arranged a super early breakfast time with the very convivial host who brightly let us know that everyone staying with him was a competitor in the event and therefore breakfast was going to be a busy affair at five a.m.

We then double checked that we had the right gear with us (bikes, helmets, cycling shoes, energy snacks) and jumped back into the van for the ninety kilometre or so drive down to Killary and the official registration centre for the event.

Well, I drove hard and took my chances on a few tight corners, in the dark and on unknown roads. I noticed Chris gripping the edges of his seat and occasionally reaching for the dashboard or pressing his right foot down hoping to have some effect by using the invisible brake pedal on his side of the van. In any event the journey seemed to simply take forever, and we began to grasp rule number two, nowhere is close on the west coast of Ireland!

In the end we reached Killary slightly frayed and wide eyed, it had been many hours since we'd caught the flight off the Isle of Man and many of those had been spent driving all too quickly just to get ourselves set for the event. But here we were and just in time to show our ID's and sign the compulsory waivers, get route maps, race numbers and a short verbal briefing from the race organisers on what to do next.

Somewhat crazily 'what to do next' was another drive back along the shores of Killary Fjord and around to the far side via various thin country lanes. The mission we had to accomplish was to find the bike drop off and transition area, an essential part of the preparation for any multi-sport race. Indeed, if your bike wasn't there then it really would be race over so it just had to be done!

So, Chris and I once again blasted our way along the lanes in a sort of good humoured but 'this is getting tedious' mindset. No navigation was necessary as out there in the wilds of Connemara late this Friday evening there was now a long snake of car headlights frantically winding their way to drop bikes off. We dutifully took our place in the line and made sure to respect the distance from the car in front mindful that we'd all be in the same place sometime in the next hour!

It was around eleven p.m. when we finally hauled up at the small parking area, a site of feverish activity with cars coming and going, bikes being unloaded and head torches lighting up the short walk down to the transition field. It seemed to be quite some distance from the kayak landing spot on the fjord shore. Dropping the bikes wasn't a big job, but most certainly an essential one, hanging it on the make-shift scaffolding racking, each arranged neatly in fish bone style suspended by their saddles with all other necessary cycling gear by the front wheel or alternatively clipped to the bike in a small waterproof pack. In the dark it was hard to define just how close to the fjord shore we were and also to get a full mental picture of the field and how many bikes were now racked. For the triathletes reading this you'll know that having some idea of where your bike is at transition is pretty bloody important — and here we were in the pitch dark in an unlit field hoping to goodness that we could quickly retrieve our bikes when the moment came in the morning and particularly as we would be approaching the transition from the water rather than the road with no mental picture of the overall layout.

All done we were quickly back in the car and tear-arsing our way back to Westport once again in a trail of fast-moving, frustrated adventure racers all united by the despondent reality that it was too late for a beer!

Back at the bed and breakfast we parked the car neatly and headed directly for our cosy little room for a serious late-night session of kit faffing. As many of you will know, this is an ever-essential element of any race or event — fussing over what to wear, what to carry and the dilemmas of what extras to take along — additional weight that could either prove absolutely useless or an absolute god-send.

On this occasion we were pondering the variables of a really early start — breakfast at five a.m. and then on to a coach for an hour's drive to the start line on Glassiluan beach back at Killary. There'd be a bit of milling around waiting for the actual start and then the first trail run section along the coastal path which would soon warm us up. At the end of the run would come the kayak section across the Killary Fjord which would in turn reunite us with our bikes racked in some distant wet field on the other side and the additional dry kit that we'd optimistically left by the front wheel.

The forecast wasn't wonderful — windy with low cloud and temperatures hovering around ten to twelve degrees, it'd be a day to keep moving and perhaps have a thin layer as a spare cover up, definitely no risk of sun stroke along the way on this occasion.

And so, it was that we boarded the coach at six a.m. wearing our running kit and the addition of a small bum-bag holding a thin, windproof, compulsory buff and a few energy bars. We figured we'd just tough it out before the start and then quickly get warm once underway. "Start cold" is the mountain law and that seemed the sensible choice.

The race was massively popular, as I've mentioned something like one thousand, six hundred competitors which necessitated the organisers letting people go in waves over an extended period of time. We were not by any means the first wave — even having caught the six-a.m. coach, some had left at five a.m. and others at five thirty a.m. — this was set to continue right through to nine a.m., wave after wave of willing victims throwing themselves at the Atlantic coast and anything that the elements could throw back at them.

It was all just a little too commercial and most certainly underwhelming — fifty or so lycra-clad 'athletes' assembled under an inflatable start line on a blustery west coast morning waiting for the starting signal. There were lots of bending and stretching going on, eager people doing shuttle runs up and down the soft sand — and then Chris and I stood there exchanging the odd sarcastic comment. Many years earlier I'd waited at the start of the Manx Mountain Marathon with good friend John Matthews — who I was in awe of as he waited a similar starting gun. On that day John watched all the limbering up and seemed unimpressed. I, on the other hand, was deeply concerned for him and his total lack of pre-race activity.

"Aren't you going to warm up Johnny?" I asked as I eyed the others all looking super keen.

"Plenty of time for warming up John!" came his instant and calm response. And of course, he was right, with thirty-two miles and something like twelve thousand feet of climbing ahead of him, why would you bother warming up? — There was little chance or indeed sense in a sprint off the start line.

So, we ambled around and waited for the allotted time, the ever compulsory briefing urging us to be safe and look after one another and then to the blare of a gas foghorn we were unleashed on Gaelforce West.

I'm at risk of stating the obvious to many who will know what comes next in these events. Every time, for me at least, there's the rush of the crowd, the excitement of finally being underway and the initial tow that simply gets you going far too fast. I rarely take the sensible option of settling down early, watching my pace and managing my heart rate — oh no, I'm away with the elite boys somehow thinking that the pace is sustainable that some miraculous training effect has kicked in and I really can run like this for any sustained length of time! Of course, I can't and all too quickly, perhaps two to three minutes in, I fade very quickly and a steady stream of far more sensible runners starts to pass me as I gasp and splutter once again a victim of my own ambitious imagination.

Every time I do this, I think of Kevin Gale, one time head of the Isle of Man Fire Service and a fell running friend.

I passed him going up Peel Hill one day in the winter hill league and I could hear him muttering to himself "too fast, too fast" as he realised that he was ahead of himself and it was all about to go very wrong.

Stage 1 — Trail Run to Kayak Start

The initial run section of eight or so miles were absolutely beautiful and actually mercifully flat. After a short and energetic sprint away from the beach we hit a small climb before being dropped down on to a major path that skirted briefly around the coast before turning inland along the banks of the fjord. The solid cart track made for decent running on its firm grass and hard-packed stone. Chris was constantly just ahead of me — I'm sure he's practiced this to perfection over the years — teasing me with what seems like a distance I can cross to be back besides him but actually never letting me catch up and so in effect making me run harder and faster than I normally would. I have spent bloody years chasing him and like some enthusiastic puppy dog (even though I'm the older man) I keep turning up and trying again. I can clearly recall our first ever run together. I'd already got many years of running in my legs and had plenty of fell races under my belt — Chris by comparison had not long before given up smoking and quaffing large amounts of beer with his Christian Biker mates. He'd asked me if I could take him for a run and so we did and from the very start he rather depressingly just sat on my shoulder all the way — I knew then that he was a natural born runner and within weeks it was me starting to chase him as he became ever stronger and ever lighter.

The fjord side path eventually trended right, up and away from the water, climbing for some distance to a tarmac road and then a hard left back towards a forest. Fast downhill running then followed on soft, needled pathways as we dropped back to the waters' edge and a final short distance on the shore to the kayak 'get in' signalling the end of the first leg.

I was surprised to see a line of competitors ahead of me, maybe twenty or thirty runners all lined up but close together sharing a bit of warmth on what now had become a windy, grey and drizzly day. Chris and I arrived together, courtesy of his charitable nature, and we joined the line to wait for a double sit on kayak to become available. I'm sorry to say that this was simply poor organisation — too few kayaks for too many runners. The fjord was maybe one and a half kilometres wide and was filled with kayaks heading one way 'outbound' with people paddling furiously and then a gaggle of rescue boats 'inbound' towing empty kayaks and laden with paddles.

I think that we waited for around forty minutes by which time were very cold, the sweat of an eight-mile run long blown off us and our thin fell running cagoule doing little to retain warmth when standing still. I became increasingly frustrated by what seemed to be a simple logistical cockup — but there was nothing to be done but wait and jump around on the spot with every stitch of spare clothing pulled on.

Stage 2 — Kayak leg

Eventually we were ushered forwards to a free sit-on and given two soaking wet buoyancy aids to pull over our heads adding misery to our already cold torsos. We then grabbed paddles and pushed away from the shore — a teaming, shouting, splashing scene as people left and boats arrived all at the same time.

Away from the rocky beach we settled into a smooth rhythm being sure to measure our effort for a windy crossing on a choppy section of water. The conditions were not overly threatening but equally we were very conscious that a casual unwary moment could see us taking an unwelcome and very cold dip. A few people did and were being hauled out by the various rescue boats and either opting to go on or being shuttled back to the shore for an early exit from the race.

Perhaps twenty minutes or so of steady paddling saw us reach the far bank, making our exit from the kayak and up over a rocky beach through a ticker tape funnel. The large rocks were very slippery and everyone's haste to get out of the water saw lots of slips and tumbles, again nothing dramatic and only knee-deep but still pretty chilly and annoyingly unsettling.

It was then a very short clamber up the beach and into a wet field following a well-worn path through the tall marshy grass. This was wet running and pretty soggy as hundreds of feet had already trampled their way across the unsuitable running terrain. The transition field with our bikes was quite a distance, clearly the dark of the night before had fooled us into thinking that it would be a quick sprint from kayak to bike — but it now showed itself to be a muddy stumbling jog of a mile or so and most certainly not a sprint.

Into the transition we had to identify our rack, to find our bikes and gather equipment for the coming sections of the race. Many of the bikes had already gone, earlier competitors had been through and fortunately the confusion had been suitably lessened. We homed in quickly and wasted no time in preparing for the cycling section.

Stage 3 — Bike leg, Fjord side to Croagh Patrick

The organisers of Gaelforce West are very clear that the cycling sections are suitable only for mountain bikes or cyclocross bikes. There are sections of tarmac, gravel and even a few quite tricky, rocky descents. As you now know, we had borrowed our cyclocross bikes from a friendly Belfast man and had taken the time only to ride them up and down his street enough times to adjust the saddles and make sure our cleats matched his clip on peddles. He had talked about the different gearing ratios on each bike, and I think, being a more regular cyclist than Chris, I opted for the bike that had the more demanding set up — not that I really understood what he was telling us at the time.

So now we alight upon rules number one and three. Never borrow a bike from a stranger for an event and never ride it in anger for the first time at the event!

From the get-go of the cycling leg, I realised that whoever owned the bike I'd borrowed most probably had legs the size of a rugby prop forward with a power ratio far and above that of mine. I struggled at every incline — the easiest of the bikes gears still demanding that I stood up in the peddles and toiled my way up hill at probably three to four miles per hour. Chris had long since disappeared ahead, I couldn't blame him as I was embarrassingly slow, and the miles were not slipping by quickly. The route was very hilly, crossing open countryside which under any other circumstances would have made for a beautiful ride. On this occasion however and with this bike — superman's bike, it was feeling like a very long way!

I can recall the final five or so miles where the course took us across a high open moor on a gravel drover's road or farm track. The wind had steadily increased as the day lengthened, and every rider was working hard to retain their momentum not just on the rough surface but also into a strong breeze blowing directly into our faces. It was simply painful, slow, frustrating and not enjoyable.

After what felt like forever, the route turned right downhill off the moor and through a farm steading on to a narrow country lane underneath the banks of Croagh Patrick, the holy mountain standing at a rocky seven hundred and sixty-four metres.

The transition area was not far away, and I pulled in feeling absolutely shattered. Chris was sitting waiting looking quite frustrated. He immediately began muttering at me that I had quite clearly 'bonked' and was a fool for not eating and drinking enough on route (Lesson number four I hear you say!) He was clearly aching to get going straight away and stood round impatiently as I pulled my cycling shoes off and put on the wet and muddy fell running shoes retrieved from the small backpack that I had been carrying. He thrust energy gells at me and full water bottles of pre-mixed glucose drinks.

"Get these in you as quick as you can," he grumbled before turning for the off on to the hill and our next Gaelforce challenge.

The route was quite literally straight up the side of the fell. No footpath to be seen and intimidatingly steep. There was a string of 'runners' (no one was!) heading uphill contouring to the left and the right but ultimately into the low hanging cloud and onwards to the summit. The rules were pretty straight-forwards, every competitor had to dib in at the start and end of each section and here we were required to reach the summit, dib in, and turn back for a quick decent to our bikes for the next section heading ever onwards to Westport.

Stage 4 — Croagh Patrick fell run

Now organised we headed off — on to the fell side, and upwards. Chris, in a softer moment offered to carry my drink which seemed a very generous gesture particularly because he was so clearly frustrated with my speed. The plan was for me to take some more food on board as well as to get my head together for this next section, ever upwards into the cloud — and I guess to get plenty of fluid into me as well.

The plan and the action were however very different. Chris clearly pumped up by his run-away emotions, headed briskly off up the hill and within minutes was fifty or more metres away. Perhaps he was attempting his usual tactic of pulling me onwards or perhaps it was just frustration burning through his legs — whichever the net effect was that he had my drink and was not near enough to me to be of any use at all!

Frustrated I shouted up to him in words mainly beginning with 'f' — to explain that he needed to slow down and what was the point of carrying my drink if he wasn't going to be anywhere near me. Chris by return answered in words ending mainly in 'k' but thankfully did concede to stopping and waiting. Good friends can indeed 'do stupid things in anger!'

We regrouped and headed on in momentary silence none the worse for our little moment on the hill!

And so it was as with many hills that you toil upwards with eyes alternating from the grass at your feet to the skyline and the route ahead. On Croagh Patrick we were quickly into the cloud and then not too far ahead we picked up the tourist track and turned left towards the summit. The track was significantly wide, kicked to death by the feet of millions of catholic pilgrims. This was after all 'the holy mountain' and it had clearly suffered for being so, resulting in what now was an uncomfortably stony surface with long, shallow steps that served to break your rhythm.

We joined a mass of people heading both up and down in the cloud. It was the proverbial tourist motorway. Older women in bare feet carry sturdy wooden staffs that I guessed had been up this mountain more than once before. Runners were everywhere some heading up struggling to find a pace even if they could run and others heading down wanting to allow their momentum to gather with the aid of gravity but then having to navigate through the crowds being sure not to wipe out the unsuspecting and fragile pilgrims.

It actually wasn't a particularly long climb, albeit there wasn't much fun to be had that day. We arrived at the summit church along with many others and in thick clouds. In my ignorance I simply hadn't expected there to be such a substantial building at the summit and it did seem just a little surreal to see a formal building in such an otherwise wild space.

Croagh Patrick, nick named The Reek, standing at 764m

Wasting no time, we 'dibbed' in and turned to run off the hill the same way we had come up. We were exhilarated to be on the way down and exploited the full width of the path to pass the holy masses and plunge down out of the clouds as quickly as possible.

We arrived back at the bikes in no time at all and I was now feeling so much stronger, the benefits of food and fluids having made their helpful way into my energy system. The transition area was a simple field and it was easy to tell that we were well down in the race as the vast majority of the bikes had departed leaving just a small number to be collected by weary stragglers.

Once again exchanging fell shoes for riding cleats we readied ourselves for the off and the bike journey onwards towards Westport and the next transition area at a small harbour somewhere near the town.

Stage Five Croagh Patrick to Westport — bike leg

Much rejuvenated and with far better mental preparation for the cruel gearing of my bike we headed off along the narrow lane and down the valley away from the mountain. Westport wasn't far away, no more than eight kilometres by the most direct route, but then it was doubtful that the race organisers would be taking us that way!

Not far down the tarmac lane we spied a large black arrow on a yellow background (aren't all race signs such) that pushed us assertively off the tarmac and on to a rutted old drover's road that crossed the moor towards a rocky descent. The terrain became increasingly challenging however I'd finally found my pace and began to revel in the technical demands of the ride and adopted a pretty carefree attitude towards the bike. For the first time in the race Chris dropped behind and I found myself passing a good number of more cautious competitors choosing my moment to roll past them as they hesitated above a small drop or put their foot down in caution.

As many a rider will tell you, speed, within reason, is your friend on rocky surfaces. The wheels will more often than not simply roll over an obstacle (of reasonable size) and there's a discipline in looking far enough ahead to plan your route in advance of arriving. Looking directly down at your front wheel and worrying about the obstacles that are in the 'here and now' only serves to slow you down and make the ride nerve-wracking and somehow fragmented. To a degree it pays to let the bike go, call upon your confidence that you'll cope, look ahead and trust the kit to do its job!

I found myself on a real roll now, enjoying the rocky descent and the thrill of actually passing people. It was the first time in the race that I'd actually managed to make up some ground — I'd been dropped by people on the first run, on the long bike leg and even slogging up Croagh Patrick, but now I finally felt like a competitor even if in reality I was probably battling my way up from eight hundred and something to seven hundred and something!

My new-found adrenalin continued as we swept off the moorland track and back on to tarmac. Whilst it was another country lane it definitely started to have the feel of a road that was heading towards a major town and that town could only be Westport. I slowed my pace to allow Chris to catch up and before long he hauled himself up at speed from behind. We cycled on then in unison now joining a long line of cyclists all heading the same direction.

I have no idea as to what the rules might have been about 'drafting' in an event such as this however in my head it's just bad form. For me that thirty per cent. gain in efficiency is okay on a long sportive or during a group ride — especially when the people on the front are quicker than you — but in a triathlon its certainly illegal and here it just didn't seem right.

Chris and I cycled pretty much side by side chatting about the day and reaffirming our deep friendship after the 'difference of opinion' on the slopes of the mountain. We either passed slower riders or got passed ourselves but there was now little sense of urgency. No pelotons formed and no one seemed interested in any mutual support and that was just fine by us. Actually, I think most people were just getting their heads down and thinking of the finish which was not now too far away.

The route took us through the outskirts of Westport and down to a small and very pretty fishing harbour, the piers made of local stone and wrapped by a beautiful grassy bank. Here we were directed to a marked compound where a growing mass of bikes had been hastily laid down leaving their riders free to then once again don their running shoes for the final leg to the finish.

Wasting no time Chris and I dropped our bikes amongst the melee and followed suit, dumping cycling cleats next to the bikes and pulling on wet trail shoes to be ready for the off within only a minute or two. Chris was, of course, back in his true element and immediately set a pace which was at the top end of sustainability for me. I don't think that either of us had any idea how long the leg was, in my mind it couldn't be far as we were in the town, and it seems crazy to think that the organisers would drag this all out for much longer.

Stage Six Westport Harbour to Finish

The quaint harbour surround was quickly behind us, and the tarmac surface turned to gravel and then to narrow coastal footpath as we made our way around a forested headland, through the trees and then variously on to cart tracks and muddy terrain heading into a secluded bay. It was all very lovely spoilt only by the fact that I was feeling bloody buggered and was once again chasing my light-footed friend whose energy seemed to have returned with vengeance.

And so, it was that we rounded a final corner to spy a large manor house standing within lawned grounds sweeping to the shoreline at the head of the bay. We caught the first tell-tale sounds of announcements being made from a public address system and floating to us on the afternoon's gentle breeze, the compulsory flags fluttering — all beckoning us on to the finish and the end of a great day out.

As we reached the lawned area and the taped finishing funnel I could hear our names being announced in that beautiful melodic southern Irish accent. No one in particular was paying any attention and that was absolutely fine, we were pretty far down the field and, save for our own, any excitement had long since died. We crossed the finish and in our usual tradition turned to one another and shook hands. The marshals encouraged us towards a small gazebo where the race timing print outs were being handed out alongside medals and hoodies.

I can recall events many years ago where finishing times and positions took days to publish — sometimes getting posted to you and that being the first time you'd know just how you'd faired in the race. Of course, modern day events see us wearing dibbers on our wrists, or even now they're often embedded into your race number — and results are instant with split times.

Perhaps the most influential book I've ever read with regards to running is entitled 'Running Free' by Richard Askwith. Richard is a journalist who escaped the London rat race and moved his family to Keswick in the Lake District so that he could train for and then successful complete the infamous Bob Graham Round. Having achieved this, he turned somewhat more philosophical about why we run and his own reflections upon what it might mean and our underlying motivations. The book struck numerous chords with me but the one that stays with me permanently is about attitude and enjoyment. It's my own interpretation but I think of it as reminding oneself that you're better for enjoying the run, where you are, the scenery and very often the company of good friends. That if you've toiled to reach the summit of a hill or mountain then there is no shame in stopping to take in the view — pause for a moment and look around. As he advised — no one will really care if you finish two minutes later, it might be the difference between eighty-fifth position and ninety-fifth position — but then who really cares so 'get over yourself' is how I interpret it.

So I remain interested in how I've done in the race but my sights have moved from an overall race position to an age category finish. Over time however I've become more focused on the overall approach that I first and foremost set out to enjoy the event, the nervous anticipation, the self-management of finding your own pace early on, the varying terrain and the independence brought about by carrying the right kit to deal with the changing elements. The finish is just one part of the overall experience.

Gaelforce West will long stay in my memories of adventure races. It's a commercial event for sure, super well organised and inviting you to travel through some amazing terrain and Atlantic scenery. Looking back, I'm pretty sure we created quite a few additional challenges ourselves — getting there late, not having our own bikes, not perhaps feeding properly during the race and allowing circumstances to split us as a team travelling together. That said, it was a great day out and as their own slogan says:

"Gaelforce West — No Certainties Only Adventure"

Four Peaks by Bike
Summer 2013 — In memory of Andy 'Parky' Parker

Nine men, four mountains, four hundred and forty miles of cycling and thirteen thousand feet of climbing

The British Three Peaks is a well-known challenge that has been tackled by many thousands of people from the fittest of fell runners through to corporate groups comprised of people for whom the challenge is perhaps the biggest thing they've ever undertaken.

The traditional challenge is to climb Ben Nevis in Scotland standing at four thousand, four hundred and thirteen feet followed by Scafell Pike in England at three thousand, two hundred and nine feet and then finally Snowdon in Wales at three thousand, five hundred and sixty feet. All of this and the very unpredictable driving between the mountains has to be completed within twenty-four hours.

I haven't ever come across a rule, formal or otherwise, that states whether this should be undertaken North to South or vice versa, I doubt that really matters! One debate I did once have with a friend of mine, when we first attempted the Three Peaks with a corporate group, was whether the timings could actually end when you summit upon your last mountain? Strictly speaking that's the challenge — to summit the three highest peaks — but most purists would include the walk back to the vehicle which you left at the foot of the last mountain.

All of that however is merely detail as in 2014 we had developed a new permutation of the challenge which included bikes and allowed us to both start from our home base on the Isle of Man and to include Snaefell (Snowy Mountain) at two thousand and thirty-seven feet as our first and smallest peak. We concluded that we could do that first to add the Manx element before heading off on the Isle of Man Steam Packet ferry to Liverpool and the traditional British Three Peaks.

Common to some other stories that I've written about adventure challenges, there is a consistency as this one also stems from having a great bunch of friends who relish a challenge and me having a job running a charity that could underwrite the costs of the trip in full knowledge that the eventual returned sponsorship would easily put the charity in profit.

I had worked for 'The Children's Centre' as Chief Executive since August 2000 and, over fourteen years, had encouraged the fundraising team to develop adventure events as a reliable means of charitable income generation. Indeed, their enthusiasm and the charity's investment had grown to the point that we employed a dedicated 'adventure events' fundraising team member. On several occasions the charity had organised traditional British Three Peaks walking trips and I'd had the fortune to go along on at least two of these to help guide the various people up and down the peaks. These had been great trips but, by 2014, they were becoming common place and so alongside a group of likeminded friends we started to ponder how we might do it differently — and the idea of "Four Peaks by Bike" was born.

There were nine of us in total who came together around the idea, all had a depth of experience across a number of events, and all knew each other well enough to know that we could get along throughout a journey which would certainly present some challenges.

In no particular order, the team consisted of:

Phil Drowley, a senior officer in the Manx Constabulary who had recently summited on Everest and had a depth of cycling years to call upon. His colleague and even more senior police officer, Kev Wilson, carried a few tummy pounds extra but had legs bursting with well-toned muscle and a deceptively slow but powerful cycling cadence that made him a fine fellow to tuck in behind on the long straights at twenty miles per hour.

John Swindlehurst and Dave Isherwood were great all-round triathletes, fell runners and open water swimmers. Juan Owens was one of the quietest but arguably the fittest member of the team, he'd been a part of the Land's End to John O'Groats non-stop relay team from the year before and was turning his mind to Ironman events. Matthew McSevney, another quiet soul who has very sadly since left us, had a core of steel, had cycled LEJOG solo and made little fuss about anything, a true 'just do it' character.

Paul Warburton had masterminded our first ever LEJOG adventure and had since continued to log many thousands of miles on his bike. Finally, excluding myself, was Rob Parker — the youngest team member but with a raft of Ironman finishes to his credit there could be little doubt of his ability to go the distance that this challenge required.

Sitting centrally in my job at The Children's Centre, I was able to coordinate people over the winter of 2012 / 2013 to first set the dates necessary for the event, to then recruit two support drivers into the role that is so essential for such an event and to book the various ferries, vans, hostels and other necessities that sit behind eleven people being in the right place at the right time over a seven-day period.

Bill Collister and Andy Parker were the driving and support crew. Bill had been CEO of Isle of Man Post and was a seasoned fell runner with a mental map of the Manx fells and a wisdom that made him an absolute pleasure to be around. I'd first met Bill when we walked the traditional Three Peaks several years earlier. It's a mark of the man that he'd decided to do this during the summer of his retirement from Isle of Man Post and to ask all of his staff to sponsor him for The Children's Centre rather than buy him unnecessary retirement gifts. We instantly got along and started fell running together straight afterwards. I clearly remember one late autumn afternoon up on the hills and in the clouds a few miles from his house in Glen Vine. It was starting to get dark and I'd become totally disorientated. Bill was a dozen or so metres behind and when he appeared at my shoulder, he calmly pointed towards a wall junction which, to me, seemed to be in totally the wrong direction. Of course, he was not only right but absolutely spot on in taking us back to the main path and a long tree lined descent home. It wasn't to be the last time in our running relationship that he did this!

Andy, by contrast, was the unassuming landed gentleman who pretty much played for a living. Cancer has since taken him from us, but his humour was legendary as were the sessions in his rather large home gym where many a Manx athlete gathered for a personal training session with Parkey that truly tested you to the limit. In many ways it was this wonderful charismatic person that was the link between us all — and alongside Bill his presence as support crew was fundamental to the trip's success.

'Crewing' as it is more modernly called, demands that people are pretty much selfless. They need to be in the right place at the right time day or night, moving ahead of their competitors far enough to be sure that they are ahead but not too far to risk leaving their team unattended for long stretches. This of course becomes more and more a matter of judgement as the race progresses. One time on the Devizes to Westminster Canoe Race — one hundred and twenty-five miles of kayaking and over seventy-two lock portages — we lost our support team in the middle of the night. We didn't see them for around two and a half hours by which time we were pretty despondent, and very hungry. In the end they had decided to jump seriously far ahead of us and then to wait it out knowing that we'd have to come through at some time — and indeed we did, but by then we were pretty pissed off!

Of course, as crew you have to be constantly positive, have food and drinks ready, pamper to grumpy athletes, be amusing and equally knowledgeable about the route and the conditions, give updates on who's 'been through' and what the weather is supposed to do next. Andy and Bill were the perfect combination — Andy totally the comedian who could lift our spirits in a split second and Bill the ever-organised and calm sage.

Day 1: Snaefell Mountain Isle of Man (two thousand and thirty-seven feet) a ferry journey and Snowdon (three thousand, five hundred and sixty feet)

It all began as we gathered ourselves at the ferry terminal on the sea front of the Isle of Man. Nine cyclists, two support crew, a few family members as well as the local media. Dave, a member of the staff team at Isle of Man Post, had managed to persuade them into some sponsorship of the event which included an attractive and functional grey 'Four Peaks by Bike' hoody that we now sported with great pride.

Once done with the media — which didn't take long — we loaded our various bags of personal equipment into the large box trailer alongside spare bikes and bike parts, food, water and a scutch of other 'just in case' accessories. We didn't know it at the time however that the trailer, which would be classed as a very large 'load lugger', was to be our saviour on more than one occasion in the coming days. It served not only to hold our belongings and spares but was also a place of refuge, a little oasis from the elements, where we could stand and drink hot tea or change whilst out of the weather. God bless that load lugger!

Pictures done and without any further fuss we all climbed aboard our bikes and headed off on the short journey out of Douglas and up on to the Mountain Road towards the tram station which is the natural stop from which to walk up to the summit of Snaefell.

This was absolutely the shakedown ride, we rode along with a false sense of joviality that only served to mask a secondary layer of nerves tangible around the group. We fell into an orderly cycling pattern and steadily tapped our way up the consistent but perfectly groomed tarmac of the TT course, many of us instantly regretting being overdressed as the heat of the day rose from the road to meet us.

Perhaps only thirty minutes later, having been buzzed several times by the support vehicle with cameras hanging out of windows, we reached the tram stop. Propping bikes against the trailer and van we quickly changed from road shoes into fell shoes before together heading off up the well-trodden path which climbs to the radio tower and trig point on the summit of Snaefell.

Snaefell is famous amongst more than just the Manx people as the place from which on a clear day you can see the four kingdoms — west towards Ireland and the Mountains of Mourne, north to Scotland where the Merrick Hills of Dumfries and Galloway sit, south east towards Wales — Angelsey and the Great Orm and finally east towards England and the wonderful fells of the Lake District.

Sadly, for most of the year, like many peaks, Snaefell sits in cloud and I've found myself running across it more worried about finding the path off than enjoying the view! It's also a very windy spot where the prevailing summer westerly air flow rises quickly up the mountain slopes and blasts across the summit. Worse still are the winter north easterlies that seem to cut through you and chill you to the core if you dawdle for any length of time. It's infrequently a place to hang around perhaps other than to 'dib in' or punch your card to prove you passed through on your route to a fell running finish.

However, on this day, and perhaps to celebrate the start of a great adventure journey, the sun had come out to meet us as we skipped our way together — thrilled to be underway and in anticipation of what was to come. Up on the summit and gathered around the trig point we had our first picture taken in earnest as proof that we'd been there together and then off we skipped once more to run back down to the waiting van, cycling shoes and downhill rush back to the ferry.

At the Snaefell Tram Station with Sky cyclist and Olympic Gold Medalist Peter Kennaugh Snaefell summit in background

Down at the van as we all changed, we were pleasantly surprised to be joined by a group of Manx cyclists out on a training ride who pulled in at the tram stop to take a drink and a rest and no doubt to also check out what was going on. Imagine our surprise to find the group was an elite cross section of top end amateur and very top end pro riders including Olympic Track Gold Medalist Peter Kennaugh, Commonwealth Games Mountain Biker Elliot Baxter and various other Manx youth riders destined to be picked up by the GB talent squad. Like most occasions on the Isle of Man, someone knew someone and very quickly a joking, friendly conversation broke out amongst what was now a big group of lycra-clad men. Parky took the opportunity to snap the moment and the picture above captures not just the group but the summit of Snaefell behind us and the balmy nature of the day.

The programme for the day had been carefully timed to ensure we could pack our bikes and change before boarding the two forty-five p.m. 'boat' to Liverpool. The super sea cat, an impressive looking water jet-propelled catamaran, was to whisk us across the Irish Sea and deposit us upon the UK mainland by late afternoon, allowing us enough time to then drive down to North Wales and ascend Snowdon to round off an initial great day.

From the Liverpool ferry landing, the van journey down to Llanberis in Wales was uneventful and we quickly found our overnight bunkhouse to change for the walk, up Snowdon. Within half an hour we had made some sandwiches and packed our hill sacks before being dropped at the Pen y Pass Cafe from where we were starting the walk, up Snowdon. Our intention was to use the tourist track or Pyg Track as it is best known to climb the mountain and then to descend via the Llanberis track which would take us directly to the town and straight to the comfort of the bunkhouse.

It must have been late afternoon or even early evening by the time we started walking as my memories of the ascent are sketchy. As with Snaefell I'm sure that we would have set off at a good pace still high on the early spirits of the adventure and bouncing off one another's humour. The Pyg Track is a pretty straight-forward ascent, used every year by hundreds of thousands of people. There are no navigational challenges, sadly the mountain has been brutally trampled, 'kicked to death' and aside from the sections where the path crosses massive slabs of rock there is generally a clearly defined route throughout.

Snowdon summit in the falling darkness.

We summited in the falling dark and gathered around the trig point to take a second 'we've been here' photo before then turning to pick up the path that initially follows the mountain railway back down in to Llanberis. John and Ish, with their usual boyish energy, pushed on ahead having reassured us all, but in particularly me as the sole qualified Mountain Leader, that they had walked this route before and well knew the way down! I, by contrast, had not used this route before, having only ascended and returned via the Pyg Track or the Miner's Track both of which approached the mountain from Pen y pass.

Before too long and now with nine head torches piercing the dark night sky, we dropped away from the company of the mountain railway and descended quickly. The lights of LLanberis disappeared from view and I began to feel twitchy, however both John and Ish were by now well ahead. In my mind the lights of the town would be the obvious beacon guiding us to our ultimate destination. They were now however blotted out by an increasingly large amount of dark mountain skyline. John and Ish plunged onwards down this track visible only by their combined torch light and I became increasingly questioning as to why we couldn't see Llanberis? For sure the track had swung down away from our intended route.

It took too long for us to shout for the leading two to stop and wait. I wanted to regroup and review the map. Eventually gathered together under the lights of our head torches we quickly defined that we were in fact on the Ranger's Path and indeed heading to a different car park in a different valley from Llanberis. Faced with the challenge of either reascending a good portion of Snowdon or heading onwards we opted to continue down this path and, in the fashion of our modern era, simply phone the support van and ask them to drive round and pick us up at the new road head. Not good at all and a very quick lesson to 'be in control' on the hill and to discourage the adrenalin-fuelled motivation amongst the group to run on ahead and split the team. There was no doubt that Scafell Pike and Ben Nevis could easily be more demanding as we would be fatigued from our rides and the forecast for the coming days was nowhere near as good as the one we'd just had.

Sometime after midnight having reached the road and located the waiting van, we drove back to Llanberis and the hostel before quickly dropping into bed. We had however agreed a departure time of seven a.m. to be on our bikes and riding out of Llanberis. Our destination would be Ambleside, close to the entrance to the Langdale Valley. Easy to say and now easy to reflect back upon — but the challenge then was a one hundred- and seventy-six-mile ride and none of us had ever ridden that far before!

Day 2: Llanberis to Langdale (One hundred and seventy-six miles)

I've never been a heavy sleeper and on any trip such as the Four Peaks by Bike I find myself lying awake from the very early hours waiting for the first signs of movement. There's a mental conflict between the warmth and comfort of your sleeping bag and the dark of the dormitory set against the knowledge that the departure time isn't going to move, and you have the tasks of both eating properly and well enough ahead of time as well as sorting and packing essential kit for the day.

Soon after six a.m. everyone was up — no doubt to the annoyance of every other hostel user — and we all busied around getting organised. Bill and Andy kindly made porridge and tea and then steadily we drifted outside to the van and trailer waiting in the nearby carpark. Bikes were unloaded and the essential last-minute faffing began, which is a fundamental part of any day out and is mastered much more speedily by some than others. Tyre pressures, chain oil, checking spare kit in packs under the saddle, water bottles and various drink mixes, how many pumps do we need, does anyone have a first aid kit — the list goes on!

That said, our target time of seven a.m. was achieved and the nine of us rolled out of town on the long ride North. The weather was overcast but dry with no rain forecast and spirits were high for the day ahead.

We had agreed a very simply riding pattern. Five miles on the front maintaining a speed somewhere around seventeen to eighteen miles per hour with the other eight riders tucked in behind, no dropping anyone on the hills. After five miles we would swap around meaning that any one person would only have to spend five miles on the front in every forty-five miles covered. Putting that system into a one hundred- and seventy-six-mile day meant that you'd only be required to ride four times at the front throughout the day — simple really.

And so the pattern formed, admittedly on the quieter country roads we'd ride more as a pack or in pairs, however as necessary we'd quickly fall back into our pattern. In addition, we did have the luxury of the support vehicle which would meet us at suitable locations either by distance or if there was a convenient large pull-in area where we could all safely get off the road and take a drink, drop or gain a layer of clothing or do any essential bike maintenance.

It seemed like no time at all before we reached the North Wales coast and began the steady swing eastwards along the Dee Estuary past Shotton Steel works and other industrial sites that lined the waterside. The traffic grew in intensity but there was no sense of threat amongst the group as we cycled along in a close-knit pack, our, by now well-practised formation helping us to make good miles.

There is something addictive to riding within an organised group, a sixth sense that seems to connect the riders often with just inches between their wheels but a confidence of knowing and anticipating what those ahead and those behind would do in most situations. With the effort of the riding pace and the concentration for the road, the traffic, potholes and essential navigation we would cease from talking for lengthy periods and yet remain somehow connected in our thoughts and in recording the mileage between successive people dropping off the front and a new person taking up the strain. This could all be done in silence or with a simple nod or hand signal. The flow of the group and the ride, the teamwork was a joy to be part of.

And then at one comical point in the late morning I was riding second or third in line with John Swindlehurst behind me. I sensed and could occasionally hear him grumbling about the speed that we were travelling and voicing concerns that 'we'll never get there at this rate'. Bemused as to what was his problem I did try and question him, however the road noise and focus on riding effectively meant that we didn't really connect in our conversation. Sometime later, having done my stint on the front I dropped away and left John to pick up his five miles. By the time I'd free wheeled to the back of the line and regained the moving pace of the group I was shocked to find myself having to dig deep and significantly pick up the pace! What the hell was going on? This was typical of John I thought — to totally disregard the pretty straight-forward group rules and ones that everyone else had adhered to all morning. Suddenly, at his discretion we were now riding at around twenty-one miles per hour and that was simply not sustainable.

Within minutes, even if that long, a shout went up across the group, the waving of arms, riders sitting up in their saddles and looking around to one another gesticulating. Soon, at the next safest stopping point John pulled in and we all followed, assembling into a crowd around him.

"John man, what's going on?" is possibly the polite way of re-phrasing the general question that rang round the group aimed at our tall, athletic and currently not so popular friend Mr. Swindlehurst.

"Well, it's about time we pushed on, you lot have been riding at fourteen miles per hour all morning — and we'll never get to Ambleside today at that rate!" came his animated reply.

There was confusion for a moment or two as we all looked to one another to validate what speeds we felt that we'd been leading at, and it was only then with the confidence of one another's insight that the penny began to drop.

"So John, who calibrated your computer? Have you checked it for accuracy recently?"

Smiles started to appear as John rather sheepishly started to excuse himself for not having the most accurate of bike computers and for never really checking it 'in anger' against anyone else or indeed anything else. So whilst we'd been riding between seventeen and eighteen miles per hour John had been grumbling along thinking that we were doing something closer to fourteen miles per hour. As soon as his turn came on the front, he had of course lifted the speed up to his own version of eighteen miles per hour which was closer to twenty-one or twenty-two miles per hour for the rest of us!

Enough said and with some thoughtful guidance from the rest of us John resumed his turn on the front and led us at fourteen miles per hour (!!) to the Ferry terminal in Birkenhead where we would be catching our very own 'ferry across the Mersey'.

Once on the far side in Liverpool, we met the support vehicle and stopped in the shadow of the Liver Building to eat a sandwich and have a hot brew kindly prepared by Bill and Andy from the mobile kitchen in the back of the trailer. It was early afternoon and we had lost some time waiting for the ferry and now, casually eating our late lunch, it began to feel like the day was beginning to ebb away quicker than we were tackling the miles. So it was with a renewed sense of haste we all did the necessary afternoon 'faff' routines — finding a toilet, rechecking the bike, stuffing a few snacks in to jacket pockets, changing tops, refilling water bottles and ensuring that at least one person has a grip on the route immediately ahead.

We cycled out of Liverpool initially though atmospheric old dock roads, huge dirty stone industrial warehouses towering above us and derelict pubs on street corners with boarded up windows. With a quick succession of errors, we found ourselves crisscrossing a number of streets before finding the most direct arterial road out of the city and northwards.

Away from the busy roads our morning riding routine was re-established, and we got our heads down for the long afternoon and evening riding that lay ahead.

My memory fails me of much if any detail of what followed, perhaps that's because it was a monotonous slog, I'm not sure, following the wheel of the bike in front of you calculating your distance and anticipating their slight changes in speed, exchanging the odd words but overall, just keeping your legs turning (the rest will take care of itself!) In amongst this all I can remember stopping on the old A6 just south of Lancaster. We were all feeling very tired after twelve or so hours on the road, but now with a growing sense of anticipation that the Lakes were literally just around the corner. Standing with the team munching on a banana and exchanging meaningless conversation we also consciously acknowledged that whilst we needed a break and a refuel, we also needed to keep going, to not allow ourselves to stiffen up or prematurely think that we had actually achieved the distance — because we hadn't. We needed to get through Lancaster and then up into the Southern Lakes close to Kendal before then making the final run through a hillier section into Ambleside and out the other side for the final few miles up the Langdale Valley and the Old Dungeon Ghyll Hotel car park.

In anticipation of the soon-to-be dark, we dug out our bike lights and fitted them as necessary. Then it was off again and once more heads down for the final session. Just before we headed off, I called my great friend Mark Hatton who was generously hosting us all that evening at his house in Ambelside. His wife Sandy had been press-ganged into making us a very welcome curry and then we could bed down for the night in the warmth and comfort of his beautiful lakeland home. Better still Mark had agreed to guide us over Scafell Pike from Langdale the next morning. This was a route that he knew well, and it would also mean for myself that there were no worries around navigation and route-finding with a foggy mind after such a long day in the saddle.

It was dark by the time we reached the Old Dungeon Ghyll Hotel car park. The end of what had been all-in-all a pretty impressive day. For me, my legs had been feeling heavy and tired over the last twenty or so miles and I had progressively dropped behind the main group who had accelerated at the thrill of finishing. The undulations of the low lakeland fells had really taken their toll and I was mighty pleased to see the van but also mighty pleased with our day in the saddle — it remains the furthest that I've ever ridden in one session, oddly I recall that it left me wondering how a two-hundred-mile day might feel?

We quickly passed the bikes to Bill and Andy to carefully pack and pad in the trailer. All of the riders selfishly jumped into the warmth of the minibus and sat waiting like a group of tourist riders in Majorca waiting for the morning shuttle out to the start of a ride. In our case Ambleside was just fifteen minutes away and Mark had called to say that the meal was ready and cold beers waiting in his fridge, surely there is no greater motivation for a tired 'athlete' than the thought of food, a hot shower, fresh clothes and a cold beer, "sheer bloody luxury" as Mark would often say.

Day 3: Scafell Pike and then cycling from Borrowdale to Abington (One hundred and two miles)

There were definitely to be no sleeping in on this trip and mindful of another big day ahead everyone was up and at it early the next morning. Whilst the bikes could remain packed, it was time to liberate our own mountain walking gear from kit bags and get sorted for the healthy walk out of Langdale and over the tops including Scafell Pike before dropping down into Borrowdale to join the support van and the bikes for our ride North.

The forecast was not good, low cloud, rain and high winds dictated that it was full mountain kit and a good deal of spares to be shared across the group — especially for those for whom this 'mountain malarkey' was entirely something new.

Mark was in fine form. In his usual generous manner, he handed out lunch provisions from seemingly bottomless cottage cupboards, chocolate snacks, fruit, crisps and rolls with fillings to accommodate everyone's choice all appeared and were willingly taken and packed for the walk.

We made an interesting sight as we assembled next to the minibus readying for the off. The range of hill kit was diverse if not impressive. From Phil who was sporting some of his almost professional 'Everest' garb to John and Ish who'd never been truly up on a mountain and had simply fashioned their best cycling kit to look something like walking gear. Their footwear was running shoes and whilst this wasn't a problem it made an interesting contrast to the boots and gaiters that others had on.

Bill and Andy delivered us all to the spot that we'd stopped riding at the evening before and we tumbled out of the van before donning our rucksacks and heading off. The route 'chosen' was initially along the 'Cumbrian Way' following Mickleden Beck towards the steep climb up Rossett Gill, Angle Tarn and on towards Esk Hause. We would then skirt around Great End before heading over Broad Crag and finally our last climb up to the summit of Scafell Pike.

The weather was pretty much as forecasted. Almost immediately as we began our ascent, we stepped through the cloud base and the drizzle began to make its inevitable way into and through people's equipment. Perhaps it's just me, maybe I've suffered all of my life from a poor kit budget or just made bad kit choices, it could even be that I've been tight when it comes to spending on good kit but I simply cannot remember the last time that I had a full day in the hills during bad weather when I actually felt properly dry!

This day was no exception and slowly, slowly the damp

crept in, through poorly taped seams, up cuffs that didn't Velcro tight enough and down necks where the stitching was coming away. This was all fine whilst you were moving but far less so in the wind when anyone stopped, heat was lost desperately quickly and those cold shivers down the spine were never far away.

By contrast to the weather, Mark was a real champion as he knew the route by heart and time spent navigating was an absolute minimum even in the swirling clouds. He set an assertive pace and we all set to keep up with him, many of us suffering heavy legs from the day before and the new test of the contrast between yesterday's rotational motion and today's striding. On we went covering the ground quickly and without much of a sense as to where we were, Mark constantly ahead just visible in the near distance but checking to see that we were following — us all once again forming into our familiar line mimicking our road chain gang but up on a hill! Was this to be our life for the coming days? Simply following one another in a line hoping that the person at the front knew where they were going!

We stood on the summit of Scafell Pike (nine hundred and seventy-eight metres) jubilant that we had now scaled three of the four peaks. There was no view to speak of, the wind still had a cutting edge to it and the cloud foiled any sense of height or Lakeland vista. Other day trippers were variously sitting eating sandwiches, taking photos and enjoying the high point of their day. By contrast we felt very much in a hurry, partly spurred on by the thought of a one-hundred-mile ride that had yet to be tackled but also by our thoroughly damp thermals and soaking wet outer layers. Predictably this meant that once again, other than to take our own mandatory picture and grab a snack, we were off and almost literally running down our ascent. Mark had elected to take us via 'The Corridor Route' and past Styhead Tarn before descending Grains Gill to Seatoller at the foot of the Honister Pass and the waiting van.

Back out of the cloud I have a memory that the rain stopped, and some weak sunshine filled the valley ahead of us. It began to look like a nice afternoon for a ride and Mark set to making a few phone calls to his wife Sandy and friend from Ambleside organising that he and friend 'Steve' could join us for some of the route up to our overnight stop Abington.

Down at the van the team grabbed kit bags and quickly changed from wet hill gear into the almost mandatory brightly coloured cycling lycra. Bill and Andy fussed around, pleased to have something to do having been sat in Seatoller for several hours. The trailer was open, food was out to graze on, and a hot drink was ready waiting for us. Much as the sunshine was weak it was nevertheless blissful, warming limbs and drying the road surfaces of the lakeland lanes that we were about the ride along.

Within thirty minutes we were all changed, fed, trailer repacked, bikes variously checked and ready for the off. I think it was around one thirty p.m. but then it could have been later and by comparison to the previous day's one hundred and seventy-six miles, the afternoon's ride of one hundred miles didn't seem intimidating! Spirits were high as we rolled out of the car park together — or so we thought. Gently making our way along the first mile or so from Seatoller into Borrowdale we became aware of a distant barrage of shouting coming from behind. We slowed together and quickly realised it was Phil Drowley — one of our Isle of Man Constabulary colleagues who was peddling hard to catch us up and using language that was certainly not becoming of a police officer. Indeed, so bad was the abuse that he was comically hurling at us that a local resident shouted back at him to 'curb' his language! Phil's head dropped and his shoulders hunched in embarrassment. It turned out he left the car park only seconds after us but headed right instead of left, an easy mistake that had quickly put him at the start of the tortuous climb up Honister Pass. Whilst he hadn't gone far up the hill before realising his mistake, Phil had nevertheless immediately punished his already heavy legs and he was not happy!

So we were off, heading first into Keswick and then on towards Penrith and Carlisle — the usual backroads to avoid the tourist traffic and heavy goods vehicles. We quickly fell back into our routine of five miles on the front although with two new riders, Mark and Steve, there seemed to be more time riding two abreast and enjoying some conversation and the afternoon sun. The pace was certainly up and on the long straight sections of the old A6 from Carlisle towards Gretna we sustained long periods of plus twenty miles per hour.

It is a reflection of many multi-day rides that I've been involved in that your body is quite incredible at adapting to what you ask of it. On the Land's End to John O'Groats trips for sure the first two to three days are hard but then your body suddenly clicks as if in realisation that all you're asking of it is another day sat on a bike turning your legs and making progress. "Steady away" as many a runner or rider would say, or as someone else once said to me "You just keep turning your legs and the rest will take care of itself".

Here now on the old A6 our little peloton had firmly found its groove and we made excellent progress north, through Gretna and onwards across the Scottish countryside. Paul Warburton had the route plugged into his Garmin so, for the majority of us, it was as simple as riding and chatting interspersed by a navigation instruction from somewhere back within the group. Head down, peddle, peddle shelter behind big Kevin Wilson and get dragged along, occasionally pop out and do your stint up front and toil a little harder watching your speedo' to be sure to maintain the average!

Fifty or so miles in we pulled into a road side lay-by where Mark and Steve's wives were waiting to pick them up and whisk them back to his lovely warm house in Ambleside. The rest of us had plenty more miles to knock off but we stopped anyway to wish them well and thank Mark in particular for his local knowledge of Scafell Pike that morning. We also took the opportunity to find and fix on our bike lights ready for the fading light of the evening and to grab a little to eat from out of the trusty trailer, refilling water bottles and stowing an extra layer ready for the inevitable temperature drop. These intermittent meetings with the van and of course Bill and Andy were always great for group morale. Andy, in particular, had a wicked sense of humour and a fine sense of how to keep motivation up within the group. With his sharp wit and roaring laugh, he was always a welcome sight stood next to the park van up in the distance.

Again, time fades the clarity of my memory around the second half of that afternoon and evening's ride. I know for sure that we reached the services at Abington on the M74 (via the backroads of course) around midnight and feasted on fish and chips from the restaurant in the motorway service station.

The group had broken into two smaller bunches over the final miles and I had been hanging on to the tails of Rob Parker, John Swindlehurst and Dave Isherwood. My front light's battery had died, and I clearly recall plunging down a long tree-covered lane into Abington village guided only by Rob's rear flashing red taillight. Charged both by the adrenalin of the moment and also the fact that the day was all but over I was whooping and shouting as we sped along, myself virtually unsighted! There's been many a time that I've reflected back on that descent, leafy road surface, dark, no light — and concluded that I might have been better advised to have tackled it in a more conservative way!

Rooms had been booked at the small service station hotel and we wasted no time in retrieving kit from the trailer, stowing bikes and heading for a well-earned shower and then bed. The truth of the matter — even though it had been a great day — was that we needed to be up and about early ready to ride to Fort William — one hundred and fifty miles away!

Day Four: Abington to Fort William — One hundred and fifty miles via Glasgow, Loch Lomond and Rannoch Moor.

After an uneventful night and early morning service station breakfast we were off again cycling out of Abington Services and over the top of the motorway towards our country road north, the little known and lonely B7078. For those reading that might know this section you'll know that it's a poorly paved surface pretty much left to its own devices now that the motorway has been built. It has a consistent uphill gradient as you battle your way up to a wild and open watershed. Few vehicles now use the road, albeit in its day it must have been the major route north. Now it's only the occasional farmer that roars along it in their pick-up with dogs barking wildly in the back. The road offers little shelter as it roams across the wide-open rolling hills — allowing the wind to slowly nip at both your temperature and energy. It's a very unsatisfactory route to Glasgow but from Abington there are few if any other choices. Once over the main watershed there's lots of twisting and turning on country lanes through unattractive villages that motivate you only to keep going with the anticipation that Glasgow's not that far away — but it is and I recall it seeming to take forever to reach the outskirts of the city and to feel that we were actually making some decent progress.

We skirted the city from East Kilbride heading then westwards towards Paisley to pick up the city cycle network. We navigated ourselves onwards to the Erskine Bridge and then to Dumbarton with a renewed energy as we left Glasgow behind and began to anticipate the opening up of the wonderful Scottish countryside almost immediately out of the city. We had arranged to meet the van at a service area on the outskirts of Dumbarton where we knew there was a large Costa as well as a shop to re-stock on snacks.

Road-side cafes are dangerous places when out on a long ride. They offer hot drinks and tasty treats as well as shelter and soft seats — but the temptation that pulls you in then seems to speed up time and before you know it forty-five minutes has passed and you're pondering a second drink and more banter with your riding mates in the luxurious comfort of the cafe. The truth however is that you're dropping time and therefore miles, and on a long day that begins to matter.

The forecast that we had was for deteriorating weather as the day progressed and so we resisted some of the temptation to stop for long and managed a more considered rest, just one coffee, and a pit stop to buy some chocolate.

Back on the bikes we revelled in leaving Glasgow behind and now knowing that we were heading into some of Scotland's finest scenery, Loch Lomond, The Bridge of Orchy, Rannoch Moor and then Glencoe before eventually arriving in Fort William itself at the foot of Ben Nevis.

I was personally now on very familiar territory and thriving at riding through such amazing scenery with a great group of mates. Scotland, in my humble opinion, is truly God's own country and I need little excuse to head up there whether for a family holiday or a 'boys adventure' such as this.

The Four Peaks by Bike team were back in their well-formed routine and we made good time along the banks of Loch Lomond to Tarbert where the road divides going either left to Arrochar and further to Inveraray or right, as we were, to head on to Crianlarich and Tyndrum. This section of the road gets pretty narrow and is often wet either from rain or from 'run off' cascading down from the hills to the Loch side. The traffic is compressed along this section then further agitated by endless tourist coaches making their way north or south with wide-eyed passengers watching the beauty whisk by through their coach window. Cars, cars and caravans, mobile homes and coaches all meet head on and battle to make their own journeys' progress — cyclists holding them up only makes their frustrations increase.

From the end of the loch there's a steady but long climb.

It takes you up Glen Falloch and over another less impressive watershed before then quickly descending down into Crianlarich — another tempting cafe stop famous for its train station and converted old train coach cafe. We resisted though as we'd set our sights on the next village of Tyndrum some seven miles further north. The skies had greyed considerably, and the wind was picking up — the forecasted weather was indeed arriving, and we had the most exposed and toughest part of the day yet to do. Little did we know at that point just what an adventure this next section was going to be!

At Tyndrum we re-grouped outside the world famous 'Green Welly' shop. The rain had started albeit only lightly and the wind was certainly starting to make its presence known. I have a vivid memory of putting on my waterproof cycling jacket in anticipation that we were about to climb firstly out of the village and on to a long section leading to the Bridge of Orchy after which the road climbs again on to the wilds of Rannoch Moor. Kevin Wilson watched me pulling my jacket on with an amused scepticism. He commented, questioning me as to why I was 'over dressing' and I gave a rather short response that 'if it's windy and wet down here, it's going to be bloody wild up there!' Little did I know just how accurate that comment was!

As you leave Tyndrum the A82 splits immediately, heading right the road climbs immediately sweeping underneath the cover of a tall forest that shelters you to your left. It's great tarmac but people were cold after the stop and the day's toils had begun to set in. Almost immediately the group scattered, the stronger climbers pushed on ahead and of course those who were slower dropped behind. I ended up somewhere in the middle, a bit in 'no-man's land' neither quick enough to stay with the climbers but, at that point anyway, slightly stronger than the back markers. So I plodded on alone eventually enjoying some speed down a long steady descent on the good surface that runs you quickly through to the Bridge of Orchy. There, sheltered in front of the hotel and huddled under the canopy, the faster riders had waited, and we once again re-grouped now realising that the weather really was going to be a challenge. It seemed to be that we had reached that point in the ride where simply keeping going to stay warm against both the wet and the driving wind was the most sensible option. Indeed, at the Bridge of Orchy, it was the only option as the van and trailer were nowhere to be seen.

We waved the back markers through encouraging them not to stop but to keep turning their legs and heading ever northwards. The wind had picked up a notch or two and was now sweeping in menacingly from the west, buffeting our left shoulders and threatening to drive us out into the main carriage way towards the oncoming traffic. Spray flew off tyres, and the wind pulled at our rain jackets, it was now proper serious weather and I imagined with a grim smile what the drivers of cars passing us must have been thinking. I knew for sure that the next climb would splinter the group again, it's a good half mile or more up a steep gradient switching back on to the 'Black Mount' and then Rannoch Moor itself at three hundred and forty-eight metres. The summit of this next sweeping climb ends at a large viewpoint affording a magnificent vista back down the valley that we'd thrashed along.

The rest area is usually packed with tourist vehicles

stopping to take pictures of the views or for a snap with the ever-present Scottish Bagpiper who stands gloriously against the elements playing for his supper. Today however there was none of that. The rain had driven the bagpiper home and the coaches and cars pressed on hurrying their way to Glencoe or more likely Fort William and its multitude of pubs and coffee shops.

Now strung out but within distant eye-sight of one another none of us stopped, we just kept our heads down and battled the elements. The road swings west and, as it did, that took us firmly into the teeth of what was now for sure a full-on gale. The day had become an 'every person for themselves' affair.

Personally, I was determined and still managing to cycle with John Swindlehurst and, I think, Paul Warburton? Half focusing upon the soaking road and half anticipating the next major gust, I also endeavoured to keep some cognisance of the wheel just ahead of me. John and Paul were leaning to their left at a pretty heavy angle, shoulder into the breeze and taking the gusts as they charged across the moor. The rain was now painful, stinging through thin cycling jackets that no longer offered any real protection. The strongest gusts that came through literally skittered us sideways across the carriageway, thin tyres battling to retain a grip on the soaking road surface when our body weight was no longer sufficient to maintain their traction against the strength of the wind.

We battled on making slow progress but at least the effort was keeping us warm whilst we were still moving. I knew this road well and therefore had a very good idea as to just how far we had to go. After the summit of the moor and the complete wild desolation of the beautiful empty space we began the steady descent down past the Kings House Hotel, the landmark pub in the middle of the moor. It was mostly significant to me that day as it was the first time ever that I'd had to cycle downhill to maintain some form of momentum — so strong was the headwind! Through the rain and spray — much of which was being generated by cars albeit passing us cautiously — we glimpsed the white outline of the minibus and trailer parked up ahead, a glorious sight and one I'll never forget. Bill and Andy had parked at the foot of the 'Devil's Staircase' where the road swings sharply left and heads into the top tight section of Glencoe proper and then the steeper descent on towards the village.

Our spirits lifted with the promise of some respite from the elements, and we pushed just that little bit harder closing the gap towards a hot drink, and dry clothes. Minutes later when we arrived it was instantly apparent that Bill and Andy had parked the vehicle absolutely perfectly. The nose of the minibus was directly into the prevailing wind and the back of the trailer was wide open — downwind — affording a haven of shelter. Wasting no time we propped our bikes against the trailer, more laying them down than standing up, and then jumped into the trailer itself...

"What the fuck was all that about..." were the first words that I heard from John and Paul. Andy and Bill were roaring with laughter but equally setting about getting people dry as they arrived. The faster members of the team were by now already changed and preparing for the off which made good sense as the trailer was filling up with wet cyclists and a highly amused support crew!

We dived into our bags and unceremoniously threw off wet kit, no shame amongst soaking cyclists before pulling on dry layers, thermals, cycling lycra, new dry replacement waterproofs and a thick jacket that would at least do the job of warming us whilst we sheltered and ate for a few minutes. Meanwhile the trailer was literally rocking in the breeze, the rain beating against the fibreglass shell seeking any weakness in its thin skin to get at us. Spirits were high, adrenalin pumping and jokes flying — it was proving to be the most memorable of rides and we were by now in sight of the end of the day in Fort William just some twenty miles distant.

As any athlete will know, there quickly comes a time during a recovery stop and getting dry that the realisation dawns of 'getting back out there'. I certainly, even having changed and wearing a decent down jacket, knew that I had to move on pretty quickly. Stopping any longer would just allow my body to start stiffening up and we were stood upright in the draughty trailer with the elements constantly reminding us that they were out there ready to greet us as soon as we left its shelter. No amount of deliberation was going to get me through the next section, it had to be done no matter what the weather, so I found myself exchanging a brief peak communication glance with John which said 'let's get going'.

Paul opted to stay on and to wait for the stragglers so without any further ado John and I stripped off our down coats, pulled on a dry beanie and then our cycling helmets ready for the off. Maintaining this momentum, we immediately were then out of the trailer and picking up our bikes. I can't even recall Bill or Andy emerging to help us, I think they knew they'd simply get wet and that we'd be gone literally in seconds after emerging back into the wild Scottish elements.

So we were off again and it remained utterly brutal. From the Devil's Staircase the road climbs briefly before then descending towards a tighter section and an 'S' bend passing a large lay-by and scenic viewpoint known as 'the meeting of the waters'. On many a trip north with young people I'd stopped here to let them stretch their legs and be out of the minibus for a while, the coming together of several impressive waterfalls at one point usually made for a good stop and great pictures — however not today. We found ourselves once again back into peddling downhill territory as the wind being channelled through the cut in the gorge became even stronger, endeavouring to push us back up the hill. It was bordering on reckless but was absolutely exhilarating at the same time I found myself simultaneously grinning and gritting my teeth, not cold or scared but simply in awe of what we were riding through.

Thereafter is a long descent through the main body of Glencoe valley and much of it a blur of spray and managing gusts of wind buffeting us as were ploughed on. Alone now, separated from the front riders and with no sight of those behind, John and I headed on exchanging a few shouted messages over the wind. I proposed that we keep moving until we reached the actual village at Glencoe where I knew there'd be the opportunity to take shelter at the hotel. In theory we could wait there for the others to catch up. I thought that John had heard me clearly and I passed him shortly before the hotel itself and then swung in off the road and on to the forecourt of the Glencoe Hotel itself.

Just feet behind me John followed suit and we swiftly jumped off our bikes and took a few hurried paces to the hotel front door and into the lobby of the bar. We were absolutely sodden, water running rather than dripping from our clothes, gloves ringing with water as we clenched our fists and feet squelching in riding shoes. The joy of our waterproof socks was not lost on us as they had become water retaining socks at least giving us a pool of warm water to keep our feet tucked within.

Once in the lobby I stood there, too polite to go further into the main bar and hotel reception. The area was crowded, people sat around tables in friendly group huddles all with inviting looking pints of beer and glancing at us with incredulous looks. Steadily the water dripping from both of us started to create an actual pool of water on the floor around our feet and a decidedly wet looking area of carpet began to spread outwardly from us.

It was at this point that John muttered something about now just having to wait for the van to arrive and wondering where the other faster riders were? He seemed to have become relaxed and, leaning against a warm radiator, he began to strip off his soaking outer layers.

"What are you doing John?" I asked him.

"Well, I'm starting to get out of this kit" came his indignant reply, "We are done for the day, aren't we?"

It dawned on me that against the wind and the rain, the spray and road noise, John had mistakenly heard or thought that this was indeed the hotel at the end of the day. To be fair to him he'd never been to Scotland before and had no idea as to actually where he was. For all I knew he might have even been thinking that this was average Scottish weather. With that in mind it wasn't overly surprising that he'd relaxed and let his guard down and I guess was already figuratively ordering his first beer at the bar!

My response was probably not the most sympathetic, in short and descriptive words I explained that this was by no means the end of the day and that we had both Ballachulish and Onich villages to ride through before the final eight-mile section into Fort William itself and the proper end of the day.

With a sullen look John pulled his 'waterproof' back on and we silently walked back outside to get back on our bikes. It transpired that our timing was awful, as we left the front door of the hotel, we noticed the back of Juan Owens who had just flashed past us head down against the wind, he didn't hear our shouts and simply cycled on alone in his own little world of survival.

As we walked towards our bikes Matthew McSevney appeared coming down the road, a second lonely figure in as many minutes and this time with advance warning we were able to wave him down and he peeled off the road and into the hotel car park. He, like us, was soaked through and had a slightly manic look about him. Matthew had cycled the entire stretch by himself having quickly been dropped on the first climb out of Tyndrum. Whilst there was never any doubt as to his steely determination — indeed in later years he repeatedly proved himself to be above and beyond in endurance events — Matthew had stubbornly seen through the gruelling ride totally alone.

So, after a brief exchange of stories and short updates, we rode on together now picking up the shores of Loch Leven to our right and swiftly on through the village of Ballachulish towards the famous bridge over the entrance to the loch and the tidal race that lay below.

Ballachulish is an interesting and pretty little community nestled as it is along the shoreline of the loch. On this road, well-travelled by myself I had stopped there on many occasions whether it had been to allow children time out of the minibus or to buy supplies at the local village store. Once we'd used the impressively large local garage and road recovery services to re-weld our kayak trailer and on more than one occasion to put a new tyre on to a wheel rim that had been damaged somewhere on the single-track roads of the west coast. My most significant stop here however had been many years before when we'd been camping with a group of young adults at the Glencoe campsite. They were a rowdy bunch and needed constant entertainment and any energy sapping activity to help them sleep soundly at night. As the youthful leaders, we ourselves decided that it would be a 'great idea' to take a group out by kayak and sleep on one of the small burial islands which lie just a few hundred metres off the shore. Quite why we thought that this would be a good idea — I can't now recall — but I do have vivid memories of kayaking out under the weak beams of early day's head torches with rucksacks full of sleeping bags and roll mats to then sleep wild not far from a cluster of ancient gravestones. This bizarre trip — especially for the teenagers who came along — was made even the odder in the knowledge that the islands there are famous for being the burial ground of witches, taken there to be buried 'offshore' for the safety of the local community.

Needless to say — we didn't have a great night's sleep on those burial islands — and I'd struggle to explain in a court of law as to why we even thought it was a good idea in the first place!

Back on the Four Peaks by Bike adventure, we resumed our very wet and soggy toil along the road but now at least had the enjoyment of a new dynamic, with increased company and the fact that we had descended out of the worst of the elements. The road runs tight along the shores of Loch Leven and serves as one of the main drags north to Fort William, so the traffic moves fast and the subsequent spray expelled from passing cars and trucks was both intimidating and depressing. We hadn't been going for too long, certainly well before the road swings right to cross the Ballachulish Bridge, when we spotted a lonely figure sitting at the side of the road. The figure was quickly identifiable as Juan Owens, hunched over against the elements and seemingly to be stopped for no apparent reason. We closed upon him quickly and he looked up with a weak smile as our brakes squealed us to a halt alongside.

Juan was sitting munching on a banana — in the rain and all alone. He looked a most forlorn character, bedraggled, hunched and shivering it seemed the most obscure of places to have chosen to stop — because there was nothing of relevance there, not even a bench to sit on.

"What are you doing Juan?" we asked in a rather polite British way.

"I decided to stop and eat and to have a serious word with myself" he responded his weak smile becoming a beaming grin. "I am absolutely spent, needed a rest and needed some fuel" he continued.

"You look absolutely bloody freezing," I said to him, "Come on, get back on your bike and we'll all ride this last leg out together, only nine miles or so to Fort William."

Without question good old Juan hauled himself up off the grass verge and remounted his bike. Experienced athlete that he was, not to mention Manx Lifeboat Engineer — he knew how to look after himself and knew that riding would soon regenerate some essential body heat especially if he could draft someone else and grab a little bit of a tow for a while.

And so, we pressed on — four of us now, over the Ballachulish Bridge and on through Onich. Psychologically this was a challenging village to pass through as we'd booked ourselves in to the Inchcree Bunkhouse for the night and this was here in Onich and required us to ride — soaked and chilled — past the front door and on for a further eight miles. However, after all we'd just encountered our determination was absolutely firm and we stuck together, not riding particularly fast, and just kept going.

At some point along that final section the van passed us and Andy called out that they would be waiting at the main car park on the seafront as we entered the town. We pressed on, almost home and ready to stop, to pack our bikes into the trusty trailer, to get warm in the minibus but most importantly to get back to the bunkhouse and have a long and very hot shower!

I've some memory of the car park and of Andy and Bill energetically taking our bikes from us and encouraging us straight into the van. We somehow had all arrived within a reasonable time of one another and as such there wasn't any significant waiting around before doors were shut and we sped off for the short drive back to Onich.

It began to feel like it was all about to be over, we had after all now done all the necessary riding, the weather had thrown just about everything at us, and we were all here in one piece and still managing to make light of the adventure. But of course, and I didn't compute this at the time, there was every chance that the rain we had been battling all day had most likely been falling as snow up on the slopes of Ben Nevis and that particular challenge remained waiting for us the next day!

Day Five: Ben Nevis and a time trial back to Onich (four thousand, four hundred and thirteen feet and eight miles respectively)

There wasn't much life and energy left in anyone that evening — having managed to shower and sort our respective equipment, we ventured to the bar of the fabulous Inchcree Bunkhouse and ordered food. Isn't it great when you are at an event such as this that you can eat exactly what you want in the evening — if you've just spent the day using over nine thousand calories, then there's really little reason for holding back? My favourite food — at that time anyway — was cheese burgers, in fact I was known for my love of a cheese burger and that evening was no exception.

Almost inevitably however our early evening bravado was soon snuffed out by the warmth of the bar, our food intake and a beer or two. The soft downy feel of a sleeping bag and potential of a good few hours in a horizontal position became overwhelmingly attractive and it didn't take long for the first of us to bid the others a good night and head off back to the dormitory. The ice had been broken and quickly everyone followed — bed was most definitely the place to be. Even the loudest of snorers couldn't have kept anyone awake that night — we were well and truly buggered but we laid our heads down with that warm satisfied glow of achievement — what a day it had been.

So day five began for the team bright and early. We were by now very comfortable in each other's company and the deluge of jokes and well-intentioned personal insults formed a consistent undercurrent of conversation. As the slumber of the night was shaken off, people began the task of dressing and packing for a mountain day. Cycling kit was put to one side and exchanged now for walking trousers and mountain jackets, fleeces and hats. Unlike the cycling, where we were all much of a muchness with regards to strength and endurance, the range of experience in the hills for walking was radically different. As I've mentioned Phil Drowley was not long back from summiting on Everest, Matthew McSevney was well at home in the hills, and I was a qualified Summer Mountain Leader which sort of gave me the responsibility as leader for the day — or so it appeared from the way in which most of the group quizzed me about the mountain. By contrast John Swindlehurst, Dave Isherwood and Rob Parker were as good as mountain virgins and I worried as I saw them putting simple running trainers on their feet for what could well prove to be a demanding and wet day. Even more disturbing they were using a pump bag as their rucksack and their cycling windproof jackets were now substituting as their outer mountain layer.

We were quickly away, being self-sufficient for breakfast and into the minibus for the short drive back through Fort William and up to the car park at the bottom of the tourist path for the Ben. Bill had decided that this was his day and he looked thrilled to be leaving the van and trailer behind having been pretty much attached to it for the previous four days. As a tight group we set an early considered pace 'trending generally upwards' as the Scottish Mountain Guide would say.

Things were relatively uneventful, we walked and chatted, toiling upwards and began to enjoy the views as we gained elevation and the countryside opened up behind us. For sure it was windy, and the temperature steadily dropped as we climbed — I think the general rule of thumb is minus one degree for every one hundred and fifty metres climbed. In my mind the well-known 'tarn' that lies on the route right next to the footpath always feels like a sensible midway stopping point and it was here that we did indeed take a few minutes to regroup and assess how people were doing. There was now certainly a split forming in the group with some people labouring harder than others after the previous four days of flat-out endurance activity. Juan, Matt and Phil were chomping to get on with things and some of the others — certainly the less well-equipped people were starting to feel the cold and, I sensed, to be a bit spooked by the mountain itself.

We resumed the walk upwards together, however Juan quickly pulled ahead and to my frustration disappeared into the cloud. For those who don't know the Ben tourist path, the tarn is quickly followed by a long series of switch backs that ascend steeply up to the summit plateau. The end of these 'zig zags', where they exit the climb and join the plateau, is a very important place to be able to find when retreating from the summit. The plateau itself has various gullies, the most famous of which is 'five finger gulley', that drop precipitously away and have claimed the lives of several unsuspecting people who literally walk off them in bad weather and through poor navigation, route planning and mountain knowledge.

Not far up the 'zig zags' we crossed the snow line and Juan rather frustratingly pulled ahead disappearing into the cloud and was then both out of sight and shouting contact. Led by myself the others all plodded on but now in the snow, the path became less well defined and progress slowed. John and the others in trainers had wet feet and were also slipping on the surface making their walk frustrating and even more of a worry for myself as the 'leader'.

I'm not sure just how many of the zig zags we'd completed however there came a point in the gathering wind, the cloud, the wet snow and the dropping temperature that I stopped the group and asked their view about continuing. As you might guess, there was a mixed response — Matt and Phil were all for continuing, however the others very readily volunteered that this was far enough and that turning back was totally acceptable. They didn't seem to have any doubt that their sponsors back at home would honour their payments for the challenge — forgiving them for not reaching to top of Ben Nevis by perhaps two hundred to three hundred metres.

From my point of view, I was most certainly worried about the less well equipped and those who had no mountain knowledge to draw upon. I had a quick conference with Phil and Matt who were sure that they wanted to complete the mountain themselves and we could also not forget that Juan was ahead of us and no doubt continuing to the summit. It seemed wise to have some people go up and rejoin Juan to ensure that he was brought down safely. In addition, the fact that both Matt and Phil were in full mountain gear — and that Phil had only recently submitted on Everest left me feeling pretty confident that they could look after themselves.

So, Phil and Matt continued up and I turned the others around — which didn't require any persuasion whatsoever! Indeed, John Swindlehurst almost started running back down so happy was he that we were now descending.

Before long we were back at the tarn and we again briefly stopped to gather our thoughts, have a drink and a bite to eat — and then we descended onwards, our steps lightened by the fact that we were benefiting from gravity, the air was warming and we were out of the cloud and enjoying the fantastic views.

And so we descended and eventually with heavy legs rejoined Andy and the van parked beside the bunkhouse-come-bar and cafe. It was beginning to feel like the adventure was all over and there was a light mood amongst us all accepting that there were still three of us upon on the hill. We gathered together in the cafe and ordered coffees and food — exchanging stories of the hill and of the past four days, the weather, the distances, our individual lows and highs, the personal demons we'd battled and our mutual amusement and amazement as to just how much we'd achieved in a relatively short space of time. The air was thick with stories and laughter the time passing quickly before the heavy wooden door of the cafe door was thrown open and the final three of our team joined us flushed with the personal sense of achievement of absolute completion.

There was however just one final challenge that we fancied — before our last evening together and the inevitable plan to enjoy a few beers with no pressure to get up early and spend a full day walking or cycling or even both — and that challenge, relatively tame, was to ride the ten miles back from here, the base of Ben Nevis back to the bunkhouse at

Onich. Juan, John, Ish, Kevin, Rob and I all decided that we fancied that final ride and as such we retreated back to the van and faithful trailer to find our cycling kit and unpack our bikes for one final time.

It started as the most innocent of rides cycling at times in single file and at other times two abreast along the busy A82 from Fort William heading South along the shores of Loch Linnie. Whilst our legs were tired from the long days in the saddle, they were also road conditioned and after the first few miles of gentle warm up I could sense a steadily increasing pace spreading almost naturally through the group. The road surface was excellent — new tarmac providing us with some of the best riding we'd had. It was impossible to say where or who was pushing the pace — no one was breaking away however just like runners sitting upon one another's shoulders and the group pace increasing so we steadily climbed through the mph readings until we were pretty much flat out and into some kind of road racing mode.

Now I'm no speedster on a road bike and I must admit to have spent much of the time hanging somewhere within the little peloton enjoying the benefits of other people's labours. It was totally exhilarating, and our speed was only very occasionally interrupted by some short undulation in the otherwise flat and perfect surface. With a glimmering sea loch to our right and extensive mountain and forest scenery to our left the ride was beautiful but punishing. As I am prone to do on such occasions, I found myself chuckling high on the adrenalin of an adventure with great friends and the inner celebration of achievement.

For years back at home in my garage I'd used a training

DVD on my turbo trainer — a Carmichael Train Right Road Race programme to be accurate — that had helped me significantly in building my strength. I'd mounted a TV / DVD player on the garage wall and would retreat there two to three nights per week over the winter months to push myself and privately sweat in the hope that I'd reap the benefits sometime in the spring and summer. To this day I can still hear the final sprint section of that DVD, the outright push to the finish line, where the trainer — ever present in the DVD itself — begins to scream:

"You've been waiting all day for this, don't get dropped now, dig, dig, dig!" — and I'd done so many times all by myself in that garage sweat dripping off me and gathering little pools around the bike on the training matt.

And so here we were just a few short miles from the bunkhouse and almost at the end of this incredible adventure. I simply couldn't resist. I pulled out of the peloton and made my charge to the front past the initial unsuspecting riders and then up and past the shoulders of those at the front who had by now sensed that something was changing. As I did this, I found myself screaming — in a wild banshee sort of way — "You've been waiting all day for this, don't get dropped now, dig, dig, dig" — and I put everything I had through my legs and into my pedals.

The pace climbed dramatically as each and every one of the others rose to the challenge and within seconds, I could sense them bridging the short gap that I'd put into them and getting back on to my wheel. Head down and still smiling I searched within myself to find just a little more silently willing the driveway of the bunkhouse to appear around the next corner so that I could win this now flat-out sprint.

However, as we rounded the corner and took in a short incline, I realised that I had gone far too early, made an ill-informed jump, and as the road snaked ahead into the immediate distance there was no sign whatsoever of the bunkhouse.

The others had quickly sussed out my tactics and now quickly and with no mercy they overhauled me one at a time hanging on to each other's back wheel, within seconds — as cruel as cycling can be — they dropped me and sped off down the road. I was broken and they'd gone!

Only minutes, perhaps even seconds later, I rounded the next corner and could see the group pulling up at the end of the driveway laughing and gesticulating back in my direction. I valiantly closed the distance between us and joined them smiling — "What?" was all I could think of saying feigning a look of total disbelief and ignorance as to what my initial burst of speed might actually have caused.

What a way to end — laughing, sweating and on a total high of adrenalin, the Four Peaks by Bike completed!

The Four Peaks Team: (Left to Right) Rob Parker, John Knight, John Swindlehurst, Juan Owens, Dave Isherwood, Kevin Wilson, Matthew McSevney, Paul Warburton. Picture taken by Phil Drowley.

The Arc of Attrition
Cornwall, February 5th & 6th 2016

(In memory of Matthew McSevney 1974 – 2017)

What is it that inspires people to run a long way? I don't mean a marathon; I mean a truly long way like one hundred miles! Then there's the added challenge of it not just being one hundred miles of road but rather one hundred miles of trail, of ups and downs, of twists and turns and of exposure to the elements for every minute that they're out there.

Inspirational ultra-runner and film maker Billy Yang challenges us as to whether we want to end our lives with well-preserved bodies that haven't been tested or taken to the limit, or whether we wanted to hand over a body that had been truly used, that knew about positive adrenalin-fuelled suffering and limitations?

"What will you do with this one wild and precious life?"

In 2016 I got a glimpse of an incredible endurance race, possibly the toughest of its kind in the UK and it was a joy to be involved as support for two inspirational friends and runners in what turned out to be an amazing adventure.

Even by the relatively young history of adventure racing the "Arc of Attrition" is a very new race with the inaugural event only happening in 2015. The 'Arc' is described as "a point-to-point extreme coastal race from Coverack to

Porthtowan" along the Cornish Coastal Path. There is an outside time limit of thirty-six hours staggered along the way with four compulsory check points and associated timing gates. Runners have to pass through these gates within a pre-set time or otherwise be disqualified and withdrawn from the race due to their lack of adequate pace to finish within the allotted time. They can of course continue by themselves but would not qualify for 'a finish'. Oh, and by the way, there's the added challenge of four thousand and ten metres of climbing along the way that I shouldn't forget to mention!

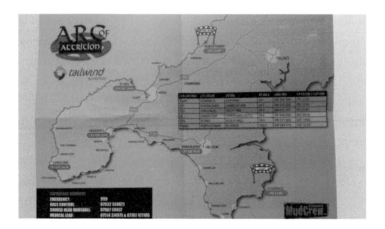

To say that the South-West (Cornish) Coast Path is brutal would be an understatement. I've had the fortune over the past eleven years to holiday at least once a year down near Padstow and have run various sections of the path. It is a wild and beautiful environment, often windswept with the sea pounding on one side and open pastureland on the other. The path winds its way high and low, dropping to remote coves and beaches then climbing quickly back to cliff tops through gorse and broken undergrowth along twisting shady paths or up wooden and stone steps all of which seem to be just that little bit too high to raise your legs comfortably. There are so very few flat sections for any respite and my experience is that no sooner do you think that you've found a steady breathing pattern then the path once again rises or plunges and you're once again fighting for breath or trying to ignore burning legs. In any weather it's a simply incredible place to run particularly as the path draws you on mile after mile just to see what's around the next corner.

Back in 2016 and in my usual say "yes" and think about it later approach, I'd offered to act as support crew to a couple of friends who'd entered the race. I'd been watching them both on Strava all winter building their respective miles and noticing their dedication to training at the most inhospitable times of night and in all weathers. Both of these factors are of course essential elements of the 'Arc' if you're going to complete it.

I mainly knew Matthew, a great sailing, cycling, open water swimming and triathlon buddy from the Isle of Man who had found out about the event whilst scouring the internet for something challenging to do. Having found 'The Arc' Matthew had been able to on-sell the idea to his long-standing friend Dave who was from Reading. Matthew's motivational up-sell to Dave was something along the lines of, "Well, if we're going to do a one-hundred-mile race, we may as well make it the toughest!" and hence their winter training had been undertaken very separately and in totally different geographies. Whilst Matthew had been pounding out the miles on the Isle of Man Coastal Path which literally passed his front door, Dave had been having to find forest trails in the vicinity of Reading.

Whether Matthew had even bothered to fully research the Arc and its potential challenges I really don't know, however the reality of one hundred miles of Cornish Coastal Path in February was enough to make most other friends simply ask the 'why?' question. Added to the unforgiving terrain, with barely a flat section to be found along the route, the winter weather patterns sweeping menacingly across the Atlantic added a very vicious extra element. In the end the reality for the 2016 race was that it fell perfectly into the middle of one of those Atlantic storms and the thirty-six-hour running window was set to be truly wild.

Matthew's rise to ultra-running had come about in quite an unexpected way. Although I knew him well, mainly from sailing yachts together and the odd long day out cycling — it was only when we undertook the Rat Race Scottish Coast to Coast in 2012 that I noticed the birth of his love for endurance events. On that race, and that's a whole other story, we were deep into the second day running a fourteen-mile trail section along a historic path called 'General Wade's Road'. Earlier that morning we'd knocked off a lengthy mountain bike section from Fort Augustus into Fort William before exchanging bikes for fell shoes and heading out westward bound towards the final kayaking section on Loch Leven.

Matt and I weren't attempting to be quick and there were a few chunky climbs to conquer — but I recall distinctly noticing that the longer the day went on the stronger Matthew became. He never had much to say, but was nevertheless wonderful company, as we plodded along next to one another looking out across the mountains and soaking up the surrounding grandeur. At some point, I can't remember where, I turned to Matthew and commented that he seemed to be in his element: "This sort of event seems to be your thing Matt" I said, "You're getting stronger with every step!"

In his usual understated way, Matthew simply grunted and continued. We finished together not much later that day — enduring the final and very uncomfortable one-and-a-half-kilometre paddle in a poorly set up sit-on kayak crossing Loch Leven from beneath the Mamore Lodge Hotel across to the 'Lord of the Isles' hotel in Ballachulish.

From there-on it seemed Matthew's focus upon 'going long' seemed to gather momentum. He changed his diet, set up a structured training routine (which he stuck to), lost a lot of weight and started entering events that left us mortal others quaking at the thought.

The 2016 Arc saw a total of one hundred and seven runners at the pre-start kit check and briefing in Porthtowan. My first glimpse of the field revealed the usual mix of those that 'look like' ultra-runners, generally over six feet tall, skinny but plenty of leathery like sinew, and then others who you wondered or even might worry about. These are the people that look like it's their first race or that they've entered the wrong event and are now just realising it — oversized rucksacks, kit that somehow doesn't seem to fit, running shoes that would be better kept to the roads… and so forth. That said, these 'unexpected' athletes can often be those that surprise you the most and have that special ingredient (usually mental resilience) that just gets them through to the bitter end.

What I particularly admired about Matthew's preparation had been the high number of totally unsociable late night runs he'd been doing. With a full-time job, wife and two young boys both under five years old, Matthew clearly had certain parameters that he'd have to train within. It is a mark of the man that he'd do a full day's work, then come home and spend time with the family, eat tea and do the bedtime routine before then pulling on his fell shoes and heading off in to the dark for a not so short eighteen miles and over two thousand feet of ascent! Those of us fortunate to call Matthew a close friend already regarded him as tenacious, single minded or even just plain bloody stubborn and his Strava output that winter only served to underline that we were right!

At that time, I couldn't have claimed to have known Dave anywhere near as well as I did Matthew, however again our mutual friend Strava confirmed that a marathon a month — road and trail — served as his regular running digest. Let's just say that it was clear he had plenty of miles in his legs even if they weren't mountain miles. Going into this event I had him down as the stronger of the two physically but equally hadn't any indications of the mental demands that this challenge would throw at every competitor.

You can always tell a quality event from the very outset. The accuracy of the pre-race information, the clarity of the route planning, thought around support, kit checks and the knowledge and experience with which the organisers talk. The Arc was and remains a very high calibre event, every runner had a GPS transponder taped to their pack at registration, which would then provide a live ongoing feed as to their position on the coastal path and indeed therefore their position within the field of runners. The event management team and ourselves as support crew could get this read out via our smart phones twenty-four seven — providing a massive help to locate our runners and give them the necessary support they need particularly throughout the night.

True to say that this technology was somewhat hampered by the ruggedness of the coastline as the runners twisted and turned, dropping and climbing in and out of the remote coastal coves often with no telephone signal — and then reappearing as if by magic out of the darkness like ants set against the grandeur of the wild and rugged coast.

With a thorough kit check done, the competitors were then given a very full safety briefing about the course, any last-minute changes and the weather forecast — which was ominously severe. Then it was on to a couple of coaches for the journey across the Cornish peninsula to the start point at Coverack. The route then headed west around The Lizard, Land's End and on through St Ives, Hayle and eventually back to Porthtowan one hundred tortuous miles later.

The forecast was indeed severe. Storm Imogen had been ravaging the East Coast of America for most of the previous week and was now heading menacingly across the Atlantic, no doubt gathering moisture as she travelled towards landfall at Cornwall. Imogen was due to arrive late Saturday afternoon and provide a genuinely wild night of gale force winds and associated driving rain. Just to add insult to injury the forecasted direction was straight into the runners faces and would last throughout all of the night time running hours!

Myself and my fellow crew member Julian had the keys to Dave's pristine Audi A4 Estate which was to serve as the support vehicle for the thirty-six hours and carry everything;

food, water, head-torches, umbrellas', spare clothes, extra running shoes and other emergency equipment including sleeping bags should we actually get the chance to 'sleep' in the next period of time!

Our additional and unanticipated package in the car was the inherited presence of another 'support' crew member — but for a different team! Most bizarrely this team had managed to organise a support person but not actually managed to organise a support vehicle and thus we ended up offering "Kenny" a lift along the way so that he could provide some kind of skeleton support for his friends as long as they were somewhere near our team. To this day I still struggle with that concept — you plan and train to run a one-hundred-mile foot race, you have the equipment, and know how to pass through scrutineering, but then somehow do not manage to bring a car along through which to gain support from the person that you've organised to be there and help you!

So at the eleventh hour we inherited Kenny, and through him both Rob and Ben as a second running pair with a predicted completion time of around thirty hours — significantly quicker than Matthew and Dave's anticipated time. Ben was actually already known to us and was another Manx athlete, with over twenty ultras already bagged, he'd met Rob whilst successfully completing the Thames Towpath Race of one hundred and eighty-five miles in 2015, so we knew they'd be strong and probably also quite fast.

Runners, friends and support crews all gathered around the village green in the very picturesque village of Coverack for the twelve-noon start. The weather had decided to remain kind, at this point anyway, with clear skies and a gentle breeze, all seemed to be very settled for a good initial afternoon of running and walking. The start was inauspicious, just one hundred and seven very fit people all kitted up, and bundled together at the only road junction on the tiny seafront. No warm-up shuttle runs or random blasts of energy being expended pre-start (plenty of time to warm up on this race!) and then there was a quick countdown, a blast of a foghorn and away they all went en masse in a jolly, no rush sort of manner chatting their way along the thin village road that hugged the coast supported by a magnificent stone walled sea defence.

It tickled me that some local people watched with interest at the "little race" that had just got underway, and I heard one comment to another as to whether they'd all be back before tea-time?

With the runners all gone the various support teams headed back to the small village car park to get kit organised, sort their vehicles out and then quickly study OS maps before heading off to the first potential meeting point about five miles down the coast. Julian, new recruit Kenny and I all obediently did exactly the same, although we had to re-organise a little more to accommodate the added kit required to support Ben and Rob. With Ben's suitcase, Kenny's own rucksack and significant food and water supplies the big Audi wasn't feeling so spacious any more and a new off-road running shoe aroma was also starting to make its presence known!

The early miles in a race such as this don't actually require much in the way of support. Each runner's compulsory equipment includes spare food, waterproofs, first aid kit, a bivvy bag and other essentials which actually provide them with a high degree of self-sufficiency for a decent period of time. What drives the support teams is the fact that many of them are comprised of enthusiastic runners who relish the opportunity to follow the race and to perhaps even do a little of the event themselves. Many run out to greet their friend(s) as they wind their way along the coastal path, in some ways the support role is an indulgence of being deeply involved in

David and Matthew, early race stage — Arc of Attrition 2016.

something but with the convenient option to dip in and out of the pain when you fancy!

The field quickly spread out with an early group of five

runners setting a formidably strong pace considering the distance and time that they were facing. Rocky cove after cute fishing village, after harbour after headland draws the runners on, they provide dozens of convenient 'next step' targets and allow the competitors to stop and refuel, change socks or shoes or grab a dry top without too long waiting for the next opportunity. For them there must also be the pleasure of seeing people cheering them through the next road head or village. Everyone supports everyone and no runners go through without someone offering them a sweet, some water or even, as I witnessed in the 2017 event, a can of Carling Black Label which was politely declined, despite the locals enthusiasm to pass it on.

We weren't long into the afternoon before it became obvious that Ben and Rob were indeed going to be quicker than Matthew and Dave — and so covering both pairs for any length of the race would prove impossible. After the first hour they were twelve minutes ahead and then by The Lizard, the gap had increased to thirty minutes. Indeed, as we pulled into The Lizard car park the guys were actually passing through and we missed the opportunity of offering any support. Kenny, who as it turned out was a GB age group triathlete, decided that the best thing he could do was pack some spare gear and food into his own sack and set off down the coastal path after them. He figured that being fresh he'd soon reel them in and then run with them to the first compulsory checkpoint at Porthleven (mile 24.5) and then wait for us there.

Sometime later, and having seen Matthew and Dave safely through The Lizard checkpoint, Julian and I then pushed on to Porthleven where my plan, inspired by Kenny's enthusiasm, was to throw on my own running kit and head out to meet them as they approached. It was still a pretty decent afternoon, the light beginning to fade and only the first signs of the forecasted winds were showing. The rain hadn't yet arrived and — for these ultra-competitors — the distance covered so far at just short of a marathon — wasn't yet enough to cause them too much discomfort.

Hot food and respite from the weather at Porthleven

We ran into Porthleven together where the check point was in a harbour-side pub. There was wonderful hot food, energy drinks, snacks to refill running pouches, course updates, sports massage treatments for tired muscles and first aid for blisters or chaffing.

Having eaten heartily and been warmed through, Matthew and David exited into the early dark of the February afternoon — the rain had now arrived and the wind was blowing into their faces with far greater intent than when they'd arrived twenty minutes earlier. Water bottles refreshed they'd donned running cags and head torches alongside fresh socks and warm gloves before resuming the long run out towards Praa Sands, Marazion and then Penzance where the next check point awaited with a 'no later time gate' of eleven forty-five p.m. and a total distance covered by then of thirty-eight point four miles.

Julian and I kept hopping ahead of them and the weather continued to deteriorate as the Atlantic storm arrived with vengeance having swept the three thousand miles from the American east coast. When you add together the winter, the dark, strong winds and associated driving rain then it makes an unpleasant night for anyone. Add to that the knowledge that you're going to be out all night — have over sixty miles still to cover and the forecast telling you that the weather is only going to get worse — then you can perhaps start to imagine the resolve that these athletes needed to have. Their mental toughness was most certainly going to be tested perhaps even deeper than their physical toughness.

Much of the night from there on fades into a blur — of moving on then meeting up. Of handing out snacks and drinks, exchanging head torch batteries, finding dry tops and endeavouring to stay one step ahead whilst not going too far and placing Matthew and Dave in a position where they had miles to run with no support.

I recall parking at Praa Sands — the wind by now buffeting the car and driving the rain incessantly against the windscreen. Every few minutes either Julian or I would jump out of the car and steel a quick look eastwards along the beach only to see a line of head torches coming in our direction. Other support crews did much the same, or huddled in the door of the public toilets, one guy boiling up water on a camping stove to give his runner a hot drink as he came through. The weather was by now so utterly miserable that standing outside for any length of time simply rendered you soaking wet and bitterly cold. The runners however just kept coming in their dribs and drabs, hooded figures stooped against the weather many using walking poles to steady themselves and passing quickly through the lonely beach car park. Their motivation focussed upon keeping warm kept through their own relentless momentum.

Matthew and Dave came through in much the same fashion — quiet, determined and heading for Penzance where food, warmth and some dry respite awaited.

Around this time, we managed to get a call through to Kenny, trying to have an update as to where Ben and Rob were, anticipating that they would be well down the track. What we discovered, and much to our amazement, was that Rob had withdrawn from the race and had been picked up by a family member to go and get dry and changed. Being relatively local to Cornwall his intention was then to come back with his own car and support Ben who'd decided to push on alone. Quite where Ben was now was anyone's guess, we could only hope that Rob was able to turn himself around quickly and get back to look after Ben through the long, stormy night hours and into the dawn.

Through Penzance, Newlyn and Mousehole the race continued, and the weather became ever fiercer. There was little time for idle chatter as 'the boys' came through. Standing behind the tailgate of the Audi provided almost no shelter and the wind soon whipped away any body warmth. We had flasks of hot water, collected at pubs and cafes throughout the day — so at least a hot coffee was available to be quickly knocked back before turning once again into the night and pressing on. Time and motion became as if one and there was nothing more could be done than pass out what was required and wave them back off into the dark. I was deeply impressed by their fortitude and resilience against the extreme conditions.

And so on to Treen, a sandy cove with a remote road head through what seemed to be a private estate. The gates were open and our motivation to stay near the team far exceeded any concerns about upsetting any landowner who would most likely be tucked up in their beds oblivious to the trail of hardy runners traversing their land in the wild depths of the winter's night.

Julian had by now succumbed to the need for sleep and so we agreed, having parked up, to grab fifteen-minute naps whilst the other stayed awake and spotted approaching head torches. At this point, so far into the race, a pattern had emerged and as a head torch or two appeared at some distance support teams would emerge en masse out of their respective vehicles and make their way to the path side and wait until the runner arrived. Of course, on most occasions it wasn't your runner and so you'd turn and retreat to the shelter of your vehicle only to see another torch coming across the headland or descending the cliff path. It was a somewhat boring and repetitive task but of course essential, and it fuelled the paranoia of closing one's eyes and missing the vital moment that your team came through and you'd miss them.

At Treen however we were in for a big surprise as when David arrived just on the heels of Matthew he walked directly to the car, threw his poles and sack into the back and promptly dumped himself into the rear passenger seats.

"That's it," he said firmly "I'm finished, fuck this!"

And he was, that was it. No amount of cajoling or motivational prompting could get him back out. He even pulled his sleeping bag from the boot of the car, unzipped it and wrapped it around himself. Matt and I stood lamely outside the car once again exchanging glances and, I think, both expecting Dave to suddenly crack a smile, laugh and get back out — but he didn't, he was indeed properly out of the race and Matthew was now officially on his own.

It was so dark and so wild, I can recall feeling deeply sorry for Matthew as he tried one last time to tempt Dave out of the warm embrace of his sleeping bag — but perhaps already resigned to the fact that he would either have to continue alone or retire himself.

Matthew was killed on his road bike in the early hours of Thursday October 5th 2017.

He was riding to work, and the autumnal morning sun was low in the sky, blinding drivers who were approaching from behind. One driver, young and inexperienced misjudged the conditions and didn't spot Matthew until it was too late, hitting him at speed from behind and causing his death.

At his funeral, Dave and Julian, his lifelong friends and with whom we'd shared the Arc 2016 race, spoke of their love for this quiet and understated man. He was determined and stubborn, with a quiet resolve lying deep at his core. Matthew was absolutely a family man, dedicated to his wife Rebecca and two boys Finbar and Orry who were just six and four when he died. Matthew loved nothing more than his family, being a husband and a father — coming home, eating with the family, reading bedtime stories and then heading out to train but only when everyone else was all right and all chores and duties had been done for the day. At his funeral he had a guard of honour from the Manx Fell Runners and over three hundred people attended from almost every adventure sport pursued on the Isle of Man. It will be strange for all of us who knew him and loved him — to think of an adventure event and immediately want to enter with friends but realise that Matthew can't any longer join, whether it be running, sailing, swimming or simply being outside — we'll carry him in our thoughts!

Matthew's resolve certainly came to the fore back there on that stormy night in Treen, he quietly asked me for a new head torch, pulled up his collar (metaphorically speaking) before turning away and thoughtfully shining his torch up the steep incline that led away from the cove and on to the next headland. Land's End lay ahead and in his own inimitable way — he simply departed back into the darkness.

Again, I have no concept of time, but it felt like we sat at Land's End for hours watching head torches come and go. The depths of the night meant that we easily found a park right next to the coastal path allowing us to watch runners passing without leaving the relative safety of the car. The buildings were adorned with large spotlights permanently lit facing out across the grass and cliffs and which helped us to identify people. By now it had become a sombre trail of lonely, hooded figures leaning forwards against an invisible force which challenged their every step of progress. Their various coloured running gear immediately helped to identify them, not by name of course, but by style or running gait until they were close enough to show their face and give us a benchmark against which we could estimate Matthew's arrival.

I had walked the next section of the path twice before from Land's End to Sennen Cove where the race schedule promised shelter, food and the opportunity for runners to re-group and re-focus. Matthew passed through Land's End without incident but spoke of his wish to get to Sennen and take a good rest, eat well and have his feet looked at. In the big scheme of things, the distance was relatively small and so his momentum never ceased. I passed him an energy bar, a fresh drink and walked with him for a few hundred metres whilst he drank a luke-warm, sweet coffee.

The feed station at Sennen Cove was a scene to behold. Soaking wet runners, in various states of undress, and assuming a variety of positions; sitting, lounging, lying and all poses in between. Race officials and support crews buzzed around, high on the atmosphere working on redressing people, covering blisters, serving hot food or re-filling water bottles and sack pouches.

Matthew lingered at Sennen for a long time, possibly too long but then who could blame him? Dave was fast asleep as was Julian, so I ministered to Matthew as best I could, ensuring that he had a meal, that his feet were stripped, dried and given plasters where they'd rubbed raw. Most of this time Matthew simply stared ahead blankly looking into the near distance with a remote 'the lights are on but no one's home' sort of way. Whatever his mindset or demeanour he showed absolutely no signs of any desire to retire — but that was Matthew for you! In his own time, he regained his feet, readjusted his dry clothing, pulled on his refreshed pack and bid me a polite goodbye. He resumed the race which, by now, had truly become 'The Arc of Attrition'!

Much later at the atmospherically named Pendeen Watch Lighthouse, high up on a rocky outcrop in the dark and above the crashing Atlantic waves we waited once again in the car tucked behind the high wall of the lighthouse compound but gaining little respite from the elements. The car was literally being physically moved by the gusts of wind and the rain, battering against the windscreen, and beating any efforts that the wipers could make to give us a view of the coastal path and approaching runners climbing up from below. It continued to be a truly merciless night and we struggled to even imagine what it must be like to try and make headway against the elements now over twenty hours into the race. But come through he did — and once again only the briefest of stops, a few words, shared glances and raising of eyebrows in the beam of head torches and the need to get on. There was however I recall a sense that dawn was breaking, that slow creeping of new grey light and a lift in personal optimism that perhaps the worst was over, and the new day might bring with it some respite in the weather.

What we did know was that the next section had the reputation of being by far the loneliest and toughest. Some fourteen miles of path that provided no easy opportunity to offer support. At Matthew's current pace that was easily four hours of walking and we began to wonder whether reaching St Ives by the compulsory two p.m. cut off was possible. It was a long way, he was utterly exhausted, once again wet and now more visibly cold. He asked for his full hill walking waterproof as running seemed to now be a distant memory and walking steadily much more the order of the new day.

So, again we equipped him to move on. Another dry top, a change of shoes, more food, a hot drink, words of encouragement and advice which came from 'a good place' but fell on to exhausted ears that no-longer heard. We waved him goodbye, and this determined but empty man departed, alone again on 'the path' which would afford him no mercy whatsoever.

Up ahead and unbeknown to us our friend Ben Scott had brought his own race to an end just as the last darkness of the night lifted and the new grey dawn began. Ben, alone since late afternoon the previous day, had made good progress. A seasoned ultra-marathon man — his lythe race-tuned physique had taken a real battering during the storm ridden night hours. Tired, wet and fatigued Ben had made a number of wrong turns losing the coastal path and adding frustrating extra distance to his race. Demoralised he finally spotted the lights of a farmhouse to his right and decided to go in search of some respite from the weather and the chance of using their phone to call either us or his team mate Rob to come a rescue him. Ben regaled his story to us later that same day as we sat drinking a beer and sharing experiences of the last forty-eight hours.

He'd knocked on the farm door and been elated when it was opened by a woman, clearly suspicious of just who would be knocking on her door at dawn after such a wild night. She found, stood in front of her, a wiry athletic man drenched to the very core with sunken eyes and an expression that immediately softened her heart.

Ben had asked if he could briefly come in and use her phone, perhaps get warm — just for a minute or two — or even wait with her until a car came to collect him?

"You can do more than that young man" came her reply. "You can come in, make your call, then go upstairs, strip off your clothes leave them outside the bathroom and get yourself in the shower. I'll dry them for you whilst you get clean and warm and then come down for some tea and breakfast".

Ben couldn't recall just why he started crying, it might have been the fatigue or perhaps the relief, or even the generosity that this stranger was showing him — but it rushed over him and he wept. They still exchange Christmas cards to this day and Ben visits them when he can, particularly after he completed the 2017 Arc in twenty-eight hours, five minutes and fifty-four seconds and in doing so gained one of the coveted Gold Buckle's that only sub-thirty-hour runners are awarded.

For Matthew, still out there on that lonesome section, the day was now brightening, and the rain had turned to just the occasional shower driven by the strong wind. Dave and Julian had rejoined the land of the living and we drove well ahead before scrutinising the OS map to find a place from where I could drop down on to the coastal path and work my way backwards towards Matthew. I reckoned that he'd welcome both something simple to eat but perhaps more so the company of a friendly face for a mile or two.

With a bag of high energy goodies in hand I descended a rocky path, stepping carefully from stone to stone and over the occasional larger boulder endeavouring to avoid the deep puddles that had formed during last night's storm. It was tricky going, hard to gain any momentum and certainly no significant pace, even here the path twisted and turned finding its way to the main coastal path. I grumbled to myself about the lack of progress that I was managing to make eager to find Matthew. I was of course relatively speaking very fresh from being in the dry and warmth of the car all night. I imagined that the terrain would be another demoralising blow for Matthew, fatigued, wet, lonely and still more than thirty miles from the finish.

I found him after perhaps a mile and shared a few sweets with him as we walked mainly in silence back along the way I'd approached. The few words he stuttered were mainly curses about the terrain and his frustration at not being able to go faster. He was buried deep behind his hood which was pulled forwards to protect his head and face from the wind that now blew from the west. He walked with two poles, going much more slowly hampered by the inhospitable path and his own deep tiredness.

It was hard not to get the sense that this could well be the beginning of the end. St Ives, perhaps still six miles distant, was the last compulsory check point and also the final opportunity for food and to get rewarmed. What followed then was a further twenty-two miles through Hayle, Godrevy and Portreath before reaching the finish at Porthtowan.

As my path junction arrived and I turned up towards the where the car was parked, I bid Matthew farewell and promised that we'd all be seeing him soon at St Ive's. He was motivated by the thought that Dave would be there to cheer him on, that we'd have a hot flask, and the car would be close enough for him to access dry clothes before getting to the feed station proper. I left him stumbling ever onwards, trying stubbornly to get a rhythm as the slippery rocks gave him no traction or he kicked a loose stone and stepped heavily forwards to regain his balance. Our anxiety for Matthew had been well founded — the race had been tough from the very start and it wasn't offering any let up even now after nearly eighty miles!

Back at the car I updated Dave and Julian and we did some quick calculations around time, distance and current pace — it seemed now unlikely and exceedingly cruel that Matthew was going to miss the two-p.m. cut off at St Ives', and would be withdrawn from the race by the officials.

We drove ahead and found a place to park as close to the coastal path as possible on the outskirts of St Ives. The occasional rain shower still blew through but now, to add insult to injury there was a hint of sun in the sky and what was left of the day seemed to have promise. In the bay the sea continued to drive heavily in, crashing on rocks and pounding the sandy beach. For the committed surfers it made for a great afternoon, and we watched for a while amazed at their resilience of the cold.

After waiting for some time, we all set off together walking away from the town and outwards in the direction from which Matt would be arriving. The odd runner came past us, familiar figures now all actually walking and, to the person, they were withdrawn into their own world wrapped tightly in their waterproofs, heads down and focussed upon maintaining their rhythm.

Eventually and after what seemed an age, we spotted a lonely figure walking slowly towards us. The undulating path meant that for a short time we would see him and then he'd dip down behind a coastal bluff out of sight. It was like our time stood still as we waited for him to reappear, of course eventually he did and whether he spotted us or not it was clear that his pace was now at rock bottom and that time and distance had got the better of him.

As we all drew together there was a chorus of encouragement and applause of admiration. Matthew gave a grin, his face shadowed by the extent of his hood which protected him from the elements. His spirit remained, his resolve undiluted by the fatigue of so much time on his legs and a night alone on the wild coastal path. He was still able to share a joke and showed no hint of resentment in accepting that this was the end for him. So, we all turned and walked slowly back to the car reflecting just how brilliantly he'd done — and already hearing Dave and Matthew plotting their entry for 2017 and what they'd do differently! Julian and I just looked at one another and shook our heads — time to find our hotel and think about warmer things like showers, hot food and perhaps a sneaky late afternoon beer!

The 2016 Arc of Attrition saw competitors run and walk through a bitter February night, long hours of darkness and a severe Atlantic storm. There was a seventy-five per cent. drop out rate, only twenty-eight of the one hundred and seven starters actually finished and these some of the toughest endurance runners that you could possibly wish to meet. Having been there and endured that night, even from the safety of a warm car, it impresses me that twenty-eight managed to get through to the finish. An incredible achievement.

Late afternoon, the blustery conditions soon became wild!

As for us, we did drink beer that night and amazingly Dave and Matthew joined us for a few. Ben even showed up and shared his tales and made us laugh as he described his tears with the farmer. Over twenty-four hours of running and braving storm force conditions hadn't dampened their enthusiasm for a night out and as with all these things, we swapped stories and plotted for the future which pretty soon included a healthy intent to be back at The Arc.

Perhaps in 2017 the weather would be more kind!

Matthew enters St Ives after 78 miles and a wild Atlantic night

September 2018
Seventy plus through The Lhairig Ghru

So, many moons ago I knew a couple in Newcastle upon Tyne. Bob was an engineer and a staunch wee Scotsman. Sarah, his partner, was another Scot and we'd all come to know one another through a mutual love of squash. On one of many evenings out drinking and telling tall stories Bob announced that he was off to walk through the Lhairig Ghru with a group of friends intending to take two days and spend the middle night in a bothy around half way through. Being honest, I wasn't much of a fan of Bob, he was a pretty arrogant individual and seemed to relish generating arguments just for the sake of it. His favourite was to wind up our mutual accountant friend by rubbishing his profession and his most outrageous was claiming to know what it felt like for a woman to orgasm! As crazy as this seems to even be writing, it's true, and he stuck to his position which was quite clearly ridiculous. His saving was that for some reason Sarah loved him and most of us loved Sarah — so he got away with more than he should have. But I found Bob's description of the Lhairig Ghru absolutely beguiling, and it stayed with me for the best part of thirty years. Throughout that time, I never lost the desire to go and see this place, indeed it grew to be an ambition lodged firmly in my head, an absolute must do!

The Lhairig Ghru is a glacial valley cutting through the Cairngorm mountains in the heart of the Scottish Highlands. It runs generally from south to north covering a distance of around twenty-one miles between Braemar and Aviemore. At no point is the valley terrain particularly steep, the high point is at the watershed known as The Pools of Dee, a boulder strewn moonscape broken up only by one or two small lochans from which streams flow in either direction. A well-defined footpath runs through the entire valley; navigation is not tricky and the imposing mountains either side create an undeniable sense of wilderness whilst giving a clear sense of direction leading you seemingly ever onwards — it would be hard to stray from the path without quickly realising something was wrong! But the Lhairig Ghru is equally a desolate and potentially dangerous place. At the centre you're a good eleven miles from civilisation and the weather whips through the valley giving no mercy to the poorly equipped. Things can change quickly in the Lhairig Ghru!

The valley's geological grandeur is undeniable — looking ahead, looking up and looking behind, the view grasps hold of you, and it feels a privilege to be a part of it if only just for a short while.

Bob eventually departed the shores of the UK to work somewhere in the UAE, a well-paid engineering job which understandably took him away and demanded that the pair marry thus allowing them to move together on his visa and that's where their part in this story ends. I remain in debt to Bob for so vividly described his walk and drawing my attention to the fact that such a place existed.

Moving on several years I stumbled across the world of fell running. There is no doubt that I'd always far preferred off road running. During my competitive badminton days my default inkling was to head out and train along local forest tracks. Once I could drive, I'd get myself out to Hathersage and run routes on to the moors and along the edges, Froggatt, Burbage and Surprise View as well as many others which always felt so much kinder to my body and forgiving for my joints, not to mention the sense of freedom and motivation generated by the wild open spaces and distant views. It was during my fifteen years of living on the Isle of Man and making such great friends with cyclists, triathletes, adventure racers, sailors and open water swimmers that the ambition once again surfaced in my mind of journeying through the Lhairig Ghru. A fell run with best mates, a big day out enjoying the grandeur and finishing no doubt with a few celebratory beers. In truth the plan had come and gone several times over perhaps three or maybe four years.

Finding a date that everyone could do was a struggle, then when we had what seemed like a firm date, one of the group very sadly had a family bereavement and we all agreed that it would be wrong to go without him — and so the plan once again took some time to become a reality. Strangely for me, with my persistent hurry up drivers, I felt oddly relaxed about the delays, good things are best not rushed and having the right people there was a big factor, time in the mountains with friends is indeed special time. So it came to pass that the stars finally aligned — well, our diaries matched — for late September 2018 and a group of seven were committed to make the journey north and spend a long weekend of adventuring primarily centred around a run through my own little field of dreams.

The group was made up as follows

From the Isle of Man; John Swindlehurst — Manxman, Ironman triathlete, fell runner, swimmer and general "I'll have a go at that" person. Dave Isherwood — Manxman, understated athlete, always willing to go along for the ride but endeavours to play down his abilities. Ian Large — Manxman, support driver, mountain biker and logistics. Andy Gosland — Scotsman, triathlete and adventure racer, but injured and somewhat sceptical of the journey at that time of year due to the threat of poor weather.

From Cumbria: John Matthews — long-standing adventurer friend, ultra-distance runner, loves his planning and never caught out with the wrong kit. Jonathan and Roy — friends and work colleagues of John Matthews, and then me — the eternal optimist and convenor of said group.

The overall plan was to meet up at Aviemore Youth Hostel on the Friday afternoon / evening with kit for both running, a night on the hill and also mountain biking if the opportunity arose.

We would then get shuttled on the Saturday morning down to the south end of the Lhairig Ghru near Braemar which would leave us free to run through the valley and back to Aviemore. The options were to do a straight run through or to carry kit for an overnight in the bothy and perhaps extend the route on day two by adding a leg into another valley.

The group all arrived as planned up in Aviemore and the Scottish Youth Hostel made a warm welcome for us with shared rooms but importantly a small bar, hot showers and enough space to get kit sorted in the warm and dry.

We obviously wasted little time in identifying a suitable pub to go and discuss plans for the next day, luckily finding a big high round table with stools that allowed us to catch up on old times and recent adventures. The group had last been together (well some of us) riding the West Highland Way the previous year, these September adventures were becoming a habit and long may they last.

The forecast for the next day was absolutely horrendous, with southerly gale force winds gathering during the day and then joined after lunch by heavy rain no doubt being driven by the seventy plus mile per hour gusts. John Matthews description of the bothy where there was a chance that we could overnight didn't really inspire any of us to want to carry sleeping bags, stoves and food for forty-eight hours and so it became a quick and easy decision to run straight through. Although this pushed us close to twenty-six miles distance, we agreed that there was no rush and if we opted for a south to north route choice then the elements would be helping us on the way!

And so it was settled, we'd leave fairly early and take advantage of the generosity of Ian Large who would shuttle us to the start at the Linn of Dee and then loop back to Aviemore in the van. Andy decided that he wasn't fit enough for the full day and was also sceptical about the weather — he'd walked through the valley before and feared that it could turn out to be a pretty rough trip particularly if we weren't moving well with him in tow. So the group became six in total — all well experienced in the hills and mountains and all with a glint in the eye for a great day out whatever the weather.

The drive around to Braemar through the hills took far longer than I'd anticipated and of course this only gave plenty of time for my head to play its usual pre-adventure games… "it's so far, can I really do this, isn't the weather changing, it's getting worse…" the stream of negatives, the self-questioning all played around at the forefront of my consciousness. Fortunately, such self-indulgent questioning was more than countered by a steady stream of jokes and ribbing that flowed around the van. Up front Ian was driving, and Andy sat alongside him, both safe in the knowledge that their day would be one of relative warmth, coffee shops and a degree of anticipation around our arrival. The rest of us were packed in, ready dressed in running gear with light-weight sacks ready for the day's journey.

Soon after ten a.m. the van rolled in the public car park at the Linn of Dee and we all tumbled out relieved to finally be free of the van's confines. It was dry but already windy, actually a good day to be running especially as our strategy of running south to north was looking to be absolutely spot on. The usual almost ritualistic faffing then took place, toileting, adjusting kit, last minute changes and the inevitable "shall I take this or not" changes… and then we were off.

The Linn stands at three hundred and seventy-three metres and our highest point of the day was The Pools of Dee lying at just eight hundred and twenty metres. In old money that's a climb of around one thousand five hundred feet — so not a major climb at all and particularly as that ascent is spread over some nineteen kilometres or around twelve miles. This was all round good news as it meant that the route was quite literally all runnable and therefore simply to be enjoyed from start to finish.

"Steady away" has become my running philosophy particularly in recent years and especially when there are many miles ahead and hours on your feet. So steady it was as we jogged out of the car park and through the forest heading initially westwards along the banks of the River Dee on a well packed land rover track. The group splintered slightly as people started to find their own pace, no worrying gaps just social running in two or three small clusters getting properly warmed up and revelling in the early exhilaration of the journey. The mountains stood tall to our right and I knew, having studied the route many times, that we'd soon be turning right and heading into and through those very hills, winding our way through their remoteness and looking up at their craggy profiles which would shadow us throughout the day.

After around four and a half kilometres we regrouped at the White Bridge, our first significant route marker of the day. It was here that we left the made-up track and took to the easily defined but narrow footpath still following the Dee but now turning north skipping over grassy tussocks, small boulder gardens and wet boggy sections. The river was full as it tumbled southwards alongside, the valley ahead started to take shape characterised by the steep slopes of Sgor Mor to our right and Cairn Geldie to our left. There was no escaping that I was absolutely loving it, having thought about this epic run for so long I now found myself totally energised — the way ahead was so clear, the mountain scenery so dramatic and the camaraderie so evident, we were all in our element!

Ish, Swin and I found a common pace which was not really surprising after so many years of running together. I have many vivid memories of us open water swimming, cycling and then chasing each other around the lake in Mooragh Park on the Isle of Man during a sprint triathlon training session. Ish always won but there was adrenaline-fuelled exhilaration to be had knocking out seven-minute miles for a short time before I literally blew up and dropped away.

A small way back John, Jonathan and Roy slotted in together and made ground at their own pace no doubt locked in their own conversation enjoying the grandeur of the Scottish mountains.

Heading north through Glen Dee we very gradually gained height, our next significant navigational feature was the river junction where we were due to continue following the Dee but passing the Geusachan Burn which joined from the west through the incredibly formed Glen Geusachan. And what a feature this was, the Geusachan valley is brief but dramatic. Only two and a half kilometres long it ends with abrupt mountain slopes that quickly ascend to the summit at Monadh Mor standing at one thousand, one hundred and thirteen metres. Mountains stand tall to both the north and south of the valley giving it a foreboding character but one that equally seemed to call out "come run through me". John, Ish and I stood and gazed in awe up the valley. I had, at one point, thought it actually was the route onwards, but a quick review of the map and reorientation put me right. John and Ish are many things but they are not mountain navigators, so they seemed happy to take my lead as we set off again knowing that our lunch stop was just two kilometres further on at the Corrour Bothy nestled beneath the craggy lofts of the atmospherically named Devil's Point.

There was no sign of the other three, but this was of no worry to us. They had more than adequate equipment and were all experienced in the mountains. We'd agreed that we would stop and regroup over lunch at the bothy, I was also mindful of the weather forecast which warned of rain throughout the afternoon which would be unpleasant enough without the threat of it being driven by a seventy to eighty miles an hour hooley!

Corrour is a tiny bothy reached via an impressive metal footbridge that spans the Dee. A short run up a gentle slope takes you to its front door with a fine view back to the river and both ways along the Lairig Ghru. It is a well-maintained bothy by any standard, weather-proof and snug with a little separate toilet adjoining. Inside there are just two short benches and a tiny sleeping platform that might accommodate two good friends who could tolerate spooning each other all night! I imagined that the little fire would quickly warm the small space and I could imagine a snug night there if you were with a few friends and the obligatory bottle of local malt, telling stories of daring do and exaggerating exploits from across the decades!

We however were only there for a brief lunch. Although our pace had been very steady, I was nevertheless sweaty and in need of changing into a dry top. This luxury would keep me warm whilst we ate, so I pulled on my thicker new top and added my trusty buff to my head before a final layer of my heavy running cagoule which I zipped up to my neck before sitting down on the bench and breaking out food.

We chatted quietly and kept a look out for the others who soon appeared some way back along the footpath steadily making their way towards us moving smoothly and confidently against the awesome backdrop.

Outside now the weather was most definitely changing. The first drops of rain were troubling the small bothy window and the wind was beginning to drum against the corrugated iron roof. I privately reflected that the twenty or so minutes we had waited for the others added to the twenty or so minutes they would now rightly need to eat, drink and rest would indeed be expensive minutes lost to the forecasted angry weather system that was due to arrive. We were however not in any danger, or so it felt — a good footpath, decent visibility, good kit and the physical wherewithal to move quite quickly through the environment. We'd just do it whilst being vigorously buffeted by the wind and soaked by the rain!

John, Jonathan and Roy duly arrived and joined us in the bothy. Like us they changed wet tops and added new warm layers before laying out their various lunches. Now Johnny Matthews is infamous for his mountain food discipline. Over the years whilst I've settled for two-minute noodles or hot chocolate crunch, John has calmly laid out an assortment of fresh veg to cut and dice before gently frying in his Trangia lid, adding garlic for taste to produce a cordon bleu meal. When I've set out to rib him about this, he has rightly pointed out to me that my meal is cooked and eaten literally in minutes whilst his becomes an 'experience' of great delicacy set in the mountain environment where there is no rush particularly on an overnight camping trip taken with a glass of wine!

And so it was that John, Jonathan and Roy set about their lunch understandably in no rush, enjoying the bothy and their new-found shelter, a few stories and a bit of banter, thirty minutes or more slipped by and the weather strengthened in its determination to disrupt the afternoon.

When we emerged sometime later the wind had really got the bit between its teeth. It was now rattling up the valley, thumping itself against the steep mountain sides and then rushing down in forceful gusts that buffeted us as we grouped together for a photo outside of the bothy. It was then off back down the slope to the footbridge and then a short climb on the other side to regain the main valley path northwards.

Within the first kilometre we ran past three significant stones the largest of which is called the Clach nan Taillear or Tailors' Stone where legend has it that three drunken tailors perished trying to ride out a violent storm one Hogmanay night many years ago as they endeavoured to travel between Aviemore and Braemar. We were travelling in the opposite direction but with the fast-changing weather I felt at least some little appreciation of how their plight would have been in this desolate and exposed place.

Having had plenty of time to study the map over our extended lunch I had a clear mental picture of the route ahead. We would stay close to the River Dee again for a couple of kilometres before leaving it down to our left as the path crossed open hillside closely hugging the slopes of Ben Macdui. Standing at one thousand, three hundred and nine metres, it is amongst Scotland's most famous mountains. We however had no interest in its summit, instead the slopes were our handrail leading us through their gnarly topology as the footpath swung to true north and joined the tumbling burn called Allt na Lairig Ghru. From there the path rises to the mountain pass at the Pools of Dee, a boulder-strewn wilderness, a mountain saddle with two lochans and the watershed from which the Dee flows south to Braemar and the new small streams begin their journey northwards ultimately towards the River Spey. The map also tells us that it is here that we would join the Lairig Ghru proper, heading slightly west of north and dropping away towards Coylumbridge and Aviemore some twelve miles distant.

John Swindlehurst and I quickly found our legs and began to pull away — even from Ish who seemed to be struggling after the prolonged lunch stop. Consistently leading the way, I was very consciously not pushing the pace, not that I could have, and was also occasionally stopping to look back and check on the progress of the others. When I did this the full ferocity of the weather quickly became apparent. The wind was truly driving us up the valley, whistling around us and acting like a hand in the middle of your back pushing us northwards. The rain in the consistent gusts was now strong and hard enough to sting the back of your legs. Stopping to look back was literally painful, quickly we would be chilled, and the rain hit our faces like hundreds of tiny pricking pins, it was not fun and only encouraged us to turn and press on.

I told myself that we'd stop at The Pools and take shelter behind any of the large boulders that were sure to be there in order to await the arrival of the others. We could even grab a drink and maybe eat something whilst we were waiting, and they'd not be long!

Every time I looked behind me John was just perhaps ten paces back head down picking his steps carefully as we danced our way along the thin hill path twisting and turning gently up hill. There was no talking, the atmosphere had changed significantly. We were wet but warmed by our constant movement and there seemed no option other than to keep going. The Pools of Dee arrived sooner than I had expected. We'd entered the cloud now, or perhaps it had descended to greet us, welcoming us to the high pass and hiding the mountains that towered either side of us, Sron na Lairige to the west and an oddly unnamed peak to the east standing at some one thousand, one hundred and sixty-nine metres.

The Pools were not as I'd imagined them, there were no large boulders, the wind was tearing across the open rocky field, the cloud swirled around, and the rain was driving across this high point hurtling from south to north. Because the elements had been driving us onwards, we had not really noticed the ferocity of what had now become the height of the forecasted wind and there were few choices in this remote location to hide from its incessant battering. Carefully we made our way across the slippery, rocky field being sure not to lose our footing and either hurt an ankle or graze our legs. We descended a little from the high point to the side of the first lochan. Here we found some shelter behind a rock perhaps as big as a washing machine, barely large enough to shelter us both from the wind and only possible if we crouched down. I was in shorts, my warm running top, cagoule and buff, and John was still in just his shorts and a technical top, no wind or waterproof, he was ever the Irish Sea fisherman. As our body warmth quickly dissipated, I delved into my running sack to find my final dry and warm layer plus my over trousers to protect my legs from the raging elements. John did the same but opted only for his thin jacket, that was all that he had! I'm not even tempted to use the term waterproof; at best it was going to give him a little protection from the wind however it was woefully inadequate set against where we were and the weather that we were enduring. We broke out some food and I remember being slightly amused but somewhat perturbed at the sight of my own hand holding a half-peeled banana shaking so much that I struggled to orientate it to my open mouth. I was bloody cold and not enjoying the wait! I wanted to leave and to regain some warmth from movement, but we needed to regroup, and it would have been foolhardy to continue without the others.

Twice I popped up from behind the washing machine rock and headed a little way back across the rocks to see if I could get a sight of the others arriving through the cloud but on both occasions the biting wind and sharp rain quickly eroded my determination. So we waited and got progressively colder until eventually the others arrived all together and in good spirits.

Looking back, it was at this point, mentally hindered by the cold and motivated to regain some warmth that I made my first poor decision. As the others arrived, they were of course upwind of me, I shouted to them (on reflection they could probably only see my mouth moving) that we were suffering and that it would be best if they just kept going and ran straight through so we could all begin the steady descent together. I thought I saw at least one of them put their thumbs up which was all I needed as motivation to get going. So with that John and I turned and set off relieved to be underway again with the wind and rain battering our backs but helpfully pushing us towards Aviemore. The sturdy Manxman seemed to have entered a 'just follow you' mode and he stayed close on my tail, head down but speechless.

Within minutes I turned to look behind, my anticipation being that the entire group would be within eye-sight however I was wrong, the others once again out of sight, and we were once again alone in a rocky desolate place. Momentarily we stood by the path — I'd estimate we'd only run a quarter of a mile — to await their arrival but there was no sign of them. So, we decided to push on a little further and find some shelter (again!) to wait. John silently followed — the running was straight forwards and aside from the cold we were not tired, another half mile or so passed and we found a small grassy concave bowl in the valley side which provided just a little shelter. We stood there moving from foot to foot on the spot and waited but there was no sign. The cold, if indeed it had ever retreated, very quickly returned to my core and for the first time I started to wonder if we were now actually in a pretty bad place. We had not seen another soul all day and I wondered if we'd bitten off more than we could cope with? I had every layer that I'd carried with me now on my body and still I was shaking, John was neutral at best suggesting that he'd just do what I wanted, and I wasn't sure really what to do. He too was most definitely cold but was opting to say little if anything.

So it struck me that we should run back towards the others in effect quickly halving the distance between us and at least keeping us moving in the process. So we started back up the incline towards The Pools of Dee, heading in to the gale and facing the rain… it was relentless, merciless and bitter, indeed so unforgiving that within perhaps only a minute I put it to John that it was stupid to continue especially as we still could not see them.

So once again we turned and headed north, the elements back behind us, and plodded on in search of a better place to hide from the storm. I for one was now pretty annoyed both at myself and at the others whom I felt sure had agreed to run straight through and past the exposed high point. Now too cold to stop but at risk of further opening a dangerous gap we were compromised.

Over the years I've read many an adventure book and feel well informed on the matters of how a series of seemingly small errors all compound into a single much larger incident and here I was having contributed to a situation with similar potential. Maybe I should have disciplined myself to run at the back, maybe to have stopped more regularly, maybe to not have let as much time slip away at lunch, maybe to have ensured we all had good foul weather gear, maybe to have ensured my shouted message landed... maybe, maybe, maybe! And so once again we huddled behind a rock now on an exposed high section of path.

The valley had opened up somewhat, the tumbling stream now just slightly below us being fed every second by pellets of driving rain and hundreds of rivulets running down off the hillside. The route ahead meandering across it from side to side finding the path of least resistance for the multitude of walkers who'd headed up from Aviemore in this direction. Our new rock was very much a downgrade from the washing machine we'd hidden behind earlier. This one was perhaps the size of a regular tv screen and provided scant shelter from the elements.

John and I crouched behind it as best we could, he had his hood up which was pathetic against the elements and gave him a rather little boy lost look which bordered on amusing in the situation. We reviewed our options — stay and suffer the cold or run on and risk total separation — John was clear that he'd do whichever I chose and I inwardly mused whether this was because he truly didn't care or that he'd kind of given up on decision making. So, we sat tight, alternately sheltering and then bobbing up to peer back up the valley and into the rain and low swirling cloud.

Long minutes past, we shivered and chatted, tried the odd joke and mentally willed the others to arrive and of course eventually they did, a huddle of four runners all fully kitted up against the elements moving consistently together but in relative quiet as they were blown down the valley. I was ecstatic to see them and then befuddled that they claimed to have always been in eyesight of us albeit some distance behind. In truth John's windproof was a ridiculous yellow and they'd have been looking down wind and rain in our direction, we of course had been the opposite looking up the valley through squinting eyes and bowed heads!

This time we regrouped properly only briefly standing still before resuming a very welcome and warming pace downwards. The valley continued to open up and lush vegetation became our backdrop softer than the rocky terrain we'd been in for several hours. John and Ish, who having trailed behind up and over the Pools of Dee, now seemed to have found their 'get me home' legs and really put on some speed and were soon small but colourful figures scampering in the distance their yellow wind-proofs standing out against the lush green of the Rothimurcus Forest.

And so we ran onwards, now steadily losing height and being swallowed slowly into a more hospitable terrain, the path wider, more trodden by thousands of walkers many of whom will have turned back long before the real wilderness of the central Lairig Ghru. We moved easily as a little group chatting and beginning the story-telling, perhaps a little sign of easing mental states as the end of the run became palpable and spirits lifted.

The final miles were uneventful when set against the previous three hours. The backdrop was beautiful as we ran gently through the pine forest and alongside the tumbling river on soft, even paths coated in many seasons of pine needles which cushioned our steps. Eventually we crossed the widening waters on an impressive metal bridge hidden deep in the trees which swayed majestically, creaking in the continuing strong southerly wind. Aviemore was now close by — our final off-road section took us through a campsite busy with sheltering holiday makers who looked out through dripping tents flaps or steamed up camper windows as we jogged past in high spirits.

I love these closing moments to a long run or any big day out. The hard work is behind you and the thought of a hot shower, dry clothes, indulgent food and good beer is comforting and motivating to the end. The dull ache of weary muscles begins to gather, and thoughts turn to just what calves, quads and hips will feel like in the morning. They're all good feelings, addictive rewards in return for adventures and the exposure to something of the unknown and unpredictable.

A run through the Lairig Ghru — a great day out!

The Jura Fell Race 2019

"Nothing has you calling Mammy quite like your first view of The Paps: they generate a mixture of wonder and dread and offer a hill race unlike any other"

"Facing you is probably the most intimidating climb in British fell running"

Never before had a fell race, or any race for that matter, managed to unsettle my inner self like the 2019 Jura Fell Race.

The Paps of Jura looking glorious on a sunny spring afternoon.

Even when my long-standing fell running friend, Chris Kirk, suggested that we should enter I found myself doing so with the underlying hope that my application wouldn't make it through the ballot. Chris was confident in stating that annually over six hundred people apply for the limited number of two hundred and fifty places on the start line and that most of those accepted had either elite fell running pedigree or some kind of gnarly reputation built up over decades of competition. I had neither of these attributes and so eagerly anticipated an e-mail stating 'thanks but no thanks'!

Chris however had other ideas. As one of the organising committees of the Manx Mountain Marathon, he had spotted that the same person, George Broderick, was actually the originator of both races. Ever the cheeky chancer Chris made a well-pitched proposition to the Jura committee that he and I should be accepted on that basis and also added, just for good effect, our not so recent third in class and age group at the 2017 Fiftieth Anniversary OMM event in Langdale.

So I'm not sure whether my heart sank a little or just plain dropped right through my shoes when I got the 'congratulations' e-mail, we were in and the slim possibility had suddenly become a daunting reality.

Then came the start of other titbits being dropped into conversation. On one hand Chris repeatedly said that he'd only really want to run if the weather was going to be good — that if it was lashing down then he'd rather defer to having a long weekend in the Lakes. He also hinted that his research was also uncovering that many people travel to and from Jura and the race using bikes kitted out with panniers and racks so that the lithe elite runners can carry tent and other necessities for a two-to-three-night adventure only to add to the seventeen mile, seven thousand, seven hundred and seventy-five feet fell race being thrown into the middle! This was becoming a very different event and my head and heart were playing a tug of war as to just how I should be feeling about it all.

So, some background to set the scene:

The Jura Fell Race was founded in 1973 by George Broderick. It is a category A, long course event covering twenty-eight kilometres (seventeen miles) and two thousand, three hundred and seventy metres of ascent (seven thousand, seven hundred and seventy-five feet). To a very average fell runner such as myself the amazing fact is that the current course records (as at July 2019) are three hours, five minutes and fourteen seconds for the male category (Finlay Wild) and three hours, thirty-eight minutes and forty-three seconds for the women (Jasmin Paris). The reality for the average person is that it's a five to six hour long and hilly day out in wilderness terrain which demands both good mountain skills and competent navigation.

And Jura? With various derivations of the Gaelic name 'ON jur-oy' refers to 'udder island' or 'island of breasts' which neatly describes the profile of the island from afar as one crosses the open water approaching this magical destination. The island, which is surprisingly close to the Scottish mainland, covers some ninety thousand, six hundred and sixty-six acres with its highest point standing at two thousand, five hundred and seventy-five feet (every inch of which is covered on the fell race). The land is owned within seven private estates and a small amount by the Forestry

Commission. In 2011 the population of Jura was recorded as one hundred and ninety-six.

It is, of course, home to the world-famous Jura Malt Whisky, which is distilled in Craighouse, the main village of the Island and not surprisingly forms the friendly hub of the fell race. Jura sponsor the event; the Jura Hotel pretty much host the event and the distillery and its outbuildings provide home for the race hub. It's true to say that the event is indeed everything Jura.

So with around about two months to go to the day of the actual race, Saturday May 25th, there was an acceptance in my head that I needed to do a few things in focussed preparation as this was now certain to be a true 'ramp up' from my previous exploits.

Firstly, I needed to get some proper hill miles in my legs. I had vivid and painful memories of July 2018 when I'd optimistically shown up with three friends to run in the Welsh One Thousand Metre Peaks Race. This event starts on the Welsh coast along the shores of Conwy Bay and runs inland over the five one thousand plus metre peaks ending on the summit of Snowdon, the highest peak in England and Wales — having covered some thirty kilometres and over two thousand, five hundred metres of ascent. That day had taken me to some pretty dark places, possibly the darkest I'd ever experienced, and acutely pinpointed the fact that if you want to be competitive in the hills then you need to practice in the hills. I by contrast for that race had done quite a good amount of running however it had almost entirely been on the flat — and on the day the hills just broke me piece by piece. Having survived a true motivational low at Pen-y-pass where my friends picked me up with fluids, aspirins (I know, not good!) and some much needed food, I crept my way up to the summit of Snowdon and the race finish. There quickly followed the final humiliation when after eight hours of running and fast walking I had to face the brutal reality that there isn't a Snowdon Railway ride out, the runners are expected to return to Llanberis under their own leg power adding further cruel miles at the end of a long day. I recall ending with close to twenty-eight miles on my watch and legs that felt like they'd been systematically beaten with a baseball bat!

So, I needed hill miles and lots of them and I also needed a bike that had the ability to carry a decent amount of kit.

For my hill miles I set my sights on more runs out in beautiful Dovedale which lies around forty-minute-drive west from where I live. Thorpe Cloud, a stand-alone cone of a hill, became a regular evening and weekend destination and whilst it's not that high I could get there and then run / walk up, down and around it successively. On one visit I seemed to baffle the other hill users, many of whom were walking their dogs and out with their children on a beautiful spring evening — as I arrived successive times on the summit but each time from a different direction halting only momentarily on the summit before plummeting down another of the many paths to the bottom. I'd then circumnavigate myself around the base to the next path and walk back up as fast as I could.

"Mummy, what is that man doing?" seemed the common question by the various small children being dragged up the hill by their parents.

In the same area I took to running out along Dovedale to Wolfenscote Dale and then Biggindale before looping back along the Tissington Trail which never failed to be relentlessly boring and flat — but good for psychological determination. I added to the outdoor hill miles by going to the gym and spending time on a 'staircase' torture machine. This evil invention threw steps at me as quickly or slowly as you wished and had no regard for fatigue or indeed time. I'd put in my earplugs and tune into my one and only playlist time and again more so for distraction than in any attempt to find a rhythm.

In March I went back to the Isle of Man, where I'd lived for fifteen years, and went on a short and sunny evening hill run with long standing friend and fell race partner Chris Kirk. That evening alone was a stark reminder of my need for more hills with Chris quickly putting me to shame on the Manx fells — mere foothills by comparison to Jura! Then I returned again in April and took up the offer of entering the half Manx Mountain Marathon. Run on Easter Sunday, the event — in 2019 — was held in the most beautiful sunshine and a breathlessly calm day — a real hottie for every runner involved. In what could make another chapter of these adventure memories I pleased myself by getting round the twenty-two kilometre and eight hundred metre of ascent in a pretty respectable time. Although I felt drained and tired at the end, and the sun had absolutely taken its toll, my legs were definitely getting stronger.

Distance wise, as opposed to hill wise, I had been taking advantage of several friends who were getting their own miles in for various events — the London Marathon, Athens Marathon and a solo marathon run around Vancouver. So I'd managed to clock up lots of good stock miles particularly between January and April but then had to dig deep when their events all passed and many of them then temporarily backed off their weekly routines leaving me to find my own motivation to keep getting out up until May 24th!

And then there was the bike conundrum. Chris at some point convinced me that all credibility, never mind car fuel budget, pointed to the reason that the vast majority of people cycle in leaving their cars at various spots on the mainland before then ferry hopping to Jura. So I needed to either kit my existing bike out with racks and panniers or throw caution to the wind and get myself a touring bike and do it in style. Now I'm an impulsive sort of guy and so, having spent a little time trawling through second hand touring bikes on e-bay and very quickly looking at on-line bike bag offers, I went for the easy option and bought a new Boardman all weather road bike ready kitted out for touring and super sexy all in black. Cycle to work scheme it was — sometimes impulsivity is a great thing!

So the final plans were hatched and the ever-efficient and organised Chris sent me the overview:

Pick him up off the train in Lancaster on the Thursday evening before driving north to stay in a cheap motorway hotel somewhere near Glasgow. Then fairly early doors on the Friday drive to Ardrossan to leave the car and mount our bikes for the ferry to Arran. Once on Arran cycle up to the Northern end and take the short ferry hop from Lochranza to Cloanaig on the Mull of Kintyre. Then another short ride to Kennacraig and the longer ferry journey to Islay before a very short final ferry across to Jura — and the final ride over the island to Craighouse. What could be simpler? If all went to plan, we'd be pitching our tent in the evening sunshine and sipping a pint by nine p.m!

Incredibly that's exactly what happened, the day dawned bright and the plan fell seamlessly together. When we arrived at Ardrossan, we immediately joined a growing force of cyclists all leaving their cars in the long-term car park and heading for the ferry. Other cyclists arrived by road however their distinct lack of kit suggested that they were up to something entirely different. We soon got chatting to a lycra-clad Scotsman who sported nothing more than a small bladder backpack. He told us that he and many of the other lightweight cyclists were attempting the five-ferry challenge which would ultimately take them in a complete loop back to Ardrossan by the end of the day — assuming they could cover the ground quick enough to catch five ferries along the way!

As we rolled off the Calmac ferry on to Arran I enthusiastically jumped on to my bike and, for the very first time, experienced riding it in anger with fully packed panniers and my own small day sack. The truth was that more through a lack of time than any bravado I simply had not had the opportunity to ride the new purchase before then. Fortunately, it was an absolute joy and everything worked as it should. Whilst the front wheel felt a little light — due to the heavy-laden back end — and there was definitely more flex in the frame, it was a real pleasure and signified the start to the Jura Fell Race adventure.

And so the day rolled by, ferry followed by relatively short and sunny rides followed by ferry. Climbing up over the pass from Glen Sannox to Lochranza on Arran was simply beautiful with the sun shining intensely and the craggy mountains providing breathtaking scenery as an ever-present backdrop. I've heard it said many times that Arran is Scotland in miniature and that was easy to believe on such an amazing day. A trail of touring bike fell runners wound their ways over the pass and then enjoyed the long downhill into Lochranza leaving enough time for a coffee before the Cloanaig ferry arrived.

Waiting with coffee in hand at Lochranza, Chris and I were chatting in the sunshine passing the time away very pleasantly only to be joined by Isle of Man friend and fell runner Andy Watson who arrived heavily-laden on his mountain bike with various bits of kit Velcroed to crossbars and under his saddles but ultimately the majority of his gear was contained within a massive sixty-five litre rucksack on his back! Fit as he was, it gave me a degree of satisfaction that I had made my Boardman bike investment.

So on we pressed gathering additional bikers along the way. Many more joined at Kennacraig where they left their cars in the knowledge of a speedy exit on the way home. The ferry became packed with athletic looking people in all forms of lycra and outdoor kit sporting t-shirts and riding tops boasting of past adventures and challenges in pretty much every corner of the globe. New conversations sprung up and old friendships were rekindled, the sun shone and the ferry thumped along across the calmest and most beautiful of sea loch scenery, it was exciting and intimidating all at the same time.

In the early evening sunshine, we caught our first glimpse of Jura and I was immediately reminded of the sentence that heads the race directions:

"Nothing has you calling Mammy quite like your first view of The Paps: they generate a mixture of wonder and dread and offer a hill race unlike any other."

Even from this distance they were indeed awe inspiring and backed by clear blue skies they stood magnificently — geologically impressive, inviting to an adventurous spirit but equally easy to imagine how barren and windswept they could be if the weather closed in and caught any unsuspecting walker or runner out.

Head games! There seemed to be nothing steady or static either in my mind now or indeed in my stomach. One minute I'd be feeling confident, I'd done loads of time in the hills and had completed dozens of adventure races, fell races, mountain ultras and challenges that no one had made me do — and the next minute I'd be looking around at the dozens of people who seemed taller, thinner, looked faster and many of whom had clearly been here before. I'm in the wrong race I kept thinking, this isn't for the likes of me, I shouldn't be here. With every mental twist and turn so too did my stomach undulate. One minute a brick seems to appear in the pit of my belly and then next I had excited butterflies almost urging me on the 'get on with it', 'let's just go now'!

We landed on Islay at Port Askaig to spend literally only minutes waiting for the tiny ferry to Feolin on Jura a brisk ten minutes hop away across a fast flowing straight of water. The anticipation was growing, now almost tangible, amongst the group. Many had quickly become familiar faces along the way and a camaraderie had started to emerge safe in the knowledge that we were all heading for the same place and almost definitely all going to be seeing each other 'up on the hill' tomorrow.

On Jura we wound our way along the coastal road and then over a short hilly pass from Feolin to Craighouse arriving in the evening sunshine to quickly find a pitch for our tent on the beautiful green campsite in front of the Jura Hotel. For sure the midges were out in force no doubt enjoying this new influx of clean, white skin — their intimate attention only served to motivate us to make camp quickly and keep moving ultimately towards the hotel bar and a lucky seat in the bay window, overlooking the busy campsite, the setting sun and the inky calm of Castle Bay complete with yachts lying peacefully at their moorings. A pint of Guinness (essential race preparation sustenance) and nervous craic amongst friends repeatedly gazing across to the Paps which by now were starting to gather some clouds around their summits.

I was still oscillating between optimism and dread. Maybe the pint would be 'a bad one' and an overnight stomach bug might save me from the impending doom and humiliation of trying to complete the Jura Fell Race and failing miserably.

One pint in and some light-hearted banter we faced the dilemma of staying and indulging further or doing the right thing and heading back to the tent for an early night. For once in my life and motivated by the challenge that lay ahead, I opted to retreat to the warmth and comfort of the tent.

How glorious it was camping the evening before the race in front of the Jura Inn.

It was still light outside, but the sun had set and in the stillness of the evening the midges were now revelling in the human flesh of the busy campsite. The short walk to the tent afforded me enough time for a final nervous glance across to the Paps which were now heavily shrouded in cloud, the tops and upper flanks totally covered. I pondered what it might be like up there with limited visibility and vaguely hoped that the forecast might just be wrong and that the wall-to-wall sunshine of today would be repeated tomorrow. Wishful thinking indeed!

Chris and I have spent many, many nights under canvas, mountain marathons, Dads and daughter trips, fell walking and other adventures over more than fifteen years — we have an organised and embedded routine. So with little fuss we set to getting sorting out not just for the coming night but also in anticipation of a wet morning and a long day on the hill. I packed my spare thermal layers into a dry bag, filled two small five hundred millilitre bladders, tucked some spare food into pockets and ensured that my compass, map and food were all as required. It was to be my first long run in anger, wearing Matthew's Innov8 vest which I'd requested from his wife Becky, after his untimely death in 2017. It felt right and a real privilege to be able to run in his memory wearing something of his. Matthew, or Sev to his long-standing friends, was an endurance runner of remarkable determination and accomplishment, the vest kind of connects me to him and I'd be lying if I said that I never spoke to him whilst looking for energy and inspiration during a dark moment.

We awoke early, well before seven a.m. and took the opportunity to indulge in snoozing for some time. The race start was ten thirty a.m. and registration in the distillery cooperage was open from nine a.m. onwards so there was no rush both because the building was around one hundred metres away, but more so because the midges were once again out in abundance. Slowly we came to, the odd glance out through the tent flaps confirmed that the cloud remained thoroughly down, and the downbeat forecast seemed to be accurate — much to my dismay. No matter how many times we looked at the BBC weather check it only confirmed the arrival of rain and indeed their prediction slowly moved towards a perfect unison of the race start and the start of proper rain fall — all excellently coordinated by the weather Gods to occur at ten thirty a.m. prompt.

I do not know why the thought of poor visibility affected me so much because Chris and I actually run and navigate really well in bad weather. Our best mountain marathon results have been in grim conditions, and we check and double check each other really well — I guess I just like to see the views and get that greater sense of exposure to the magnificence of our surroundings. What a shame to come all the way to Jura and run only in the cloud, but that seemed to be the reality and we'd just have to get on with it.

Breakfast was a take-out tub of porridge from the campsite cafe bar and a cup of coffee, both consumed in the tent as early intervals of light drizzle passed over the gathering crowds. Then came the usual period of indecision — to take an extra layer, to add another few energy bars, to have gloves or not, maybe a spare hat, but then no that's extra unnecessary weight so let's leave it… but then… but, but…

oh sod it, I'll be okay let's just go and register and get on with this!

We left the shelter of the tent and headed to registration which included a compulsory kit check and then the opportunity to review the course on fantastic blown-up maps of the route and mountain range. Runners were gathering mostly from the campsite but others from campervans, the hotel and a limited number of local bed and breakfasts. I looked hopefully to see people that might be potentially slower than me but then I know that in the world of fell running there are few strict physical rules. Okay so the elite competitors will generally be tall, thin and sinewy but after that it's hard to spot with any accuracy how people might fare. I'm always impressed by elite runners' ability to carry the compulsory safety kit in minute bum bags and this event was no exception. There I had been pondering extra layers and energy bars only to see hardy elites in running vests and wafer-thin kit belts looking totally comfortable in the drizzle chatting idly and waiting for the pre-race briefing.

Chris and I got talking to two older ladies geared up in serious hillwalking mode, gortex jackets and over trousers, backpacks and peaked hats all ready for the hill. They entertained us briefly with their knowledge of the island and in particular the navigational challenges of the Paps — not filling me with confidence of what lay ahead. They became incredulous when we told them that we'd arrived the night before and had never previously been to Jura and most certainly hadn't scouted the route. This seemed to amaze them, and they made it clear that they thought our approach was cavalier at best — after that I didn't want to talk to them any more, I couldn't handle negativity at this late stage!

The pre-race briefing took place in early on-set drizzle, the kind of weather that one automatically associates with Scotland and that many refer to as 'dreik'. Such meteorological inconveniences are mentally blocked out by one's memories of the rare heady sunny days up in the hills. Deeply driek might perhaps be the best description of today however, the gathered group of two hundred and fifty runners were now all very much ready for the off, elite athletes lined up at the front followed by row after row of less ambitious athletes and somewhere in the middle were Chris and I — "steady away" I told myself but then I always do!

A short blast of the customary foghorn released the pack, and we were off, very briefly along the narrow village street before turning left and starting uphill on tarmac and then quickly on to muddy track and then fell side proper. With the faster runners quickly away, Chris and I settled into a large group that were moving at a pace I could sustain. There was mixed walking and running, hopping hopefully over the first muddy irrigation trenches before accepting that wet feet and muddy calves were the order of the day and there was little point in trying to protect them. In a thin crocodile line of runners, we ascended the early slopes and through the low cloud base into the waiting swirling wetness that was to be our companion for the rest of the day.

From the start at sea level to checkpoint one (CP1) the summit of Dubh Bheinn, there was a climb of five hundred and thirty metres or around one thousand, seven hundred and fifty feet over a distance of four kilometres. As with most fell races there was also the cut-off time that was clearly stated — in this case as eleven forty a.m. The time allowed seemed a generous enough window and indeed we found ourselves through the CP with over twenty minutes to spare. Such was my focus upon Jura that I'd pre-plotted the correct bearings to run on from CP to CP even adding some brief navigational notes on a folded slip of paper tucked neatly alongside my map in a waterproof sealable sandwich bag — unheard of preparation for me. As it turned out however there was little immediate need for navigating as, even in the swirling cloud, a long line of confident runners could be seen disappearing into the murk and I concluded that they all couldn't be wrong! So, with only a cursory glance at my compass and already knowing the bearing, we headed straight through and onwards now skipping swiftly down a slope and on past the reassuring presence of two small lochans.

Before long we were climbing again to CP2 at five hundred and sixty-two metres, still mixed in with a small pack of fellow runners some of whom by now were becoming familiar characters marked out by their running tops or their ultra-waistcoats or even their particular running style. Onwards through the cloud, sweating through the exertion of constant movement, soaked by the thick cloud and perpetual drizzle but ultimately exhilarated at being part of something so demanding and adventurous.

Heading westwards from CP2 we actually lost height covering a short distance of around one and a half kilometres to Aonach-bheinn. It was good running over soft ground and our little crowd of runners bounded along in high spirits.

Of course, it was the first Pap which was still gripping my mind, these first three summits were simply the warm-up, they were simply the run into the first brute of the day and the three mountains that make this particular race so iconic. This first Pap, Beinn a Chaolais, stands at seven hundred and thirty-four metres and is described in the race instructions as "one of the most intimidating sights in British fell running". For us runners it presented a one thousand, nine-hundred-foot climb and the first real test of the day.

We plunged down from CP3 experiencing the first scree run of the day and popping out of the cloud to see a welcome stream running across the mountain saddle. This was backed by the sheer rugged mountainside alternately dominated by grassy slope and rocky crag. It was big and very impressive but, I think, the low cloud base helped shield us from the full effect of the climb that we were about to tackle and the severe nature not just of the slope but also the technical route choice.

As we ran across the flat terrain and over the stream we stopped, albeit briefly, to refill our water bottles with fresh beautifully cold and clear water to quench our thirst. I decided to also get out my running poles in preparation for the monster slope to come, I figured that any advantage was worth having! Their appearance out of my small running pack came much to Chris's dismay as he was strongly opposed to running poles and had consistently ribbed me for buying them, stating that he'd have to run ahead of me to save his reputation and embarrassment. My choice to buy them only weeks before the race had been informed by supporting two friends who had twice attempted the Arc of Attrition along the Cornish Coastal Path (another chapter of my book). Matt and Dave swore by them for extra stability and confidence on steep ground, for additional propulsion and as energy saving devices. I needed no convincing, but Chris clearly still did.

And so onwards and upwards to conquer the first Pap, so

steep that grass, mud and mixed undergrowth stares straight back at you, the calves and feet of fellow runners in your direct line of sight and the occasional stop to look up, survey the route ahead, spot familiar figures in the cloud and regain a breath before bending back to the inevitable toil.

Chris pulled steadily ahead of me, always stronger uphill but always kind enough to ensure we were within eyesight of each other. He therefore made the route choice, again primarily by following the line of "runners" none of whom had any inclination now to even try to run. I knew from my many readings of the route description that we would at some point gain a little respite as the route turned sharply right along a bolder rock terrace. This came soon enough and was a reassuring navigational way marker. It lasted perhaps only a hundred metres before the faint path turned again sharply upwards and on to bouldery terrain which would now continue all the way to the summit. My poles were proving to be fantastic as long as I placed them on to a level rock surface. Not surprisingly when I pressed them into the muddy terrain, and then pushed myself forwards, they'd pierce the soft surface layer and sink making it hard to easily retrieve them and continue upwards, if I got them caught between rocks they'd jam, and the sections would separate annoyingly meaning I'd have to stop and faff on reconnecting them. That said I quickly got the hang of placing them carefully and they helped me no end... the climb continued relentlessly!

The wind was blowing strongly across the summit, a moonscape of bare rock, the cloud as thick as ever but it felt fantastic to see the terrain levelling out and catch the first colours of the brave marshal's clothing. These quite amazing volunteers were spending the best part of their day ensuring that runners safely 'dibbed' their way over the summit and continued in the right direction. They had little shelter and the elements were by now demanding to say the least, but they cheerily waved us through with words of encouragement and even a few jelly babies which we gratefully took and greedily consumed as we resumed our mountain journey. Volunteer marshals are the backbone and often saviours of many an event giving the organisers the necessary resource to run things safely with hundreds of people out in wild country. Jura was no exception, made possible through the generosity of the locals who clearly embrace the event and all that it brings with it each year.

The path off the summit was obvious enough. A good number of competitors had already been through leaving scuffed and kicked stud marks consistently in the same direction. The route stayed briefly on the mountain ridge but then plunged incredibly steeply on loose rock and scree that moved in slabs with you as you ran ankle deep, sometimes in tiny pebble-sized bands and then on to bigger rock that nipped at your ankles, shins and calves. The route drops from the summit at seven hundred and thirty-four metres down to the lochan at three hundred and seventy-five metres before then immediately climbing again — this is the challenge of the Paps!

I found myself revelling in the descents, for once leaving Chris trailing behind providing a nice contrast to the usual pattern of me chasing behind him desperate to keep up. I enjoyed the feeling of the mountain moving with me, the rushing sound of the stone tumbling together and the occasional larger rock gathering momentum and accelerating down the steep slope. "Below" would come the loud call from one runner to the next, warning of a fast-moving rock and the need to take care. "You will dislodge rocks" had been the warning at the race briefing some hours earlier and now sure enough here we were in the reality of the moment!

At the bottom of the first long descent there was a short flat saddle to cross with only momentary respite at the side of a lonely lochan before the second Pap, Beinn an Oir, loomed literally above us standing at seven hundred and sixty-three metres. The mountain waiting ominously in the cloud demanding that we climb some one thousand, three hundred and sixty feet to gain its summit.

Having revelled in this descent I looked back and felt guilty realising that Chris was not within sight. As I waited, I took the opportunity of untying my shoes in order to empty the many tiny stones that had made their way in, this coupled with adjusting socks felt like a real luxury and once reset, my feet felt comfortable, warm and ready for the next climb. I was feeling surprisingly strong, better than I'd thought I would. I hadn't even contemplated taking a gel — my intention was to not resort to such things, fearful of repeating past experiences of sugar-induced highs followed by deep energy lows once the sugar had burnt off. I'd allowed this to happen to me during the Welsh one thousand metre peaks race in July 2018 when I enthusiastically took two gels early on, had none left, and then literally plunged into a dark energy less place perhaps forty-five minutes later. Only pure determination, good support from understanding friends and a convenient food station kept me going to the finish on the summit of Snowdon.

Chris and I between summits on Jura 2019

Back on Jura, Chris came carefully running out of the cloud looking cautious as he picked his way down the last section of the steep slope and navigated his way to me. Whilst then grumbling about the scree, he set to emptying shoes and making his feet comfortable before we were once again off at our considered plod towards the lower slopes of Beinn an Oir, this race was starting to feel achievable!

I'd snatched a conversation with an Irish guy who'd passed me on the flat section whilst I was waiting for Chris. Asking him if he'd done the race before I was thrilled to hear that not only had he done so but even better he was feeling very confident of a decent finish time knowing where he was as he passed me and how long he'd taken. From there on he became my target, his red, ultra-hydration vest an easy sight to keep an eye on, and his pace well matched to that of our own. As Chris retied his second shoe, I urged him on, half eyeing the red Irish pack climbing into the cloud and zig zagging up through large boulders. I needn't have worried as we were quickly underway and soon caught up and then passed my Irish 'friend' on the steep mountain terrain.

We toiled onward, the same routine resumed, head down, one foot in front of the other, pushing ever upwards optimistic that the summit would soon become apparent. There were the inevitable occasional brief stops to survey the potential route and check the progress of others as they too pressed onwards and upwards. It reminded me constantly of my friend's reference many years earlier to a fabled Scottish rock-climbing guide that advised "trend generally upwards!" We did and pace by pace we were getting there.

Sitting here now and writing this even accepting that the race was just three months ago I have no memory of the ascent of the third Pap, Beinn Shiantaidh (seven hundred and fifty-seven metres) and little memory of the second plunging descent that took us on to this final major climb.

Somewhere on that final ascent as steady as our progress remained, I began to feel a little bit chilly. My trusty red Paramo thermal top was absolutely sodden, in truth it had been for hours, however now perhaps because of the angle and exposure of the steep mountain side or maybe because the wind had strengthened, I was most definitely losing heat. I needed to take early action and add a layer. Conveniently Chris and I were right alongside one another so I asked if he'd take a breather whilst I pulled out my spare technical long-sleeved top from my dry bag and strip down to my waist in order to get the luxury and the benefits of the dry warm layer next to my skin. I duly did so although it was an uncomfortable process stood leaning into the hillside, wind rattling around us and rain driving at us. Chris took my poles to hold and as I pulled my cagoule back on and fumbled with the zip, he set off again taking my poles with him.

It took me a few seconds to get properly zipped up and my sack all clipped together properly before I too resumed the journey. Chris was gone into the swirling cloud, chilled by my enforced stop time, and so I had to hurry walking and climbing harder to make up the lost ground. When I did start to make out his shadowy profile ahead of me it wasn't without amusement that I spied him using the poles and clearly enjoying the benefit of their aid as he crossed a narrow rocky ridge in the strong wind. I shouted out my observations and was impressed that he made no denial — even as he handed them back to me, that he could see their benefit — but that said, he'd never be buying a pair! Only time and weakening knees will tell!

I was particularly mindful of the race notes provided for the descent off the final Pap. It gave stringent advice to the runner to descend but trend leftwards as the scree runs off. The aim was to be collected some one thousand, five hundred feet below by a faint runner's path that then contoured and dropped around the mountain, heading eastwards towards the fifth and final summit of the day. Missing this path and recklessly plunging onwards further down the slope would only result in a depressing 'U' turn for the unfortunate athlete and an unnecessary one thousand foot plus climb back up! A torrid thought this far into proceedings.

So, with that in mind we descended with clear intent and I constantly glanced to my left as runners both below and alongside trended leftwards and I willingly followed their lead. After five or so minutes of twisting and turning, of floating at speed on the surface of the scree, of falling backwards with no harm and then picking myself up to move on, I spotted a small rock cairn on a large boulder and a distinct path heading off around the mountain. It helped that there were shadowy figures of runners also disappearing along the path, I was eager to follow.

Once again at the base of these tricky descents I found myself looking back up the mountainside and realising that my adrenalin-fuelled scree run had resulted only in leaving Chris behind, his more cautious approach causing him to move more slowly with somewhat less abandon than I'd shown. I waited by the cairn, and he soon appeared, yellow running top easily distinguished against the grey of both the day and the mountain scree. I called loudly to him so he could home in on me and then rather impatiently headed off along the path sometimes contouring, sometimes descending. Chris quickly made ground on me, and we were back together as we began a short boggy traverse across a flat terrace towards the sixth and final summit of the day, Corra Bheinn, in theory a relatively minor peak at just five hundred and seventy-five metres.

Theory and reality are often different, and such was the case now as the peak stood ahead of us almost entirely out of the cloud. It looked instantly intimidating, far bigger than I'd imagined and made worse by the sight of numerous runners, just small figures against the hill, making their way upwards. This was however the final big push and so I asked Chris to indulge me with a five-minute stop, to refuel, to take a gel and to gather myself before the climb.

We were easily within time and very consciously racing no one, so a break was of little competitive consequence. I found myself enjoying being still, albeit that the rain was now blowing in sheets across the moor and our bodies very quickly started to lose the heating benefits of constant movement. Chris was great, he helpfully dug into my pack meaning I didn't have to take it off and found my food, he put my folded poles away and zipped all up safely ready for another 'off' but this time to the final summit.

Head down once again we ascended, contouring to manage the steepness but equally conscious of not extending the route unnecessarily. Chris again ahead on a more forgiving and softer hillside he was strong as always on the ups and, polite to the end, he picked our way upwards until with a definite shout of celebration I spotted the coloured mountain jackets of the marshals and we were there on the top, dibbing in on the final summit and thankfully able to turn for home.

With the congratulations of the marshals ringing loudly in my ears and the elation that the worst was most probably over, we easily picked up a clear path that descended gradually across expansive moor towards the Three Arch Bridge and the final road section still some four kilometres distant from us across 'desperate trods'. The running was indeed soft underfoot, downhill and our adrenaline was up, as was our pace. I'll never forget it, Chris just ahead of me both of us able to speak already starting to share stories of the day, the elements steadily receding, visibility now fantastic and our sense of achievement growing. We even picked off three runners along the way, but I admired the fact that they were alone and had clearly crossed the Paps entirely of their own skill and confidence — could I have done that? So deep had this race dug into my confidence.

At the bridge we took full advantage of the feed station, water and welcome sweets before starting the run / walk to the finish. It was just five kilometres but I'd heard many a story as to how tough this final section was. The more competitive runners leave road shoes in bags the night before so they can change footwear or have support crew meet them with dry warm shoes ready for a big push.

In my head it was very much going to be a long slow but steady plod, however as the adrenalin subsided, I slipped in to a painfully slow trot which then descended into a walk/trot routine, which seemed to go on forever. The runners we'd passed all caught us back up and pressed on ahead, once again Chris's patience was admirable as he clearly had the legs for a swift road section home but true to his word, he stuck it out with me and we slowly reeled Craighouse village in and the finish outside the distillery cooperage. I managed a valiant final few hundred metre run, jubilant to have finished and comfortably so within the time limit allowed.

Our race time was six hours, fifteen minutes and forty-five seconds, placing one hundred and ninety-six out of two hundred and fifty-five starters. In all two hundred and forty-one runners finished and I take my hat off to each and every one of them. Considering I'd been contemplating feigning injury the night before I was happy with my big day out on Jura!

Having firmly shaken Chris's hand we went into the cooperage to get our timing print out and enjoy hot tea and sandwiches. Runners in all manner of states were standing and sitting around. Many had clearly finished hours before and were dressed and chatting casually, others were sat simply staring into space in their own world possibly reliving recent moments and feeling relieved that it was over. I had to smile and laugh when I heard the finishing announcer congratulate a local runner, the oldest competitor at seventy-one years old cross the line only minutes after us, what an achievement, many congratulations indeed.

The story of this adventure should really end here — a great day out in the Scottish hills, wild weather and fantastic friendship — I will never forget and would love to return on a sunnier day.

We rode out early the next morning and made our way back to Ardrossan in the now familiar mixed drizzle and wind-driven rain. The ferries matched perfectly for us, and I was grateful that we'd made the effort to get up and leave even though conditions were more suited to staying indoors.

By late evening we were at a friend's house in Ambleside enjoying a cooked meal and a cold beer ready for a warm bed and plenty of sleep. I had experienced the wonder and dread of the Jura Fell Race and the Paps — and it had been well worth it.

The Welsh One Thousand Metre Peaks Race 2018

The truth is that this race emptied me, never before had I been so broken and resigned to retirement and yet I look back on this particular experience with very mixed feelings.

One big downside that remains firmly imprinted in my memory is just how quickly I went from feeling 'okay' to feeling absolutely drained. Never before had I had to manage the physical and mental demons that come with that sort of fatigue, simply to see the event through. Typically, at the point I felt my lowest, we still faced the final challenging ascents of Garnedd Ugain closely followed by ascending to the finish line on the summit of Snowdon at one thousand eighty-five metres.

By contrast the upsides have been many. It was not just a very long day out on the Welsh mountains, it was time spent with some great friends and it served as a firm reminder that any event has the potential to find you out when your preparation hasn't been adequate, and you're left wanting!

I'm sure that had I not, in 2018, have encountered this personal all time racing low, then I seriously do not think I could have successfully taken on the Jura Fell Race in 2019 and seen it through with some running (just about) still in my legs. I'd learnt that you cannot train for a mountain race by running around your local fields which might build miles but takes in next to no ascent. This is stating the bleeding obvious, but somehow, I'd missed it!

Similar to many of my stories the entry to this event came about through the annual winter's telephone call with Johnny Matthews. It usually happens on a lazy Sunday evening and he calls me with a seemingly innocent question "what plans are you making for next year?" Beware that call Mr. Knight, it's got you into trouble on several occasions!

Johnny introduced me to the Welsh One Thousand Metre Peaks Race, he'd run it the previous year and championed it as a really well organised event, tough, demanding, rewarding and definitely a challenge well worth entering. Impulsively I responded quickly with a yes, I guess that's why he calls me! My calendar for the date in July was empty and, to be frank, I was missing the mountains and so it seemed like an ideal target to train towards.

Having committed myself, I called Chris Kirk, my good friend and fell running partner from the Isle of Man and he in turn called Dave Price (Spike) — so by the end of the evening we were a group of four and the scene was set. What also struck me was the pedigree of the other runners in comparison to myself. Johnny lives in the Lakes and as such his weekly training runs always include a few 'proper' hills. Chris was in a similarly privileged position on the Isle of Man where, from Ramsey, the Manx hills are close by and readily accessible. Dave, by contrast, lives down in Reading, a far less hilly geography, however what he lost in hill preparation he more than made up for in miles. At the time he was steadily making his way towards completing one hundred marathons before the age of fifty!

I have on purpose started by accurately positioning this

event as a 'mountain' race as opposed to the many fell running stories that I have regaled. The following descriptions, shamelessly lifted from the Welsh One Thousand Metre Peaks Race website, sets in context just why it is a true 'mountain' race.

"This is a navigational race so, for the most part, route selection is up to the competitor to decide. The entry fee includes a map of the route area. The map will be marked with checkpoints and out of bounds areas. Maps will be displayed one at registration and checkpoint locations are included in the information for competitors."

"For decades, mountain athletes have informally competed against each other whilst endeavouring to complete the fifteen three thousand foot mountains in Snowdonia. A more formal challenge, from Snowdon to Foel Fras, was devised by Dai Rowlands for the TA in the 1950s. This soon became an Army race, later to be joined by the RAF and civilian mountain rescue teams. In the late 1960's, Ron James, the warden of Ogwen Cottage Outdoor Pursuits Centre, along with Dr Leuan Jones, proposed a new race open to all, starting at sea level at Aber and going via all one thousand metre summits to finish on the top of Snowdon. In 1970 a trial race took place, with sixty invited competitors. The first race proper took place in 1971."

"The long course route starts at sea level near at Abergwyngregyn (652728), near the shore of Conwy Bay. It climbs to the summits of Carnedd Llewelyn and Carnedd Dafydd before a fantastic descent to Ogwyn Valley. The climb to Glyder Fawr is rewarded by flying down to Pen-y-Pass Youth Hostel, then up again to the summit of Garnedd Ugain to finish on Yr Wyddfa (Snowdon), at one thousand

and eighty-five metres."

And finally...

"The long course takes in three challenging climbs covering approximately thirty-two kilometres with a total ascent of two thousand, eight hundred metres."

A very brief summary of my race preparation:

In 2015, the year that we moved back to the UK from the Isle of Man, I had entered and completed an event called The Wiltshire Ox. It was, and I'm sure still is, a fifty-kilometre race along well marked trails and through a selection of beautiful villages.

I say fifty kilometres; however, the organisers did actually announce at the start that it was in fact a "fifty-ish" kilometre race. Ever the optimist, when he said this, I thought he may be indicating that it was perhaps forty-eight kilometres and we would be spared some distance due to their route planning. As it turned out it was fifty-five kilometres and the final five kilometres seemed to drag on forever especially when you're reduced to over ten minutes per mile pace.

I'm telling you this to make the point that I had become pretty used to longer distance events and, in the months building up to the Welsh race, I reverted to 'type' and began to put in longer miles in readiness for the big day out that was looming. I reached a point where I could quite happily run eighteen miles or so through the local fields, taking in a few gentle inclines. It seemed to be good 'time on the legs' however I now know that it was lacking in the all-important element of 'specificity'. If you're going to run — or even attempt to run — in the mountains then you need mountain miles in your legs. Ascending and, equally, descending is

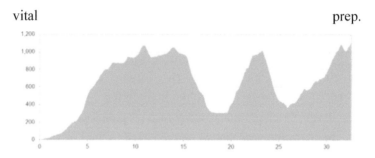

I did a little unplanned sprint training too. One dark evening out I headed on a footpath through a field of cows. In the beam of my head-torch I could see that they were a good distance away and thought nothing of heading out from the stile along the boundary hedge towards the next gate perhaps some three hundred metres away. I alternated my torch beam from lighting up the grassy path in front of me to looking across the field at the large herd of cows that seemed now to be heading in my direction. Their evil eyes glinted in the beam of my torch, and I was in no doubt that they had decided that I was an object of interest. My speed picked up at probably the same rate as my heart which started thumping impressively in my chest. I alternated between run, look right at cows, head down, run faster, look right at cows getting closer, run even faster, look ahead at far gate, am I going to make it — NO, OH SHIT!

As I was now in full flight so were the cows and in the dark, I could make out that it was an impressive herd, their glinting eyes now joined by a very healthy thudding of multiple hoofs as they homed in on me. I kid you not, it was bloody terrifying. Now, probably within ten metres of me, the cows showed no sign of slowing down and I began to mentally ponder that a brave but necessary dive into the thick and thorny hedge might just be my only way out… and then just ahead appearing out of the dark I saw a metal gate in the beam of my torch, to my left and within striking distance. Once again, I lifted my pace, the cows were no longer silhouettes, they were present in my space, damp air pluming out of dilated nostrils as they rose to the thrill of the chase.

I reached that gate with only feet to spare and threw myself over it with wild abandon, not caring about style or potential injury. My feet touched terra firm on the far side just as the herd arrived blowing hard and slamming their own brakes on, straight legged and hooves sliding in the mud around the gate.

Safe now at least from those beasts, I noticed that the new field I had vaulted into had its own shadowy herd not too far away. "For fucks sake" I muttered to myself. All I wanted now was to get out of these fields and go home, the fun of this night time run was long gone. I figured that stealth was my best bet and so I doused my torch and stood very quietly tucked into the hedge by the metal gate and waited — partly to catch my breath and let the jet of adrenalin ebb away.

Heart and breath settled, I left my little thorny alcove of safety and started walking directly back along the hedgerow, torch off but eyes firmly fixed on the new herd still some distance away and seemingly uninterested in my rude arrival into their field.

In true terrified fashion I walked deliberately on a direct line towards the next gate and a potential safe haven — but only to a point where I judged that, no matter what, the cows would not be able to catch me before I reached the exit gate, and at that point I launched into a new, flat-out sprint, tense with nervous excitement. I surged across the final metres giggling to myself like some crazed convict evading capture.

I remain firm to this day that cows are bloody terrifying!

Race Day

Our little team gathered the evening before the race in the town of LLanberis which also serves as the race hub. Chris flew in from the Isle of Man to Liverpool airport from where I collected him and enjoyed a very sociable drive down and much needed catch up. Spike travelled up from Reading and had secured a room in a local hostel whilst Johnny drove from the Lakes and found digs just outside of the village.

Pre-race discussions had helped us to conclude that our approach focussed on having 'a great day out with good friends' rather than some adrenaline-fuelled, lung-bursting assault on the Welsh mountains. I think that we all knew just how that would end, most definitely with differing variations of being beaten by the mountains and it wouldn't be pretty! This easy-going approach suited me just fine and as such I felt no guilt in having a beer or three with Chris and Spike the evening before, whilst surveying the route map and pondering the all-important weather forecast.

Pleasant as that was, we were soon back in our respective rooms to undertake the all-important kit preparation. I've spoken about this at length in other chapters so will not dwell on it too extensively here. It's accepted that you must carry the compulsory gear, the conundrum is just what else do you put in your tiny pack for a twenty-one-mile mountain race? The forecast was for heavy cloud, perhaps a few showers but generally humid temperatures. Food and drinks essential, full body cover compulsory, energy gels and bars, spare socks and a second warm top, hat and gloves... the list could go on as could the debate as to exactly what you do need, might need and want to need! It's all a part of the pre-race ritual of faffing with kit, packing and unpacking, worrying about unnecessary weight, uncomfortable protrusions from your pack sticking in to you, chaffs and rubs... you get the idea!

As with most long-distance events, race day itself starts very early. We still needed to undertake our formal registration, collect race numbers and go through kit check before catching the race-organised six a.m. coach from LLanberis to the start at Abergwyngregyn. All of this meant a five-a.m. start and the necessity to be well organised before dropping into bed.

The coach trip was much like any other shuttle to a race start. I have to remind myself that most probably every other runner is doing the same as I am — eyeing up the competition and fabricating weird and wonderful stories as to who they might be, how fit they are, what events they've run and whether you stand any chance whatsoever of beating them! It passes the time and helps a little to calm the nerves that course their way around my body on these pre-race trips. What often crosses my mind at moments like this is "I'm on the wrong coach, I've entered the wrong race, these people all look fitter than me, indeed, how did I get myself into this and why am I here?"

Once in 'Aber' we were led as one mountain running contingent from the coach along increasingly narrow lanes to a gathering field. Here an efficient race volunteer had erected a makeshift taped off starting compound typical of most fell and mountain race protocol — very little, if any, pomp and ceremony. The holding pen is usually accompanied by the obligatory race official in high vis jacket with a loud hailer who makes the final safety announcements, notice of route alterations, a weather update and then the final obligatory count down to the fog-horned start.

And so, it was, we were underway, swept along far too fast in the adrenalin-fuelled first mile out of the village. The rush of the elite pack overwhelms the inner voice telling me that I'll never sustain such a pace, but the thrill of competition draws me on until the inevitable oxygen deficit and thumping heart signal an incremental halt to such tom foolery.

Within a mile the route, with no option for deviation, heads through a gate and on to the hill side following alongside a plantation and then onwards to a steep scramble past Aber Falls. This tops out quickly into a lush ascending mountain valley leading us into the Carnedd range of hills.

Taking my customary place at the back of our little group I quickly realised just how humid the day was, and the impact upon my chosen set-up for running. Caused by the bleary eyed five a.m. start I had opted to keep my glasses on rather than pop in contact lenses and I knew within that first mile that this was going to be a mistake that would haunt me for the entire day. Dressed only in a running vest and shorts I was simply too warm, sweating impressively as the still air hung in that low valley, my glasses steamed up and stayed that way for the next nine hours. It was indeed a school-boy error not to have packed a set of lenses into my backpack. We were not in any rush, and it would have been very agreeable to stop for the couple of minutes it would have taken to put lenses in — but no, ignorantly I had left them back at the B & B!

We laboured up the valley through deep heather, lifting knees high to clear each step, sapping energy as we crossed pathless terrain heading ever upwards into the low hanging cloud that covered the secondary summit of Yr Ayrg and our first check point of the race. As is usual at this stage of a race you are still very much surrounded by other runners — albeit we were all united in an aggressive walking pattern, the heather too deep for any running but the throng of people meant that navigation was not essential even considering the poor visibility.

Voices and shadowy figures signalled that the check point was close, shouts from fellow competitors to their teammates, the marshals braving the elements calling out to people for their race numbers to tick them off, knowing that they've passed through. Obediently we 'dibbed 'our dibbers and then wasting no time at all we turned for the off.

Our next target was Carnedd Gwenllian standing at nine hundred and twenty-six metres and the first true summit of the day. The heather thinned out and we joined a well-established mountain path that turned southwards and made for good steady running, a relief after quite some time wading through heather. We were off, in good spirits, plenty warm enough although the wind was now freshening, and visibility was poor as the cloud was chased by the wind across the mountain.

I can recall thinking at this point that we were now really getting into the race. Whilst there were still a good number of runners around, the feeling of being in some form of pack run was quickly diminishing further, added to by the poor visibility which only served to add atmosphere.

From Carnedd Gwenllian the route turned almost due south and we settled in, running as a tight group, to a measured pace that reflected the need to conserve energy for the long day ahead. We were now on high ground, still climbing but only gently towards the summits of Foel Grach (nine hundred and seventy-six metres) and then onwards to Carnedd Llywelyn (one thousand and sixty-four metres) the first one thousand metre peak of our day.

Along this section of mountain path, we gradually caught up with what turned out to be an older but formidable competitor. Ahead at first in the cloud we could see him variously fast walking and running, hands neatly folded behind his back tucked under his small pack, head slightly down leaning into the elements but in a manner that told of many years running in the hills. I ventured to run alongside him and exchange a few words of hilly camaraderie.

"You're going well" I started rather patronisingly, "Have you done this event before?"

The man tolerated me politely, responding modestly that this was his tenth time around this particular race and that he was in no particular rush at his age and stage. He had that gnarly look to him, carrying no unnecessary weight both in body matter and equipment, he was simply efficient in every way, a mountain machine crafted through time.

As the day progressed, we crossed paths several times. I always felt like we were travelling quicker than him across the mountain terrain but then he'd pop up again, emerging out of the cloud slightly ahead or slightly behind — he never looking rushed and, so it seemed, never even looked at a map. He just kept moving at the same pace, a mystical wiry mountain man. I mused that maybe one day I could be like him. In the end he beat us hands down!

After Carnedd Llywelyn the route steadily swung towards the west and on the Carnedd Dafydd standing at one thousand and forty-four metres. Johnny was in his element, map in hand, compass never that far away, he confidently set both the pace and the route ahead. I, by contrast, continued to struggle with my bloody glasses that were steamed up, covered in rain and generally useless. Whilst better without them on I then couldn't see very far ahead at all and quickly became frustrated at how neutralized I felt. Aside from running and taking Johnny's lead, I wasn't much use at all.

The checkpoint on the summit of Llywelyn was at the end of a short out and back dog leg. We had picked up some route intelligence that the next checkpoint was not far away along that return leg neatly positioned in a small depression close to a crumbling stone wall. It was a significant way point not just because we had to 'dib' our way through, but also because it marked the right point from which to start the long descent down in to the Ogwen Valley. Our little team decided to spread out into an extended line across the mountain side to better increase our chances of finding the marker quickly, running again at a steady pace through the tussocks of grass, eyes scanning the terrain ahead. Once again, we were fortunate to benefit from the coming and going of various other runners and the sound of their voices through the cloud as they collected together near the marshals who were hunkered down close to the dibber sheltering from the elements.

And so we turned south again, now plunging down the

mountain side running quickly whilst endeavouring to select an immediate route that didn't cause a head-first tumble. The Ogwen Valley Road runs at around three hundred metres so we were now forced to sacrifice well over two thousand feet of climbing in just over two kilometres of running. The route ahead was straight forwards as we used the shape of the terrain to guide us, a tongue of land slightly protruding, streams to the left and right as handrails and a distinct mountain tarn to most definitely keep to our right.

Down we went, heading to the next check point by a building just up from the valley road. Now well out of the cloud we could see the colourful tops of runners arriving and leaving the small table that had been set up by the marshals. Arriving breathless but elated we were pleasantly surprised to find an array of delights, orange segments, chocolate, water and other very welcome items to sustain us along our journey. At this point we were around two thirds of our way through the race and I for one was starting to feel the effects of the climbing. Never a fan of gels I had rather ignorantly used all three of the 'spares' that I carry in my pack and was now out of them at the time when perhaps I needed them most. We refilled water bottles and took on some food from the picnic table before heading off down a short section of track to pick up the valley road and a tarmac section along the shores of Llyn Ogwen. Chris and Spike were running well (not an unusual statement I hasten to add) and had pulled ahead just a little, leaving Johnny and I gently plodding along behind. I had to remind myself that this was 'a long day out with good friends' and it was fine to not be rushing — there was still a good old way to go and plenty of climbing which was going to start imminently.

Turning off the road and through a small car park, the climb ahead was lost in cloud which swirled above us and perhaps conveniently blanketed the mountain side. To a degree I was now entering more familiar terrain as we headed into the famous Glyder mountain range. Many years before I had completed my Summer Mountain Leaders training course here taking in the famous summit of Tryfan and spending time under the tutelage of yet another wiry Welsh mountain man practicing micro navigation and safety of steep ground. Great memories but of little use to me now as I began to feel the cumulative effects of the day pooling in my increasingly heavy legs.

The mountain path climbed steeply ahead, and my three fellow running mates disappeared into the cloud. The transition was gradual, at first, I could see them, then they were occasional wisps of colour in the cloud ahead, then only voices above me and then simply intermittent sounds blown back to me on the wind that increased with every metre climbed.

From memory, but distinct memory, it was at this point that I hit the proverbial wall. I found myself variously sitting by the path on large rocks watching other runners pass me as they worked their way up the stone staircase that lay ahead. I drank my water and had a good chat with myself, there was actually little choice other than heading onwards and upwards, but I felt pretty spent and it had arrived all in a rush since the valley road as if it had waited to capture me on the mountain side on which I felt pretty committed.

I recalled my friend Neil, who had spent many summers in the Lakes and Scottish mountains with an older uncle, who ate up mountains with his long stride and formidable endurance. His name was Rolf and Neil referred to their days out together as 'going Rolfing —' never a day to be underestimated. Neil also regularly quoted the Scottish Climbing Guide he had once needed to refer to in anger on a route. Calling down to his climbing partner for inspiration of which way to head next on the crag — his partner had called back that the guide simply stated "Trend generally upwards", not the most useful advice at your time of need!

But here I was faced only with the option of trending generally upwards, the summit was ahead, I could be sure of that, so I simply needed to keep moving however laboured and slow, I would get there. Rather excitingly I knew that this section ended with a short scramble up the Gribin Ridge leading then onwards to the summit of Glyder Fawr at one thousand and one metres. After toiling for what seemed like a very long time, I once again began to hear voices and see occasional flashes of colour in the cloud ahead. These gradually formed into the recognisable shapes of runners and marshals positioned at the foot of the ridge giving people guidance on the early route upwards. As I passed them, I did my best to look spritely and enthused but I'm not sure they were convinced.

The ridge was immediately a welcome change from the preceding monotonous head-down trudge up the rocky mountain path. At last, here now there was the chance to use hands and arms to pull oneself upwards and the active engagement of the brain to figure out the best route, hand holds and movement over the crag. Quickly up Gribin we were once again a little group as generously the others had waited at the top willingly sacrificing their hard-earned body heat. I apologised but kept moving, now was no time stop and let any further fatigue get into my body. I've never been that keen on stopping during a long event, I'd much rather eat on the hoof, slowing to a walk but constantly moving, it's surprising just how far you can get whilst taking on some nutrition.

On relatively flat terrain but still shrouded in cloud we initially followed a ridge and then a broad shoulder of mountain to finally raise the summit of Glyder Fawr — our third one thousand metre peak of the day. "Only two to go" I told myself!

Looking back there were a raft of momentary high points where my energy seemed to recover. The summits of course made up several of those and I ran comfortably with the 'team' as we now again descended southwards from the summit bound for Pen-y-Pass, the well-known car park and café from which millions of walkers have headed up Snowdon. It was only just over two kilometres of running, again dropping steeply from one thousand and one metres to the road at three hundred and fifty-eight metres. Another two thousand feet sacrificed by the route however there were no other options as the checkpoint through which we had to 'dib' was just where the road travels through the highest point of the pass. As we ran on and quickly the momentary elation of summiting Glyder Fawr fell away and my legs resumed their wobbly outlook on the day ahead. To make matters worse, my mind allowed those doubting demons to speak to me and I began to convince myself that if only I could get to Pen-y-Pass then I'd have done well and could catch a bus back to Llanberis.

Descending quickly, we were welcomed out of the cloud by spectacular views of the Snowdon range ahead, I even think the sun came out just a little, it was certainly brighter but perhaps that was generated in my head, now resolute that I was not far from my own personal finish at the road, just dib in, retire and call it a day.

Down at the road-side it was like we'd arrived into a town. There were cars and minibuses, hundreds of walkers coming and going from the car park, the café was open buzzing with families and friends swapping mountain stories. I sat nearby the marshals table and generally felt very sorry for myself. For the very first time ever in such an event I heard myself admitting defeat and telling the others to simply press ahead and leave me there, I'd take some time to recover and then make my way back to the B & B. Chris however was having none of it and point blank refused to listen to any of my self-pity and complaining. We'd run together for many years, sailed, cycled and shared adventures with our daughters every summer since they could toddle. He knew me well enough to switch into 'adult child' mode!

"John" he stated harshly, "Take these paracetamol, crunch them in your mouth so they act faster, drink lots of fluid and get some energy gel into you. We'll take fifteen minutes here but then we're off again, and you'll be coming with us!"

And so obediently, quite meekly I did as I was told variously drinking, eating, apologising and cursing. You simply cannot aspire to do decently in a mountain race if you haven't hill miles and climbing legs — that I knew now for sure!

So a little time passed and I gradually became fed up of watching other runners coming down out of the Glyders, happily dibbing through the check point before moving straight on to the Snowdon path. The paracetamol started to do their trick, numbing any dull fatigue that I could feel, and the fluids coursed their way through my body almost tangibly refreshing me as I sat there coming to terms that there truly was just one final ascent to be done. Surely, I could do that and especially if I just took it easy, I'd been up Snowdon several times before, knew the route well and so could visualise the challenge ahead.

With the others standing around waiting, making it clear that they were not heading off without me, I quietly packed up my little running sack and confirmed that I was up for leaving. This was not some triumphant declaration of an imminent charge, or a false bold statement of 'Let me at it!' it was rather an acceptance that I could and would go on albeit very much in a 'steady away' fashion. The obvious route was along and up the Pyg Track, the rocky tourist path to the summit of Snowdon. We jogged the flat sections and walked hard on the inclines. The thousands of day trippers must by this time have got the idea that some form of race was happening as they'd got used to an intermittent but steady trail of runners asking to squeeze by along the path and so it was that most of them politely stood to one side as our little group of four approached.

There's not too much more to say really, it most certainly wasn't a fast and athletic ascent to the coll where the path joins the mountain railway that has impressively made its way up from Llanberis. At that point we had to make a right turn to ascend the fourth one thousand metre peak of the day, Carnedd Ugain standing tall and craggy at one thousand and sixty-five metres.

Standing there together as a group we joined in a pre-planned poignant moment as Spike took out two painted stones and laid them carefully at the foot of the trig point. These had been decorated by his children in memory of our very good friend Matthew McSevney. They were to be left on the mountain as a mark of fondness and in recognition of a very special man. Matthew, like us, relished long runs, adventure sports and wild open spaces, he had discovered his deep routed ability for endurance events, raw bloody stubbornness, and had big ambitions for major races such as The Spine Race, Dragon's Back and even the Ice Man Ultra Triathlon in Norway. There is no doubt that he would have been with us on Snowdon had he not been killed whilst on his road bike the year before.

We stood quietly, only for a moment before turning back on our route and heading down the short descent back to the coll and then onwards to the summit of Snowdon just half a kilometre away standing dominant at one thousand and eighty-five metres. Battling through the throng of tourist walkers we found our way to the summit cairn, the fifth and final Welsh one thousand metre peak of the day was finally under our feet. The marshal held out the electronic dibber box and I eagerly clocked in relieved to know that the race was at an end, twenty-one miles and over ten thousand feet of climbing.

When Johnny had phoned me months earlier, he had proposed a 'big day out' in the mountains and it most certainly had been that. Never before had I come so close to throwing the towel in and never since, have I felt so drained, so empty of any motivation to carry on. It's true to say that the Welsh One Thousand Metres Peaks Race taught me a great deal. These are obvious points that I'd perhaps forgotten or become complacent about. The training principle of specificity, that to run consistently in the hills you simply need hill miles. That if you live in a flat countryside environment then you have to travel and find those hills to train in, it is no good being able to run eighteen or twenty miles through the fields, the mountains will quickly find you out.

Epilogue
This Wild and Precious Life

The work of writing these short adventure stories has been a real pleasure not least because it has enabled me to relive such brilliant times shared with great friends and to rediscover memories that had long since been stored away. I consider myself very lucky to have been fit enough to realistically contemplate each and every challenge and I remain determined to retain that lifestyle approach. For me fitness is simply a part of life, a part of being me rather than a month-long campaign in response to a throw away challenge. Such is my passion for mini-adventures that, alongside many friends, we continue to plan and then undertake both organised and independent challenges — so in time there are lots more to write about.

Alongside the pleasure of opening this 'reservoir of happy memories' my intention in writing this book was to motivate others to plan their own adventures and get outdoors. Nothing I have written about has been either complex or expensive especially when costs are shared amongst several others. Where there is a will there is a way — and there is so much to be gained in doing so... in the words of Mary Oliver.

Tell me what is it you plan to do with your one wild and precious life?